The Many Marks
of the Church

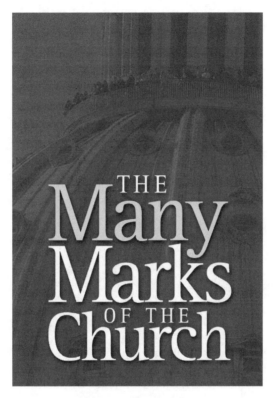

THE
Many
Marks
OF THE
Church

WILLIAM MADGES *and*
MICHAEL J. DALEY

editors

TWENTY
THIRD 23rd
PUBLICATIONS

Dedication

For Bob and Ed
For David and Diane

Twenty-Third Publications
A Division of Bayard
One Montauk Avenue, Suite 200
PO Box 6015
New London, CT 06320
(860) 437-3012 or (800) 321-0411
www.23rdpublications.com

Cover images (clockwise, beginning with upper left):
©istockphoto.com/Gunther Beck
©2006 Jupiter Images Corporation
©istockphoto.com/Chad Jarae
designpics.com

ISBN-10: 1-58595-589-2
ISBN 978-1-58595-589-3
Library of Congress Catalog Card Number: 2005936957
Printed in the U.S.A.

Contents

Introduction Michael J. Daley   1

A Historical Overview William Madges   7

Part One: The Classic Marks of the Church

1. The Church Is One   Cardinal William H. Keeler   25
2. The Church as One   Martin E. Marty   31
3. The Church Is Holy   Gillian T.W. Ahlgren   35
4. The Church Is Holy   Robert Ellsberg   39
5. The Church Is Catholic   Cardinal Avery Dulles, SJ   43
6. The Church Is Catholic   Michael Novak   48
7. The Church Is Apostolic   Mary Ann Donovan, SC   53
8. The Church Is Apostolic   Francis A. Sullivan, SJ   58

Part Two: The Church's Other Marks

9. The Church Is Active in Ministry
    Thomas F. O'Meara, OP   65
10. The Church Is Beautiful and Holy
    Alex Garcia-Rivera   69
11. The Church Is Biblical   Dianne Bergant, CSA   74
12. The Church Is Catechetical   Thomas Groome   79
13. The Church Is Charismatic   Amos Yong   85
14. The Church Is Conciliar   Michael J. Himes   90
15. The Church Is Courageous   Donal Dorr   95
16. The Church Is Creedal   Luke Timothy Johnson   100
17. The Church as Democratic and Constitutional
    Leonard Swidler   104
18. The Church Is Dialogical   Paul F. Knitter   109

19. **The Church Is Discerning** Jeannine Gramick, SL   114

20. **The Church as Domestic** Richard Gaillardetz   119

21. **The Church Is Ecological** Sallie McFague   124

22. **The Church Is Faithful** Mary E. Hines   128

23. **The Church Is Humorous** Tim Unsworth   132

24. **The Church as Immigrant** Peter C. Phan   136

25. **The Church as Intellectual** Susan A. Ross   141

26. **The Church Is the Lay Faithful** Dolores R. Leckey   146

27. **The Church as Medieval and Free** Gary Macy   152

28. **The Church Is Monastic** Francis Kline, OCSO   157

29. **The Church Is Mystagogical** Harvey D. Egan, SJ   162

30. **The Church Is Nonviolent** Thomas J. Gumbleton   167

31. **The Church Is Marked by Openness to Science**
    John Polkinghorne   171

32. **The Church Is Petrine** Richard P. McBrien   175

33. **The Church Is Prayerful** Barbara Fiand, SNDdeN   180

34. **The Church Is Priestly** Robert Barron   184

35. **The Church Is Marked by Its Relationship
    with Judaism** Mary C. Boys, SNJM   188

36. **The Church Is Marked by Ritual** John B. Foley, SJ   194

37. **The Church Is Sacramental** Peter E. Fink, SJ   198

38. **The Church Is Marked by Sexuality**
    Christine E. Gudorf   202

39. **The Church Is Sinful** Charles E. Curran   207

40. **The Church Is Marked by Suffering**
    M. Shawn Copeland   212

41. **The Church Is World-Embracing** Monika K. Hellwig   217

42. **The Church Is Youthful** Robert J. McCarty   221

Endnotes   **225**

Introduction

Michael J. Daley

A few months ago, on successive evenings, I was out with two friends. During the course of our conversations, they both asked if I was working on any writing projects. "Yes," I replied, "I'm working on a book about the marks of the church." Polite nods followed but they didn't appear to have any idea as to the nature of the project. In an attempt to give my friends an understanding of the book I was working on, I offered them the word "one." On both occasions it was met with a long, confused pause. Then I said "holy." Looking at them I could tell that they were trying to make the connection between the phrase "the marks of the church" and the words "one" and "holy." To no avail. By "catholic" it clicked though. They were able to finish it out and end with "apostolic."

More than likely we've all said them (or grew up saying them)—"one, holy, catholic, and apostolic." They are the traditional and classic marks of the church. After a lifetime of repetition, though, these words, and with it the whole of the Nicene Creed, have lost some of their meaning for many people in the church. (See Luke Timothy Johnson's piece on the Church as creedal, beginning on page 100.) Perhaps we've fallen victim to the importance of valuing memorization over lived faith. Maybe familiarity has bred contempt or, at least, indifference. Whatever the case, the marks' present "sleep-inducing" quality is unfortunate. There is so much potential for the marks to challenge and form the church. Recognized as such or not, they are said each Sunday in the recitation of the Nicene Creed during the liturgy. Similarly, they are affirmed during celebrations of the sacrament of baptism with family, friends and community. With this present state in mind, it is high time to retrieve the significance of the traditional marks of the church. Likewise, it is also time to explore other marks that characterize or should characterize the church today.

The goal of the book, then, is to offer a picture of the church that is broad, inclusive and relevant to our situation in the twenty-first century.

Prefaced by a historical grounding of the four traditional marks, Part One examines the four classic marks of the church and explores their meaning for us today. In Part Two the contributors to the book identify additional marks that either already characterize (describe, or are descriptive of) the church or should characterize (prescribe, or are prescriptive of) the church as it moves into the future. By including a description of both classic and contemporary marks of the church, *The Many Marks of the Church* should be a book that encourages a wide readership to reflect on the responsibilities of "being church" in the third millennium.

Already but Not Yet

For those generations schooled by the teachings of the *Baltimore Catechism,* it went without saying that the Catholic Church was the one and only church founded by Christ, for it alone possessed the fullness of unity, holiness, catholicity, and apostolicity.[1] Following the division of the Western Church at the time of the Protestant Reformation, the marks of the church became batons whereby each church—Catholic and Protestant ones—trying to prove that they were the one true church, beat the other into submission. Usually this was done theologically, though tragically, at times, it was done literally.

As theologian Richard McBrien indicates,

> given so many different churches vying for recognition and making various claims for themselves, defenders of the Catholic faith, known as apologists, appealed to the four marks in order to distinguish the true Church from the false churches. The supposition was that the marks would be visible to all and easy to verify, and that they would be present only in the one, true Church of Christ. The problem was that the description of the notes tended to be drawn in such a way that they would fit the Catholic Church, and the Catholic Church alone.[2]

One needs only to be reminded here of the Jesuit Robert Bellarmine's definition of church in *Disputations about the Controversies of the Christian Faith Against the Heretics of this Time* (1588) in the midst of the Catholic Reformation following the Council of Trent (1545-1563). According to him,

> the one and true Church is the community of men brought together by the profession of the same Christian faith and participate in the same sacraments under the authority of legitimate pastors and especially of the one Vicar of Christ on earth, the Roman Pontiff....The one true Church is as visible and palpable as the Kingdom of France or the Republic of Venice.

Pope Pius XII's encyclical *Mystici corporis* (1943) built upon Bellarmine's definition, going so far as to identify the mystical body of Christ exclusively with the Catholic Church. This understanding of church changed, however, at the Second Vatican Council (1962–1965). There, in its Dogmatic Constitution on the Church (*Lumen gentium* #8), one reads that the church of Christ "subsists in" the Catholic Church, rather than "is" the Catholic Church.

More recently, many, whether Catholic or non-Catholic, choose to speak of an "already, but not yet" quality with respect to the marks of the church. As much as we may want to talk about the marks being fulfilled, it must be humbly admitted that there is still a ways to go. One need not look far for evidence. Anyone who reads the newspaper today, even on an irregular basis, is tempted to begin with the "anti-marks" of the church: divided not one; sinful not holy; parochial not catholic; and, confused not apostolic.[3]

Søren Kierkegaard, the great Danish Lutheran theologian of the nineteenth century, argued for a similar starting point in his own day when speaking of oneself as a Christian. According to Kierkegaard it was self-delusional and dishonest to do otherwise:

> Imagine someone who aspired to be a millionaire but as yet had managed to earn only three dollars. Were he to call himself a millionaire because he was trying, would we be foolish enough to go along with his use of language? Would it not be better for him—simply to keep him awake and alert for the exertion—to say to himself, "I am not a millionaire." By saying it to himself in this way, would he not guard against becoming a fool?

The point is this: if there is to be any meaning to it, if it is at all permissible to take the name of something simply because you are striving toward it, then you must at least resemble what you are striving toward. In order to hide the fact that Christianity simply does not exist we say in the New Testament sense, "I am not a Christian, but I am trying." Having said that, or taking care to say it every Sunday year after year, or hearing it said, one concludes that one needs to do nothing. We are, after all, Christian.[4]

That being said, theologian Denise Lardner Carmody asserts that there is still something to be gained by looking at the church as "half-full" rather than "half-empty." She writes:

> The church itself has sometimes been idealistic, raising its gaze above the hurly-burly of its actual, empirical existence to remind itself of what it is more substantially in the creative design of God. The traditional

marks of the church express this idealism. In substance, according to the creative design of God, the Christian community is one, holy, catholic, and apostolic. Regardless of its fracture and sin, its provincialism and historic change, the church has always managed to be these good things for people of faith—people willing to grant it the prejudices of love.[5]

Whatever our starting point, though, this tension between what the church is and what it shall more fully be will always exist.

If We Image It, It Will Be

Though I saw *A Field of Dreams* some years ago, if there ever was a line that summarized the heart of a movie, it was, "If you build it, he will come." Ray Kinsella, played by Kevin Costner, hears these words one night while walking through his cornfield. Over the course of several days, fighting through his disbelief, he asks himself, "Build what?"

Then one afternoon he has a vision—a baseball field with Shoeless Joe Jackson, the disgraced Black Sox player of 1919, on it. Build a baseball field in the middle of an Iowa cornfield though? It was foolish to even give it much consideration, a sure sign of insanity to implement it. Plagued by worries that life is passing him by, that he's taken no risks and always played it safe, Kinsella throws caution to the wind and decides to bring the vision to life. He begins to build his dream.

The next day he's out plowing up his corn, his main cash crop. From a distance his neighbors watch with curiosity. Eventually, they all pretty much agree that he's a "damned fool." When Kinsella finishes building the park, he takes it all in, and says, "I have just created something totally illogical." To which his wife responds, "That's what I like about it." Then he asks her, "Am I completely nuts?" "Not completely," she replies. "It's a good baseball field."

Yet, the field remains empty. One night, facing considerable financial hardship, Kinsella decides it's time to get rid of the field. His fantasy has lasted long enough. Just then his daughter comes into the room where he and his wife are seated and says, "Daddy, there's a man out there on your lawn." Shoeless Joe Jackson had come. The dream had become a reality.

As I watched the film it got me thinking: if we can image it—the church—it will be. Perhaps some of the apathy, frustration, anger and resignation many feel toward the church today is due to a lack of vocabulary— a crisis of imagination, if you will. When suggesting any number of initiatives that the church needs to take to meet the demands of our time, so many of them are seemingly stopped cold with phrases like, "The church is not a democracy," or, "That doesn't sound very traditional to me."

Yet words shape our reality. Some would say they create it. We do or don't do things because of the power of words. As descriptive as "one, holy, catholic, and apostolic" are, surely there are other words that capture what the church is and what it is called to be. We only need to have the courage and freedom to speak these words. "If we image it, it will be." Some of these words, or marks, as one envisions the church, may seem incongruous, consoling, invigorating, aggravating, or even humorous. This is only to be expected in a faith community that is marked by such diverse theologies and spiritualities—one where Catholic Workers and Catholics United for the Faith, Missouri Synod and Evangelical Lutheran Church of America members, High Church and Low Church Anglicans, fundamentalist Southern Baptists and progressive Methodists, and still others, all seek communion with the living God in Jesus Christ.

There is a story that I think communicates the formative power of words well.[6] After a family had gathered around the table, the father asked for a moment of silence. In traditional words of thanks he said grace: "Bless us, O Lord, and these thy gifts, which we are about to receive through thy bounty, through Christ, our Lord, Amen." As the food was being passed around though, the father was far from grateful. In fact, depending on the dish, it was either too cold or too hot, too dry or too runny.

At one point during the meal, his young daughter asked him a question. "Daddy," she asked, "is it true that God hears all we say and sees all we do?" "Why, of course, it is, my dear," he replied. "Then God must have heard your blessing," she said. "Why, yes, God did," the father responded. "And he must also have heard your complaints?" she said hesitantly. Again the father said yes. "Tell me then, Daddy, which did God believe—your prayer or your complaints?"

In the church today, we may choose simply to complain or to imagine new possibilities for the church. Our hope is that this book will help people to affirm what is already good and true, and to envision that which is yet to come.

In this vein we believe this book can respond to the needs of a variety of different audiences. For general readers, this book can serve as an introduction to what the church has been or is. For high school and college students, this book can be used in conjunction with another text in the area of ecclesiology (the study of the church) to provide a more personal and narrative perspective on the marks of the church. Finally, for adult education classes and faith sharing groups, this book can provide characteristics that feed the imagination and encourage the articulation of one's own vision of church.

Of course, this book doesn't tell the whole story concerning the marks of the church. Surely, we've left out one characteristic that should have been included, another perspective that would have captured the dynamism of the church. In this sense, we see the book as a starting point to more serious study about one's understanding of church.

It goes without saying that as editors we did some but not all the work. Though the idea for the book may have been conceived by us, it became a reality due to the generosity of the contributors. A heartfelt thanks to all of them for their participation in the project. As a group, they speak with such conviction as to what the church is and, more so, what it is called to be. In the end, through their reflections, the book is truly an expression of hope rather than an exercise of despair.

We are also grateful to our respective academic communities, which continue to be such fertile grounds. We would also like to thank Twenty-Third Publications and our editors, David Lysik and Mary Carol Kendzia, for their acceptance of and support for the project. Finally, as with all projects, those closest to home bear the burdens of our time spent working on them. Thanks to our families for providing us the time, space, and encouragement needed to see this project to completion—Marsha, Katie, and Sarah; June, Cara, Brendan, and Nora.

A Historical Overview

William Madges

In the creed that Christians regularly refer to as the Nicene Creed, we profess our faith in a church that is one, holy, catholic, and apostolic. Those four adjectives have come to be regarded by most Christians as the essential attributes of the church. The Western Christian tradition regularly refers to them as the four marks of the church. They are called marks because Christians believe they are visible signs of the church's nature. They are also called marks because these four attributes distinguish or "mark" off Christ's church from other religious bodies or assemblies. In fact, the word "church" means "of the Lord" or "the Lord's house."[7]

What many Christians don't realize is that these four marks were not always used to describe the essential nature of the church nor did they always carry the same meaning in the mouths of Christians who professed them. These four marks have a history of development, which I would like to describe briefly here.

The Early Church

Although there are references to the church in the theological and spiritual writings of the church Fathers, the earliest creedal references to the church seem to derive from the early third century. Creeds developed out of the practical necessity of the Christian assembly to be able to tell those whom the assembly wished to proselytize what Christians believed. Understandably, the primary emphasis was placed upon belief in God as Father, Son, and Spirit. This belief in the triune nature of God set Jesus' followers apart from orthodox Jews, who also professed faith in the one God. The earliest Christian creeds, which found regular use in the context of preparation for baptism, were composed in question-and-answer form.

In the creeds of the first three centuries, the church is usually described explicitly only in terms of one or two characteristics. Holiness was the first mark attributed to the church. By the middle of the second century it was on

7

its way to becoming a stock epithet.[8] In the interrogatory creed of Hippolytus from the early third century, the catechumen is simply asked: "Do you believe in the Holy Spirit, in the holy Church, and in the resurrection of the body?"[9] And the Apostles' Creed,[10] although it hints at the church's unity, speaks explicitly only of the church being "holy" and being "catholic": "I believe in the Holy Spirit, the holy catholic Church, the communion of saints, the forgiveness of sins, the resurrection of the body, and the life everlasting. Amen."

In the early church, the mark of unity was closely connected to, in fact dependent upon, the mark of holiness. The church's holiness, it is important to stress, did not derive from the moral quality of its members, but rather from the animating presence of the Holy Spirit. Insofar as the church is permeated by the Spirit, to that extent it is holy. And insofar as the church is holy, to that extent it is also unified. This is the conviction that was so eloquently articulated by St. Paul in his First Letter to the Corinthians:

> Now there are varieties of gifts, but the same Spirit; and there are varieties of services, but the same Lord; and there are varieties of activities, but it is the same God who activates all of them in everyone. (1 Cor 12:4–6)

> For just as the body is one and has many members, and all the members of the body, though many, are one body, so it is with Christ. For in the one Spirit we were all baptized into one body—Jews or Greeks, slaves or free—and we were all made to drink of one Spirit. (1 Cor 12:12–13)

Just as the Holy Spirit exercises a unitive function within the trinity, binding Father and Son together in love, so too "the mission of the Holy Spirit in the world is seen as uniting believers to one another and to God in the body of Christ."[11]

The early church believed that the unitive function of the Holy Spirit was exercised in a special way through the office of bishop. In the context of threats from the outside—as in the case of persecution—or in the context of internal division—as in the case of heresy—early Christian writers stressed the role of bishops in maintaining the unity of the church. Apostolic succession of bishops became the means by which the true church could be distinguished from its heretical rivals as well as the source of the bishop's right to obedience. Jesus had promised to send the Holy Spirit to his disciples after he was gone, and the Risen Christ promised to remain with them until the end of the age.[12] This promise was believed to extend to the church's bishops. As the successors of the apostles, they were believed to have the special assistance of the Holy Spirit in the exercise of their teaching and preaching missions.

Ignatius, bishop of Antioch in the early second century, was the first individual Christian to use the term "catholic" in reference to the church. Ignatius used the word "catholic," which derives from the Greek *kata holos* (literally, through or according to the whole), to refer to the entire body of the faithful spread throughout the known world. For Ignatius, wherever Jesus Christ is, there is the Catholic Church.[13]

By the next century, "catholic" had come to be recognized as a characteristic mark that distinguished the church from sectarian, dissident, and heretical groups. St. Cyril of Jerusalem (ca. 315–86) provided an even more expansive conception of catholicity. For him it referred not only to spatial extension, but also to the fullness of the church's teaching and its virtues as well as the inclusion of all classes of people within the church. Cyril states that the church is catholic because it extends over all the world, from one end of the earth to the other; and because it teaches universally and completely one and all the doctrines that ought to come to human knowledge, concerning things both visible and invisible, heavenly and earthly; and because it brings into subjection to godliness the whole race of humankind, governors and governed, learned and unlearned; and because it universally treats and heals the whole class of sins, which are committed by soul or body, and possesses in itself every form of virtue which is named, both in deeds and words, and in every kind of spiritual gifts.[14]

From this perspective, it becomes clear why the Apostles' Creed, in confessing belief in the holy catholic church, does not explicitly state that the church is also one. Catholicity implies wholeness and unity.[15]

Beginning in the fifth century, we find the church described according to the four traditional marks. The Constantinopolitan Creed, for example, professes belief in "the Holy Spirit, the Lord and giver of life, who proceeds from the Father, who is worshiped and glorified together with the Father and Son, who spoke through the prophets; and in one holy catholic and apostolic church." This reference to the church was added by the bishops at the Council of Constantinople (381) to the creed that had been formulated at the first ecumenical council, the Council of Nicea (325). Today the Constantinopolitan Creed, which unites the work of these two councils, is popularly referred to as the Nicene Creed. From the mid-fifth century on, it became the most universally accepted of all the creeds in both east and west. It is still regularly professed by Catholics today in Sunday Mass.

It is not surprising that the marks of unity and apostolicity were added to the marks of holiness and catholicity in the creed. Christological controversy divided the church in the fourth and fifth centuries, and the Nicene and

Constantinopolitan Creeds were promulgated in the context of combating what was perceived to be heresy.[16] The desirability of church unity and the difficulty of obtaining it are underlined by the fact that the decisions of the Council of Nicea and the promulgation of its creed did not resolve the dissension between the supporters of Arius and his opponents. The controversy about the divinity of the Son continued for another fifty-five years, until the Council of Constantinople confirmed Nicea's decisions and its creed.

By the fifth century, the four classic marks of the church were not only confessed, but were also perceived to be interdependent. The church was one because it was holy. It was holy because it possessed the Holy Spirit. The church was apostolic because it was unified in its obedience to the bishops, who as successors of the apostles, were heirs of Christ's promise to send the Holy Spirit to the apostles, who would instruct them in the truth of the whole gospel. The church was catholic because it was apostolic; it had been sent into all the corners of the world ("apostle" means one who is sent or messenger) with the fullness of truth.[17]

The Medieval Church

If holiness had been the most prominent of the four classic marks in the early church, then unity was perhaps the most prominent mark in the medieval church. It was certainly a very important characteristic. For example, the Venerable Bede (ca. 672–735), whose *Ecclesiastical History of the English People* documents the history of the conversion to Christianity of the Anglo-Saxon tribes, claimed that "anyone who disturbs the unity of that holy church which Jesus came to bring together is striving as far as he can to undermine Jesus himself."[18] And it was the responsibility of those who held church office, particularly the pope, to maintain the church's unity. Maintaining the unity of the church became particularly difficult, however, around the twelfth century with the rise of schismatic and heretical sects, such as the Waldensians, the Albigensians, and the Cathari.

The challenge posed by some of these groups also pertained to the question of the church's holiness. The Cathari, whose name literally means "the pure," felt that the medieval institutional church had fallen away from the purity and simplicity of life exemplified in the apostolic period. The Cathari felt that they alone deserved to be called true Christians because they alone adhered strictly to an apostolic life, which to them meant poverty of lifestyle and repudiation of war and capital punishment.[19]

Generally speaking, however, the four marks of the church were not a topic of intense discussion in the Middle Ages. Peter Lombard's *Sentences*, the standard theological text upon which medieval theologians wrote commentaries, contains no special section on the church. Similarly, Thomas Aquinas (ca. 1225–74), the great Dominican scholastic, devoted no set of questions concerning the doctrine of the church in his encyclopedic *Summa Theologiae*. Of course, he had occasion to comment on the marks, which he identified as "one, holy, catholic or universal, and strong or lasting," in his exposition of the Apostles' Creed (1273). There he identified three elements upon which the church's unity is founded: the common faith of all members of the church, the common hope of eternal life, and the common love of God and of neighbor in mutual service. The holiness of the church derives from the fact that the faithful have been cleansed by the blood of Christ and from the fact that the Trinity now dwells within the church. The church is catholic or universal, according to Aquinas, in a threefold sense: universal with regard to place, with regard to all conditions of human beings, and with regard to time ("for it began with Abel and will last even to the end of the world....And even after, for the Church remains in heaven"). Moreover, Aquinas identified apostolicity as one of the causes of the church's strength and indefectibility. He writes:

> Fourthly, the Church is firm, solid as a house on massive foundations. The principal foundation is Christ himself: for other foundation no man can lay but that which is laid, which is Christ Jesus. Secondary foundations are the Apostles and apostolic teaching....Its strength is signified by Peter, or Rock, who is its crown. A building is strong when it can never be overthrown though it may be shaken. The Church can never be brought down.[20]

Although theologians in the Middle Ages devoted little time to definitions of the nature of the church, canon lawyers filled the void. Attention to Roman law in the nascent universities, such as Bologna, stimulated interest in church law. By the middle of the twelfth century, Gratian had produced a massive compilation of previous church law—the *Decretum Gratiani,* which sought to harmonize all the contradictions and inconsistencies existing in church rules accumulated from diverse sources. Gratian was also a papalist, who thought that the pope held supreme authority in the church. Concomitantly, he believed that ecclesiastical law was far more important than civil law. "With such a bias in favour of the popes, Gratian helped both to heighten the importance and change the character of the papacy."[21]

Communion with and obedience to the pope, at least from the perspective of many canon lawyers and theologians, became conditions of membership in the one, holy, catholic, and apostolic church. In his bull *Unam Sanctam* (1302), Pope Boniface VIII expressed this sentiment in dramatic fashion by declaring that every human creature had to be subject to the Roman pontiff in order to be saved. Boniface and his supporters imagined that the Risen Christ's final words on earth in Matthew 28:18 created a clear chain of command: all authority had been given to Christ, and he in turn gave that authority to Peter, and through him to all of Peter's successors. But what was one to do if there was more than one pope? That was precisely the problem the church faced in the Great Western Schism (1378–1417), which initially saw two men, Urban VI and Clement VII, claiming to be the legally elected pope. Eventually the number was increased to three, after the Council of Pisa (1409) failed to heal this papal schism.

The schism, which Jean Gerson (1363–1429), chancellor of the University of Paris, said was like an "incurable cancer," raised dramatically the question of the unity of the church. As each of the three claimants to the papal throne sought to bolster his own political and military power, it was no longer clear who was truly the rightful pope. The deficiency in holiness exhibited by so many of the church's leaders was exacerbated by the division of the church into competing papal parties. Emphasis upon the authority and strong role of the pope had previously been a way to counteract eruptions of heterodox thought or actual schism. Such an emphasis, however, proved inapplicable in the case of the Great Western Schism, which was resolved at the Council of Constance (1414–17) through an appeal to conciliar theory. Conciliar theory asserted that a general council, not the pope, represented the highest authority in the church. Using this theory as its warrant, the Council of Constance deposed the rival popes, elected a new pope—Martin V—and insisted that councils be held at regular intervals so as to advance a program of reform in a systematic way. Although it was initially honored, the requirement to hold general councils frequently was soon ignored. In addition, before the end of the fifteenth century conciliarism was declared heretical, as popes sought to re-establish their hegemonic authority. Despite the re-establishment of the structural unity of the church under the headship of the pope, it was obvious to many that an important early mark of the church—its holiness— was more of a possibility than a reality.

In the attempt to bring the church back to a firm commitment to holiness, some fifteenth-century reformers articulated a new understanding of the nature of the church. Jan Hus (ca. 1370–1415), who had become rector of the University of Prague in 1409, published the treatise *On the*

Church, in which he defined the church not as the Church of Rome, but as the gathering of the predestined.[22] This definition, whose immediate source was John Wycliffe (ca. 1330–84), now became a means for discriminating between "a physical understanding of the church" characteristic of the papal doctrine and an understanding of "the holy church as the bride of Christ, the congregation of the elect of God."[23] Hus's point was that one—such as himself—could actually belong to the true (invisible) church, even though presently excluded from the visible church. In short, "it is one thing to be of the church and another thing to be in the church."[24] The latter refers to external or institutional affiliation; the former refers to authentic membership as one of God's elect.

The concern for the holiness of the church was an important issue, however, not only at the time of the Great Western Schism. The conflict in the thirteenth and fourteenth centuries between the Spiritual and the Conventual Franciscans, for example, concerning the ownership of property, had to do not only with how the friars could best live out the spirit of St. Francis of Assisi (1182–1226), but also with what it meant to be holy.[25]

For many, the extent to which the church exemplified the poverty of Jesus and the apostles reflected the degree to which the church could be said to be holy. Did not Jesus say, "If you wish to be perfect, go, sell your possessions, and give the money to the poor, and you will have treasure in heaven; then come, follow me" (Mt 19:21)? But the church of the late Middle Ages seemed to be a church of wealth. The followers of Hus in the fifteenth century extended the ideal of poverty, which characterized the life of the friars, to all the clergy. And Girolamo Savanarola (1452–98), a fiery preacher and reformer, bemoaned the fact that the early church had prelates of gold and chalices of wood, but the church of his day had chalices of gold and prelates of wood. In response to the critique of the moral failures of some of the leading churchmen, defenders of the pope and the institution referred back to the early church's explanation of the source of the church's holiness. In this period, Henry of Kalteisen represents well this point of view:

> Thus also the catholic church is called "holy," not on account of the holiness of all that are present in it, since many of them are sinners, but on account of its holy offices and on account of the holiness of the sacraments that are present in it.[26]

At least since the time of Augustine (354–430), it had been customary to hold that the validity of the sacraments did not depend upon the holiness of the minister. This principle was then later applied to the church's institutional leaders: the bishops and the pope did not need to be personally holy for the church to be holy; rather, the presence of the Holy Spirit in the sacraments made the church holy. Correlatively, the pope and the bishops were entitled to govern the church and to be obeyed, not because of their individual holiness, but because of the offices they held.

During this medieval period, the catholicity of the church continued to be understood in the double sense of spatial and temporal extension. That is, the church was catholic because it was spread throughout the entire known world and because it had existed, in one form or other, from the beginning of the world and would continue to exist into the next.

In this period, the apostolic character of the church was also reiterated. According to the conventional theory, to be "apostolic" meant to be founded by, spread by, or administered by the apostles and their legitimate successors. Due to the conflict between Hussites and orthodox Christians, and between church reformers and papal defenders, however, there was no agreement on what made the church "apostolic." For some, the pope and obedience to him as successor of the apostle Peter made the church apostolic; for others, such as Wycliffe and Hus, it was conformity to the word of the apostles as contained in scripture. This clash of interpretations continued into the next period. In fact, the differences sharpened to the point that the Western church was split asunder.

The Reformation Church

After Martin Luther posted his Ninety-Five Theses in 1517, those reformers who came to be known as Protestant rejected the idea that the one, holy, catholic, and apostolic church referred to the visible church headed by the pope. The church of the four marks, they insisted, was to be found where the gospel is purely preached and the sacraments rightly administered. Consequently, the *Augsburg Confession* (1530), prepared by Philip Melanchthon, Luther's most important associate, for presentation to Emperor Charles V at the imperial diet of 1530, affirmed "one holy Christian church," which it defined as "the assembly of all believers among whom the Gospel is preached in its purity and the holy sacraments are administered according to the Gospel."[27] John Calvin, the leader of the reformation in Geneva, affirmed the same definition.[28] And the Church of England adopted the same understanding of the church in its Thirty-Nine Articles (1563).[29]

Although it was possible for Protestants to adduce credible evidence that their churches bore the marks of holiness and apostolicity, it appeared more difficult to make a convincing argument that their churches also bore the marks of unity and catholicity. Unity was perhaps the most problematic mark for Reformation Protestants, and counter-Reformation Catholic apologists made much of the apparent lack of unity among Protestant believers. Although Luther, Calvin, and Ulrich Zwingli (1484–1531) agreed on the authority of scripture and the primacy of faith over works, they disagreed among themselves concerning the proper understanding of the sacraments and the polity of the church. And the Radical Reformers, such as Menno Simons (1496–1561), the founder of the Mennonites, rejected the other Reformers' endorsement of infant baptism and their use of civil force to achieve religious conformity.

In reply, the Protestant churches distinguished between visible unity and unity of faith. Thus, the *Second Helvetic Confession*, written in 1561 by Heinrich Bullinger, Zwingli's successor in Zurich, and ratified by the Swiss churches in 1566 with a few minor changes, states:

> Furthermore, we teach that great care is to be taken wherein especially the truth and unity of the Church consists, lest we either rashly breed or nourish schisms in the Church. It consists not in outward rites and ceremonies, but rather in the truth and unity of the Catholic faith. This Catholic faith is not taught us by the ordinances or laws of men, but by the holy Scriptures, a compendious and short sum whereof is the Apostles' Creed.[30]

The Lutheran Church had previously asserted a similar line of argument.[31] Whereas the Catholic Church emphasized the unity of the church under the visible headship of the pope, Protestant churches emphasized the unity of the church under the spiritual headship of Christ. Both parties could and did insist that there is only one church, but they did not agree on how that unity was constituted.[32] The *Westminster Confession* of 1646—which became the standard of Presbyterianism in the English-speaking world, and was adopted with modifications, by Congregationalists in New England, and served as a basis of the Baptist creeds—made the dichotomy between unity under the visible pope and unity under the invisible Christ quite stark:

> There is no other head of the Church but the Lord Jesus Christ: nor can the Pope of Rome, in any sense be head thereof; but is that Antichrist, that man of sin and son of perdition, that exalteth himself in the Church against Christ, and all that is called God.

It was not as if the visibility of the church was denied. Rather, the visibility of the church was ancillary to its true nature. Thus, the same

Westminster Confession deals with the catholicity and holiness of the church, and at least implicity with its apostolicity, in the following manner:

> **I.** The catholic or universal Church, which is invisible, consists of the whole number of the elect, that have been, are, or shall be gathered into one, under Christ the head thereof; and is the spouse, the body, the fullness of him that fills all in all.
>
> **II.** The visible Church, which is also called catholic or universal under the gospel (not confined to one nation as before under the law), consists of all those throughout the world that profess the true religion; and of their children; and is the kingdom of the Lord Jesus Christ, the house and family of God, out of which there is no ordinary possibility of salvation....
>
> **IV.** This catholic Church has been sometimes more, sometimes less visible. And particular churches, which are members thereof, are more or less pure, according as the doctrine of the gospel is taught and embraced, ordinances administered, and public worship performed more or less purely in them.[33]

The Anabaptists or "re-baptizers," so named because they rejected the validity of infant baptism and insisted upon adult believer's baptism, felt that other Reformers had not gone far enough in attempting to reform the church. More than reformation was needed. The early church, with its non-violent, counter-cultural character, needed to be restored. These Anabaptists, the radicals of the Reformation, insisted that the church of Christ is visible. They did not mean, however, visible under the headship of the pope or a body of bishops, but visible by its strict adherence to the way of life modeled by Christ. Such a way of life required withdrawal from civil society and purity of heart and action.[34] The Mennonites, therefore, did not stress in their creedal statements the marks of unity and catholicity, but emphasized the mark of holiness. The *Dordrecht Confession* of 1632 states:

> We believe in and confess a visible Church of God, consisting of those, who...have truly repented, and rightly believed; who are rightly baptized, united with God in heaven, and incorporated into the communion of the saints on earth....This church of the living God...may be known by her evangelical faith, doctrine, love, and godly conversation; also by her pure walk and practice, and her observance of the true ordinances of Christ, which He has strictly enjoined on His followers. 1 Cor 12:13; Mt 7:25; 16:18; 28:20; 2 Cor 6:16.[35]

The formation of separate Protestant ecclesial bodies, begun in the sixteenth century, continued in subsequent centuries. From the sixteenth century to the twentieth century, Roman Catholic apologists interpreted the multiplication of Protestant churches as an indication that the Protestant churches could not be the true church of Christ. Against this multiplicity, Robert Bellarmine, Jesuit theologian, cardinal, and Catholic controversialist, held up the Catholic Church as the definition of the true church: "A body of human beings united together by the profession of the same Christian faith, and by participation in the same sacraments, under the governance of lawful pastors, more especially of the Roman Pontiff, the sole vicar of Christ on earth."[36] Three centuries later, *The Catholic Encyclopedia* of 1912 could remark:

> Between no two of the hundreds of non-Catholic sects is there a common bond of union; each one having a different head, a different belief, a different cult. Nay more, even between the members of any one sect there is no such thing as real unity, for their first and foremost principle is that each one is free to believe and do as he wishes. They are constantly breaking up into new sects and subdivisions of sects, showing that they have within themselves the seeds of disunion and disintegration.[37]

The belligerence and adversarial posture of the Catholic and Protestant churches, one to another, began to change dramatically in the twentieth century.

The Modern Church

In the modern period, the mark of unity became once again a *desideratum* of the churches. From early in the twentieth century, Protestants had become increasingly involved in what came to be called "the ecumenical movement." This phenomenon exhibited growing joint cooperation among the Protestant churches, beginning with interdenominational cooperation in missionary work. The World Missionary Conference of 1910 in Edinburgh, Scotland, gave decisive impetus to the desire for greater Christian unity. Out of collaboration fostered by this conference grew the International Missionary Council in 1921. Other areas of increasing ecumenical activity included youth work, Christian education, and united service to society. In 1908 the Federal Council of the Churches of Christ in America was founded, which merged in 1950 with a number of interdenominational agencies to form the National Council of the Churches of Christ in the U.S.A.

The Protestant ecumenical movement eventually broached the more difficult issue of doctrinal differences, beginning with the first World Conference on Faith and Order in 1927. That conference in Lausanne, Switzerland, gave strong voice to the call to unity:

God wills unity. Our presence in this Conference bears testimony to our desire to bend our wills to His. However we may justify the beginnings of disunion, we lament its continuance and henceforth must labour, in penitence and faith, to build up our broken walls.[38]

The Second World Conference on Faith and Order, held ten years later in Edinburgh, and representing 122 Christian churches or communions, affirmed their unity in Christ. It acknowledged division in "the outward forms" of their life, but expressed the conviction that "a deeper understanding will lead us towards a united apprehension of the truth as it is in Jesus."[39] By 1938 a provisional structure for a world council of Christian churches had been worked out. Its implementation, however, was interrupted by the Second World War. Finally in 1948, the World Council of Churches, initially including 145 churches from 44 countries, was established. The delegates that gathered for the Third World Conference on Faith and Order in Lund, Sweden specifically addressed the traditional marks of the church and the distinction between the visible and the invisible church, which had previously been emphasized in some Protestant churches. The Conference declared that, although they had unity in Christ:

> We differ, however, in our understanding of the relation of our unity in Christ to the visible holy, Catholic and Apostolic Church. We are agreed that there are not two Churches, one visible and the other invisible, but one Church which must find visible expression on earth, but we differ in our belief as to whether certain doctrinal, sacramental and ministerial forms are of the essence of the Church itself. In consequence, we differ in our understanding of the character of the unity of the Church on earth for which we hope....[40]

The Catholic Church officially remained aloof from these developments. Official Catholic sentiment in the early twentieth century continued to be guided by papal teaching of the previous century. Pope Pius IX, in his Syllabus of Errors (1864), had rejected the idea that it was no longer necessary that the Catholic Church be regarded as the only religion of the state and that there should be freedom of worship for all. In the twentieth century, Pope Pius XI, although supportive of greater understanding of the Eastern churches, maintained a negative attitude toward Protestants. In his encyclical *Mortalium animos* (1928), he declared that the only way in which the unity of Christianity could be fostered would be "by furthering the return to the one true church of Christ of those who are separated from it." This would involve their believing in "the infallibility of the Roman Pontiff in the sense of the Ecumenical Vatican Council (i.e., Vatican I) with the same faith as they believe in the Incarnation of Our Lord."[41]

Pope John XXIII (pope from 1958–63) took decisive steps to change this mindset. On October 19, 1962, he elevated the Secretariat for Christian Unity to the same level as the Preparatory Commissions that had been charged with preparing the documents to be considered at the Second Vatican Council. He also invited Protestant and Orthodox communions to send observers to the Council. Their presence at the Council was unprecedented in the history of Catholicism. Whereas it had become customary to regard Orthodox Christians as schismatics and Protestants as heretics, John XXIII referred to them as "our brethren in Christ."[42]

The Second Vatican Council produced two documents that addressed in a substantive way the relation between the Catholic Church and other Christian churches: the Dogmatic Constitution on the Church (*Lumen gentium*) and the Decree on Ecumenism (*Unitatis redintegratio*). One of the most significant aspects of the Constitution is that it goes beyond the traditional assertion that the Catholic Church is the true church to assert that Christ's Spirit is at work in churches and communities beyond the visible boundaries of the Catholic Church. Although the Constitution re-affirms the traditional teaching that the "one, holy, catholic, and apostolic" church was handed over to Peter and the apostles to be shepherded, *Lumen gentium* backs away from the simple identification of the Catholic Church with the Mystical Body of Christ, which the original draft of the Constitution had endorsed.[43] In its final version, *Lumen gentium* declares:

> This church, constituted and organized as a society in the present world, subsists in the Catholic Church, which is governed by the successor of Peter and by the bishops in communion with him. Nevertheless, many elements of sanctification and of truth are found outside its visible confines. Since these are gifts belonging to the church of Christ, they are forces impelling towards catholic unity.[44]

Instead of asserting, in an unqualified way, that Christ's church or Mystical Body is the Catholic Church, the Constitution acknowledges that Christ's church subsists—exists or lives—in the Catholic Church and that elements of truth and sanctification can exist outside of its visible structure. This statement was not an endorsement of "indifferentism," the term used in the nineteenth century to characterize the belief that it doesn't really matter whether one is a Catholic Christian or a Protestant or Orthodox Christian. Vatican II, however, did move away from the nineteenth-century Catholic position that all elements of truth and sanctification are to be found in the Catholic Church and none is to be found elsewhere. Vatican II affirmed that some elements of truth and sanctification are to be found in other Christian churches, while the Catholic Church possesses those elements in their fullness.[45]

The Second Vatican Council's Decree on Ecumenism acknowledged that baptism establishes a communion among believers insofar as "all who have been justified by faith in baptism are incorporated into Christ" and therefore "have the right to be called Christians, and with good reason are accepted as sisters and brothers in the Lord by the children of the Catholic Church."[46] This is a significant departure from the earlier language of schismatic and heretic that was directed against Orthodox and Protestant Christians respectively.[47] Echoing the words of the Dogmatic Constitution on the Church, the Decree on Ecumenism asserts that the fullness of grace and truth have been entrusted to the Catholic Church, but also asserts that the churches and communities separated from it "have been by no means deprived of significance and importance in the mystery of salvation. For the Spirit of Christ has not refrained from using them as means of salvation which derive their efficacy from the very fullness of grace and truth entrusted to the Catholic Church."[48]

The Second Vatican Council's ecumenical and dynamic approach to understanding the church's character was incorporated into official guidelines for religious education, such as *Sharing the Light of Faith: National Catechetical Directory for Catholics of the United States* (1979), and into the *Catechism of the Catholic Church* (1992). This catechism offers a concise expression of current official Catholic teaching on the marks of the church.

The *Catechism of the Catholic Chuch* affirms the traditional Catholic teaching that the church's unity is assured by the visible bonds of communion: profession of one faith, common celebration of divine worship, and apostolic succession. But it emphasizes that the invisible source of that unity is the unity of persons of the Trinity and, unlike counter-Reformation era pronouncements, it affirms the church's diversity of gifts, persons, and cultures.[49] Acknowledging the rupture of unity in the course of the church's history, the *Catechism* affirms that the "desire to recover the unity of all Christians is a gift of Christ and a call of the Holy Spirit".[50]

Drawing upon the previous tradition, the *Catechism* affirms that the church's holiness derives from the Holy Spirit with which Christ endowed the church. Although the Spirit is present in the church, perfect holiness does not permeate every member. Rather, "all members of the church, including her ministers, must acknowledge that they are sinners,"[51] who are called to lives of ever greater holiness.

In its description of the church's catholicity, the *Catechism* uses the word's denotation to explain that the church is catholic in a double sense. First, it possesses the whole means of salvation; second, it has been given by Christ a mission to the whole world.[52] In fact, all people belong to or are called to "this catholic unity of the People of God."[53] Because the church, according to Catholic belief, has been sent to be the universal sacrament of salvation, catholicity also means that the church must be missionary.[54]

The *Catechism* explains that the church is apostolic in the sense that it is founded upon the apostles, hands on their teaching, and continues to remain in communion of faith and life with its origin. Every member of the church shares in the church's apostolic mission to bring the gospel to all the peoples of the world.[55]

The *Catechism* concludes its exposition of the marks of the church by asserting that the church is ultimately one, holy, catholic, and apostolic "in her deepest and ultimate identity, because it is in her that 'the Kingdom of heaven,' the 'Reign of God,' already exists and will be fulfilled at the end of time."[56]

The Church in Prospect

As the Christian church moves further into its third millennium, it encounters a world that is increasingly interdependent, yet culturally and religiously diverse and economically and politically divided. How can the church be an instrument of Christ's ministry in such a context? That is the external challenge for the church.

But the church also faces internal challenges. Some of the challenges are perennial: how to create and maintain unity, enable greater holiness, preserve apostolic traditions, and embrace all peoples and cultures. But some challenges are new, or at least newer: how to respond to the ecological crisis of the planet, the opportunities and dangers of globalization, the privatization of religion, and the secularization of culture in the "developed" West.

These challenges—both external and internal—have already begun to evoke from the church qualities that can supplement the traditional description of the church as one, holy, catholic, and apostolic. The authors in this volume offer their reflections on what the church already is or what it needs to become in order to effectively be the dynamic presence of Christ in the world.

PART ONE

The Classic Marks
of the Church

CHAPTER 1

The Church Is One

Cardinal William H. Keeler

William Henry Keeler was born March 4, 1931, in San Antonio, Texas, the son of Thomas L. Keeler and Margaret T. (Conway) Keeler. He was raised in Lebanon, Pennsylvania, where he attended St. Mary School and Lebanon Catholic High School. He received a bachelor of arts degree from St. Charles Seminary, Overbrook, Philadelphia, and a licentiate in sacred theology from the Pontifical Gregorian University in Rome. Ordained a priest on July 17, 1955, he became assistant pastor at Our Lady of Good Counsel Church, Marysville, and secretary of the diocesan tribunal (1956–58). He was then assigned to study canon law at the Pontifical Gregorian University in Rome. In 1961 he received his doctorate in canon law and was re-appointed by Bishop George L. Leech as assistant pastor of Our Lady of Good Counsel Church. He became its pastor in 1964. As secretary to Bishop Leech during the Second Vatican Council (1962–65), he was appointed peritus or "special advisor" to the council by Pope John XXIII. During the council, he also served on the staff of the Council Digest, a daily communication service sponsored by the bishops of the United States.

After serving as vice chancellor, chancellor, and vicar general in the Harrisburg, Pennsylvania diocese he was named auxiliary bishop of Harrisburg in July and ordained as bishop on September 21, 1979. Pope John Paul II first appointed him bishop of Harrisburg in 1983 and then archbishop of Baltimore in 1989. In 1994 he was appointed a cardinal.

An influential participant in a wide range of national and international issues, Cardinal Keeler was elected president of the National Conference of Catholic Bishops (NCCB) in 1992. As part of his work with the NCCB, Cardinal Keeler developed a reputation for effectively building interfaith bonds. He is particularly noted for his work in furthering Catholic-Jewish dia-

logue and serves as moderator of Catholic-Jewish relations for the U.S. Conference of Catholic Bishops. Since 1994 he has served on the Pontifical Council for Promoting Christian Unity and the Congregation for the Oriental Churches. In addition to serving on the boards of many institutions, Cardinal Keeler is also Chairman of the Board of Catholic Charities, the largest non-governmental agency providing assistance to the needy of Maryland. He has received honorary degrees from 15 different colleges and universities in recognition of his outstanding contributions to church and society.

Reflections Rooted in Memories of Vatican II

Over the years, I have been asked to give many talks on the Second Vatican Council, usually with a question and answer period afterwards. My perspective is always that of a pastor, not an academic. I was in a small parish in a rural setting during the council, and only afterwards came to office work, but always with a share of parish obligations.

As Catholics, the council participants had been schooled in the marks of the church as one, holy, catholic, and apostolic. The underlying unity of the church was taken for granted by the council members, but they needed to find the language to meet new needs for the new times. The unity was evident in the bishops' respect for one another, in the private and public prayer (private, as so many stopped at the Blessed Sacrament altar in silence; public, in the enthronement of the gospel book and the celebration of the Eucharist that began each day's deliberations.) There was unity expressed also in the Latin of the texts and debates, and in the garb of participants, although that of the churchmen of the East brought a touch of color to the scene.

The bishops' self-understanding of their role in an ecumenical council also evidenced this unity. Even as the apostles in the Council of Jerusalem (Acts 15) saw their task as one of preaching the gospel to the whole world and, more specifically, as adapting the church of their day to this task, so the bishops of Vatican II saw themselves as meeting around the successor of Peter for a similar purpose.

At the outset of the third period of the council, Pope Paul VI commented on this mark of the church's unity:

> Recapitulating in our persons and in our functions the universal Church, we proclaim this council ecumenical. Here is the exercise of unity, here the exercise of that universality by which the Church gives evidence of her prodigious vitality, her marvelous capacity to make men brothers and to welcome within her embrace the most diverse civilizations and languages, the most individualized liturgies and types of

spirituality, the most varied expressions of national, social and cultural genius, harmonizing all in felicitous union, yet always respecting legitimate variety and complexity (Council Daybook, Session 3, p. 4).

Working toward Conciliar Unity

The Second Vatican Council gave expression to its unity in the sixteen documents it promulgated; but this unity was achieved through the process of council members listening carefully to one another and respecting the diversity of perspectives.

Although the press almost immediately divided the council participants into "conservative" and "liberal" groupings, it would be more accurate to describe the differences in scriptural terms. There were the shepherds who wanted to lose nothing of the church's precious heritage from the past, and there were the fishers emboldened to let down their nets for a fresh catch. But each participant brought an individual background to bear, and so, in the give-and-take of the discussion, was adjusting to the new realities presented by those who offered other points of view, perhaps from the perspective of another culture or another country. As a result, the conciliar documents went through significant modification in the debates, with at least three drafts required before a final, usually nearly unanimous, vote.

We could see this process taking shape in the debate about the use of modern languages in the liturgy. Pope John XXIII did well to put liturgy as the first topic on the agenda: every bishop is familiar with it and may be considered a pastoral specialist in the field. Also, so many of the bishops of the Western church knew Latin well—after all, they were conducting their debate in Latin—and had good reason to retain it as their language of worship. They saw it as a constant factor in the church's life, no matter where one might travel.

They listened as their brothers from mission countries told them that the people of those lands did not understand Latin but, even more, regarded it as a sign of colonialism in an age when newly emerging countries of Africa and Asia were leaving colonialism behind. Those from the communist bloc countries argued persuasively that church services offered the only opportunity to catechize God's people, and it would be better to conduct the liturgy in an understandable language.

In the second period of the council, the constitution on the liturgy was completed and the number of bishops voting in favor of an initial use of the vernacular at Mass grew from 1,922 out of 2,118 to an incredible 2,247 out of 2,251. In the end, after all the discussion, there were only four negative votes on the document that, of all the conciliar decisions, had the most direct impact on Catholics in the parish.

Clearly, the bishops concluded that a shift to the vernacular would not harm the unity of the church. After the council's action, the initial offerings in the languages of the people met with such approval that translations were rushed through, often without apparent sensitivity to the doctrinal meaning of the words or how well they sounded to the ear.

The council's fundamental document, *Lumen gentium*, the constitution on the nature of the church, likewise garnered almost unanimous support, the result of two lengthy periods of discussion and voting and the intense work of the Commission on Doctrine to evaluate and respond to the specific observations made by the bishops. This document complements the Constitution on the Sacred Liturgy and opens up the approaches developed more fully in subsequent documents, including those on the missionary nature of the church, the office of bishops, the role of priests and consecrated religious, and the call to ecumenical unity.

As the First Vatican Council had lifted up one principle for unity in the church, the Second Vatican Council completed the picture by describing a second, dynamic principle of unity, that of collegiality, with the college of bishops seen in succession to the body or college of apostles. With eloquence, speakers evoked the vision of the author of the Book of Revelation, of the heavenly Jerusalem rising on the foundation of the "twelve apostles of the lamb" (Rev 21:14).

In the final period of the council, 1965, three other documents were the focus of a final consensus and passage: *Dei verbum*, the Dogmatic Constitution on Divine Revelation; *Nostra aetate*, the Declaration on the Relation of the Church to Non-Christian Religions; and *Dignitatis humanae*, the Declaration on Religious Liberty. The latter two marked new insights in the development of Catholic teaching as the church reached out to those around it. With respect to the two declarations, the first drafts were rejected by the bishops, possibly because the initial members of the Secretariat for Christian Unity had been appointed from among those sympathetic to ecumenical thinking rather than elected by the council as a whole. One result: the drafts tended to reflect a particular point of view, drawn up as they were without the internal debate that came from a broader spectrum of Catholic thinking. The Secretariat was expanded by election and the drafts revised in the light of the discussion in the council hall. On October 28, 1965, the Council adopted *Nostra aetate* 2,221 to 88 and so began Catholic efforts to engage other world religions in the dialogue for justice and peace. On its last working day, December 7, 1965, the council passed *Dignitatis humanae* by a vote of 2,308 to 70, thus formally opening a new page in the church's dealing with a basic human right.

The Council's Closing Days

That same day, the presidents of twenty-four national conferences of bishops, including Cardinal Patrick O'Boyle of Washington, DC, were invited to concelebrate the closing Eucharist with Pope Paul VI. At that Mass the unity of the church in council was strikingly evident: the sun fell on the altar of St. Peter's Basilica, illuminating the concelebrants as together they recited the great eucharistic prayer. More than 2,400 bishops joined in chanting the "Holy, holy, holy" echoing the angelic chant in the vision of Isaiah the prophet. There was a deep unity of heart expressed in the varying accents and tones, a unity very hard to convey through the modern media.

Subsequently, the bishops witnessed an extraordinary act of ecumenical reconciliation. A joint statement of Pope Paul VI and Ecumenical Patriarch Athenagoras was read by Bishop (later Cardinal) Jan Willebrands with these striking words: "They (the Pope and the Patriarch) likewise regret and remove both from memory and from the midst of the Church the sentences of excommunication which followed these events, the memory of which has influenced actions up to our day and has hindered closer relations in charity, and they commit these excommunications to oblivion." At the same time, in Istanbul, at the Phanar, in the presence of Ecumenical Patriarch Athenagoras, Cardinal Lawrence J. Shehan of Baltimore was witness to the reading of the same document by an Orthodox representative.

The next day, December 8, the 2,400 council members processed into St. Peter's Square under a bright sun. They rejoiced in an incredible sense of the unity forged through four periods of intense prayer, discussion, and reflection. Also present for this final event were the observers from other Christian churches, grown from a mere handful in the first period of the council to more than a hundred, most of them witnesses to the heart-to-heart sharing of those who had voice and vote in the hall. Of these, many could say that their own observations had been voiced on the council floor by bishops who grasped their insights and agreed that others should hear them.

The task since the end of the council has been to explain the meaning and consequences of the council's actions. The task is ongoing. In 1984, we bishops of the United States met in Collegeville, Minnesota, to prepare for the extraordinary synod the following year. Beforehand, I consulted with the laity in the diocese in which I served. They told me, "The changes in the liturgy have been a blessing, but we miss the sense of the sacred we often had, and ecumenism is a great blessing, but something has happened to the clarity of Catholic teaching."

The synod of 1985 took steps to remedy complaints from around the world: a catechism was commissioned to respond to the need for doctrinal clarity, and steps were taken to be sure that our worship could regain, where needed, a sense of the transcendent God.

In his travels throughout the world, Pope John Paul II was the Lord's own tool in making the council come alive, especially in leading celebrations of the Eucharist. His encyclicals, too, pushed ahead the themes of the council, especially its missionary nature. He was the great Catholic evangelist of his day, preaching the gospel of Jesus to unparalleled numbers of people. And he developed, in ways undreamed of at the council, the themes of ecumenical and interreligious openness. I think here of his visits to the United States in 1987 and to the Holy Land in 2000. What were principles stated at and hoped for during Vatican II became ways of life: consider the extraordinary interreligious meetings at Assisi in 1986 and 2002. On both occasions Pope John Paul II gathered leaders from all major religions of the world to pray for peace.

In November 2000, at the death camp at Majdanik, just outside of Lublin, I witnessed a deeply moving service inspired by the teaching of the pope. The Romanian Orthodox Patriarch, the Chief Rabbi of Rome, the Muslim Imam of Poland and the ranking Protestant clergyman of the land helped lead the service. I had a part, reading in English the psalm with the words, "Pray for the peace of Jerusalem." The hour-and-a-half program was televised live through all of Poland. All could hear the testimony of survivors that the loudspeakers carried as we walked, some 4,000 strong, from station to station in the camp. By the end all felt the seriousness and the weight of the sad memories of the camp, and I was reminded of another reality.

When Pope John Paul II was born, his land was home to the largest number of Jews in the world. When he was ordained a priest a quarter of a century later—after the Nazis had taken the lives of millions of Jews— only a pitiful remnant remained. This priest from Poland seized the opportunity not just of a lifetime but of a millennium. The world will be forever better for it.

This is the hope and vitality of the council that continues to stimulate and enliven the fishers who want to let down their nets; this is the tradition and history that is the spiritual foundation of those shepherds who want to preserve with love the precious heritage of the church.

CHAPTER 2

The Church as One

Martin E. Marty

Martin E. Marty was born February 5, 1928, in West Point, Nebraska. He attended Lutheran seminaries, was ordained in 1952, and served as a parish pastor for eleven years. He says he cannot remember "not being ecumenically-minded," even though he was brought up in the Missouri Synod, which forbade all ecumenical contact. Since 1956 he has been involved in an editorial capacity with The Christian Century, *from which base he covered the Second Vatican Council, Third Session (which he also "crashed," as if an official observer).*

While a pastor he received a doctorate from the University of Chicago, where he taught (as the Fairfax M. Cone Distinguished Service Professor) from 1963 to 1998. He was founding president of the Park Ridge Center for the Study of Health, Faith, and Ethics, and a member of the Board of Regents at St. Olaf College, Northfield, Minnesota (1988–2001), where he was chair and where he served as interim president late in 2000. He holds sixty-five honorary degrees. Among his other honors are the National Humanities Medal, the National Book Award, and the Medal of the American Academy of Arts and Sciences. He has been president of the American Catholic Historical Association, the American Society of Church History, and the American Academy of Religion. The Martin Marty Center at the University of Chicago, the Martin Marty Prize of the American Academy of Religion— both devoted to public religion, a concept that has concerned him for decades—and the Martin Marty Chair at St. Olaf College honor his themes.

He has written more than fifty books, including the three-volume Modern American Religion. *He continues to edit* Second Opinion *and the newsletter* Context.

Marty now shares a "studio/study" with his photographer son Micah, with whom he has collaborated on five books. He enjoys and shares the interests of his musician-wife, Harriet, and the company of their extended family, is working on additional books, and does regular lecturing and consulting.

The year before the great changes came to South Africa, my wife and I spent six winter weeks in Cape Town. The change agents in the Kairos movement and the university there—both in strong dissent—were our hosts. "Schedule whatever you wish," we told our hosts, even as we struggled to get a visa. My University of Chicago ties seemed not to disturb authorities. The editorial post at the ecumenical weekly *The Christian Century* evidently appeared to be more subversive of apartheid than the academic tie.

Those hosts did what we wanted, filling our calendar with surprises. On the night we landed in Cape Town we took a walk from our guest house and, passing St. George's (Anglican) Cathedral, we saw a sign notifying passersby that Martin E. Marty of Chicago was to preach next week. That was news to me, so I scrambled to prepare. We had heard that the cathedral of the see over which Bishop Desmond Tutu presided was an imperial outpost, and that he was a hypocrite who "talked poor" but lived in the luxurious colonial bishop's house, removed from daily struggles.

The Martys attended Sunday morning. As we walked into the narthex we saw a bulletin board with a posting of the names of about two hundred parishioners whose whereabouts were unknown. They were detainees, suspects, spirited from view of respectables—but not from the prayerful hearts of the people at worship. The names did not suggest imperial splendor or colonialist homogeneity. There were Anglos, Afrikaners, blacks, Malaysians and more, designated by ethnic names chosen by some and imposed by others. Yes, the old brass plates with names of donors, heroes and heroines, and ecclesiastics were on the walls, all burnished. Many of them might not have understood or been cheered by what went on within those sacred walls late in the twentieth century, but the worshipers seemed to have had no difficulty praying for the imprisoned as well as the imprisoners of many faiths and no faith. Seldom has the ecumenical reality been more palpable.

Then, to the other extreme, same winter, same country, same peoples, but this time poorer ones. I was to preach in a Methodist-friendly mission church in one of the townships, led there by a friend who later came for his doctorate at the University of Chicago. These were not the poorest of the poor; in South Africa then it was not easy to gain access to such utterly "underclassed" and left-out ones. Still, this middle-lower-class group could not afford hymnals. When it came time to sing, the pastor would belt out a line. Then "Lucas" would play the line, after which we all sang it. On to the next line, and the next. The congregation was more homogeneous than the one the week before: mainly "colored" though, I learned, ecumenically mixed. Lucas had been a jazz pianist, and now he was "serving the Lord."

After church he and my musician wife jammed a bit, and then we went to some members' home. There in confined space lived a couple with five sons, median age twenty. All Christian. All unemployed. We visited, were served tea and cookies, and then went back to church. I remember the mother saying that, while the sons were all Christian, for a few krugerrands any one of them would "pop"—she gestured as if shooting a pistol—a police officer of the sort that had been oppressing them and their pastor. Their pastor had raised private sums to improve the sewer system in that community where, after storms, fecal material would be backed up into the homes, and the government did not care. Such fundraising as his was subversive, and our friend was regularly picked up for interrogation and harassment. Oh, how could this family afford treats for us? "They've eaten only potatoes since Thursday; we," the pastor and wife, "secretly donated the treats, so they could have the dignity of being hosts."

As at the cathedral, we were having an ecumenical experience, but did not yet have it reinforced. Back at the church, it became time to say good-bye. I hope it did not sound condescending when I thanked them and said, "You have done so much for us"—as by example they had done and still do—"now, what can we do for you." I know that's not a gracious way to receive a gift, but sometimes grace and gracefulness elude me. They did not elude the congregation: answers came from several and nods of the head from all: "Just do what you and your home congregation do for us every week—pray for us." Oh! Ask for money and we'd have some ready. Prayer? As we do every week? Here they were, thinking of us, and we in our remoteness and luxury never gave thought to them. We have, ever since.

Scene three, same winter: we also visited a Lutheran theologian in Johannesburg. He was "under the ban." Punished. For what? For writing a commentary on the book of Ephesians, a Pauline-type writing that also represented subversion. Our professor-host was not subversive. Ephesians was and is: there is too much talk in it about Christ breaking down barriers. The authorities had taken the scholar to prison and confined him with five Dutch Reformed Christians, who had demonstrated expertise in robbing banks and knowing their Bible and prayer. For them to have a fellow white—the ecumenical "I" wants to say, a *Lutheran*, yet!—there to taint them and undercut their extramural, pre- and post-prison way of life, was abhorrent. So in the chill of the prison they all had urinated on the pastoral scholar and smeared him with shaving cream, until he caught pneumonia.

The authorities, fearing he would die and thus embarrass them and South Africa, released him and confined him under the ban. We had met this practice before, during our weeks there. I do not remember the rules exactly, but they were all designed to dehumanize and prevent communication. The under-the-ban person could not make public appearances, publish anything, including a Bible commentary, or have any dealings beyond his walls. Within them, he dare never be in a room with more than two other people. Now here were we two. His daughter wanted to bring in coffee and cookies. While she wheeled the cart in, the professor, aware of surveillance instruments, stepped out, so we would stay with our allowed three. What about our driver (who doubled as a council of churches' staffer) who was listening in and sometimes speaking up? "I am black, so I don't count as a person."

Our little Bible class on Ephesians that day, with that black driver present, was another ecumenical moment across continents and across national and ecclesiastical and racial boundaries. Ephesians could never just lie there inert after that day; it has been "ert" to us ever since, a stimulant as we reckon with walls that we, or others, erect to break the body of Christ and cause divorce and separation in the human family.

Harriet and I are privileged to have such moments, whether in South Africa, Japan, Hawaii, Russia, Slovakia, or ecumenically tired and worn Western Europe or the United States. From them we draw sustenance and a new awareness of why the affirmation of "one" as a mark of the church cannot not be centrally affirmed. Technically, that mark turns us to the ontology of the church, the missing prop or goal of the church in an age of churchly marketing, "knowing Jesus as my personal Savior," going to "the church of my choice," or other ways in which the body of Christ gets replaced by "voluntary associational" thinking. Of course, Christian profession has to be personal, individual, and, of course, some element of selection and marketing is present. However, in all decisive encounters when the realization of oneness as command and promise, challenge and hope, is most vivid, what strikes us is that the "being" of the church antecedes all choice. The one-ness of the church is bone-deep in practical life and soul-deep in spiritual life. And those two "lives" are themselves wedded and one in the body of Christ, the "one, holy, catholic, and apostolic church." I could witness more, but I have to scoot off now to sing a *Te Deum*, which is more appropriate than storytelling or marketing or sermonizing when we think of this mark of the church.

CHAPTER 3

The Church Is Holy

Gillian T.W. Ahlgren

Gillian T.W. Ahlgren is professor of theology at Xavier University, where she has been teaching since 1990. Her doctorate in the history of Christianity is from the Divinity School of the University of Chicago. A church historian by trade, she specializes in the Christian mystical tradition, particularly in its medieval and reformation developments. She is the author of four books: Teresa of Avila and the Politics of Sanctity, Human Person and the Church, Entering Teresa of Avila's Interior Castle: A Reader's Companion, *and* The Inquisition of Francisca: A Sixteenth-Century Visionary on Trial. *She is currently at work on a monograph exploring the contributions of the Christian mystical tradition to a theology of sacramental marriage.*

Affirming the holiness of the church can be, at times, an extraordinary act of faith, even though we do it regularly through our creedal statements. Through the imitation of Christ and by the grace and love of God, Christians seek, in community, the fullness of the reign of God. Thus the holiness of the church is not so much a completed reality as a hope, a promise, and a form of life possible only in God. That does not mean, however, that we cannot affirm the church as holy in this, our present reality. All visible signs of the reign of God and the work of the Holy Spirit— preaching the message of the reign of God, serving others, and promoting communion—point to the life of holiness Christians can know and experience as members of the body of Christ.

To affirm the church as holy requires an operative definition of holiness. This definition cannot be merely theoretical or a listing of qualities or attributes akin to the traditional Christian virtues, as helpful as they may be. To walk meaningfully on the road to holiness—or, to be "the pilgrim church on earth"—is to commit ourselves, individually and communally, to the imitation of Christ and to taking Christ as our companion in the journey toward God. Clearly, this requires some knowledge of Christ, a knowledge not only of the historical Jesus and the message of the gospels—a message that recalled earlier prophetic challenges to justice, compassion, and simplicity, that stirred hearts and minds to deeper forms of religious life, and that ultimately led to an ignominious death on the cross—but also of Christ's ongoing, incarnate presence in humanity. It requires faithful reflection on scriptural promises like "I will not leave you orphaned; I am coming to you"[57] in light of the violence, poverty, and hopelessness that is often part and parcel of our lived experience. And it requires affirming the possibility that, in Christ and because of the invitation of a loving, self-giving God, we are graced to live in ongoing relationship with God, in and with one another. This is a relationality predicated upon the promise of Christ that "where two or more are gathered in my name, I will be with you," a unitive sharing of fullness of life, in and through Christ.

This notion of *communio*, the sharing in the body of Christ, is the essence of the church's claim to holiness. The church as the mystical body of Christ is a communion of the faithful that spans time and space. It is made up of all those, past and present, who have been touched by the word of God, have sought to walk with Christ and to live in imitation of Christ. All those who truly seek life in Christ are invited into the communion of saints by the God made flesh who came to bring abundance of life. This is the liberating message of the gospel and the reality that the church strives to make present to all. Inspired by the Holy Spirit, we are sent forth to embody the ideals and values of the gospel, to make manifest the love that makes all things new and binds all things together.

Although the term communion is perhaps the most useful and helpful conceptual term today for fleshing out the meaning of the church as holy, we should recognize that communion ecclesiology is hardly new. In fact, a notion of *communio* was alive and well in the letters of Ignatius of Antioch (d. 107), who, on his way to face martyrdom in Rome, reflected on the ways in which Christians communally manifest and replicate the incarnate body of Christ in their very being. Thus Ignatius initiates a long tradition of reflection on *communio* as a way of participating in the mystical body of Christ, the nexus of intersections of humanity and divinity within each human person and within humanity collectively. For most Christian mystics this was not an abstract question, contemplated outside the realm of concrete, historical circumstances. Nor was it a spiritual practice divorced from the grit of human existence. As the examples of Francis of Assisi, Catherine of Siena, and Teresa of Avila demonstrate clearly, the mystical life required, of individuals and of the church they loved, ongoing reform and the adoption of a prophetic voice. It meant committed engagement in and with the incarnate Christ, revealed over and over in human suffering and vulnerability.

When the model of *communio* emerged as an interpretive tool for the documents of Vatican II, it appeared to supplant the council's language of the church as the people of God, and it seemed that the immanence of God in humanity dropped out of the equation. It was feared that *communio* was a way of focusing attention on the ideal church, an illusory eschatological hope, which can never be realized on earth, and thereby deflecting legitimate concerns about the need for structural change within the institution or about the church's activity in the world as an agent for prophetic change. What I would like to argue, however, is that a proper understanding of *communio*, informed by the Trinitarian relationship— that is, of persons who are in right relationship to one another and whose relational personhood is essential to its being—is critical in helping us bridge gaps between the theory of holiness and its practice here and now.

Communio is a rich and multivalent term that allows us to merge many allusions to Christian principles and practices. First and perhaps most importantly, *communio* recalls the Eucharist as the foundational principle of union in the body of Christ. Through communion we take in the mystery of being invited to be guests at Christ's own table, to sit together there in order to partake of all that Christ and the saving knowledge of God offers us, as individuals, as communities, and as a species. A eucharistic way of being church also forces us to seek out the "real presence" of Christ in the concrete circumstances of our daily lives—that is, it requires us to commit ourselves to the possibility of God's ongoing, sacramental communication of divinity in and through the ordinary—or, as some would have it, the possibility of finding God in all things.

Second, *communio* reminds us that the mystery of being one in Christ spans all time and space. In and through this body of Christ that is the church, we are part of a larger communion of saints, a tradition made up of human persons who have committed themselves to the imitation of Christ and to the practice of gospel values, a community marked by principles of inclusiveness, interdependence, and cooperation, structured according to the perichoretic model of the Trinity, in which there is "mutual giving and receiving, without separateness, or subordination or division."[58] This understanding of *communio* as the definition of holiness allows for greater accountability and can serve as the barometer of the authenticity of our Christian witness.

Finally, *communio* recalls for us that, as people created in the image of God, we participate at some level in the Trinitarian nature of God. Thus, when *communio* defines church, we recognize the fundamental interrelationship of persons, whose commitment to one another's growth, well-being, dignity, and giftedness is the most basic requirement of membership in the body of Christ. Thus, to be a part of the church as holy is to live in reverent relationality with all of humanity—indeed, with the entire universe—as God's beloved creation. It is to affirm, through our actions and choices, the sanctity of all that God has created, reinforcing the sacramentality of life.

Understanding the church as a sacrament—that is, as a sign that makes present the reality to which it points—suggests that the inspired movement of all people to live in the love of God, graced into that reality by God's own invitation to communion with one another, is what makes the church holy. That we fall short of that reality, as individuals, as communities, and as an institution, is a constant reminder of our own fallibility as humans and our ongoing need for the grace of the sacraments, which remind us of our Christian vocation and welcome us back into the possibility of communion in Christ.

As Catherine LaCugna suggested, "The doctrine of the Trinity reminds that in God there is neither hierarchy nor inequality, neither division nor competition, but only unity in love and diversity. The Christian community is the image or icon of the invisible God when its communitarian life mirrors the inclusivity of divine love."[59] Affirming the church as holy reflects our ongoing commitment to making that vision our current reality. It is not an invitation to religious self-satisfaction, a self-congratulatory statement of moral superiority, or an endorsement of structures that promote or even tolerate division or subordination. Rather, it is an affirmation of our acceptance of the radical challenge to embody, in all our interpersonal and socio-political relations, Christ's own ministry of service to the fullness of life for all humanity. Thus the holy church models in its teachings and actions, in its internal patterns of relationship, and in its service to the world a new way of being, as persons bound together in the body of Christ, a Christ in whom, as Paul affirms, there is neither Jew nor Greek, slave nor free, male nor female.

CHAPTER 4

The Church Is Holy

Robert Ellsberg

Robert Ellsberg was born on December 13, 1955, and grew up in Los Angeles. He was raised by his mother in the Episcopal Church. His father, Daniel Ellsberg, was a government advisor who was arrested, when Robert was fifteen, for releasing the top secret Pentagon Papers to the press. Consequently, as he was growing up, the Vietnam War and issues of conscience and personal witness were prominent in his life.

Ellsberg went to Harvard as an undergraduate in 1973 but dropped out when he was nineteen to work at the Catholic Worker in New York City. He remained there for the next five years—the last years in the life of Dorothy Day. For two years he served as managing editor of The Catholic Worker *paper. In 1980, prior to returning to Harvard to study religion and literature, he was received into the Catholic Church. Dorothy Day died soon afterward, and he edited an anthology of her writings.*

After graduating in 1982, Ellsberg spent a year traveling in Latin America and then returned to Harvard Divinity School to study theology. He withdrew from doctoral studies in 1987 to accept the job as editor in chief of Orbis Books, the publishing arm of Maryknoll. He has worked at Orbis for the past eighteen years, living in Ossining, New York, with his wife and three children.

Mr. Ellsberg has written and edited a number of books, including anthologies of Gandhi, Flannery O'Connor, Carlo Carretto, Thich Nhat Hanh, and Charles de Foucauld. His interests have always involved a conversation with those he admires. This interest resulted in the writing of All Saints: Daily Reflections on Saints, Prophets and Witnesses for Our Time, *as well as his subsequent books,* The Saints' Guide to Happiness *and* Blessed Among All Women: Women Saints, Prophets and Witnesses for Our Time.

Among the four traditional "marks" of the church, holiness is arguably the most indispensable, the one that relates most directly to its very purpose. The marks of unity, catholicity, and apostolicity are all essential. And yet where holiness is absent you may have many things—but not the church of Christ. For a church that is not marked by holiness is lacking "the one thing necessary"—the visible presence of the divine life.

And yet it is not always an easy matter to identify this holiness, especially when we are so frequently reminded of the church's sins and failings. Clearly the church's holiness does not depend on the moral perfection of its members. But neither is it simply an abstract predicate that refers in some way to ecclesiastical authority, liturgy, learned theology, or expressions of piety. Repeatedly in the gospels Jesus distinguishes the path of true devotion from formal religious practice: "Not all who say 'Lord, Lord' will enter the kingdom of heaven, but only those who do the will of the Father." And what is God's will? Jesus summarized this simply: that we love God with our whole hearts, souls, and minds, and our neighbors as ourselves. The church is holy inasmuch as it reflects this love and effectively promotes it among its members.

One of the ways the church promotes this teaching is through the memory and veneration of those who most faithfully embodied it: the saints, or literally, the "holy ones." This was brought home to me when I first became a Catholic. A friend presented me with the Penguin book of saints with the inscription: "Welcome to the Catholic Church. The saints are the best thing about us!" In subsequent years I spent much time pondering the meaning of those words. Insofar as the church is the body of Christ, the saints are indeed the best thing "about us." They are those who show our best face— who show us what we could be, what we ought to be, what we are called to be, and who guide us and draw us forth by their example and their prayers.

The statement ceases to be true, however, when we think of the saints as a completely different category of Christian—as perfect people, free of faults, doubts, or personal idiosyncrasies. Unfortunately, the traditional cult of the saints has all too often fostered such conceptions. When I was a child my image of saints was largely derived from stained glass windows. On that basis I concluded that they lived a long time ago, they were usually priests or nuns; they had mystical visions, or performed miracles; they suffered and died in some gruesome fashion; they never had so much as an impure thought, and they were only happy when they were kneeling in church. If that is our image of saints, we might assume that the goal of holiness is only for the exceptional few.

And yet the teaching of the church is quite different. Saints are not a special category of Christian. Those officially designated as saints are simply those who have realized to an exceptional extent the vocation to which all Christians are called. For what does it really mean to call ourselves Christian if it doesn't mean embracing the challenge of sanctification—the process, as St. Paul put it, of "putting off the old person and putting on Christ." When we respond to this call we are simply embracing the logic of our baptismal vows, the same promises made by every Christian, to turn away from the allure of sin and turn toward God.

In the early church St. Paul addressed all Christians as saints—not just the spiritual prodigies among them. He addressed his letters to "the saints who live in Corinth" or whatever community he was writing to. The point was that all Christians could be *characterized* or *identified* by their goal, by the object of their desire and striving. And why else, in those perilous times, would someone decide to become a Christian if not to walk the path of sanctification?

A holy person, according to this view, is someone who walks the path of holiness, the path that leads ever closer to God. Some manage to progress a long way down that path. They literally *remind* us of God. And the church calls them "saints." But we do ourselves and the saints a great disservice if we simply set them up on a pedestal in some "Hall of Fame," far removed from the rest of us ordinary mortals.

This tendency began in the early church as gradually the emphasis shifted from the saint as a heroic witness to Christ to the saint as a focus of sacred power. Over time interest in the actual lives of the saints gave way to interest in the miracles associated with their intercession and their relics. Vestiges of this tendency continue in the process of canonization—particularly the way that certified medical miracles serve as an indispensable condition in the process of naming a saint.

The process of canonization often serves to put holy people on a pedestal. But when we look behind the stained glass windows and the plaster statues and get to know the flesh and blood men and women we call saints, we likely find people not so different from ourselves, people driven by the same hopes and desires, struggling with the same weaknesses and doubts, challenged as we are to find some way of living an authentic life in the historical moment in which they found themselves.

When we think of the saints as those who walk the path of holiness, at once we become more aware of all that links them with our struggles rather than all that sets them apart. Holiness, after all, is not some abstract quality. It is a resemblance to God that emerges in a person's total response to the concrete circumstances of his or her life. We recognize it not just be tallying up the quantity of good deeds or miraculous signs, but by discerning the patterns of divine grace woven into the design of their lives.

How does the story of a person's life correspond to the story that God is telling us through the life of Jesus? In light of that question we can begin to read the story of God's grace in the stories of all kinds of people who are not canonized and may never be candidates for official sainthood. And in that light we may come to recognize the holiness of the church not just in the limited company of certain exceptional people, but in terms of the larger movement of the whole pilgrim people of God, as we struggle to conform our lives to the pattern of the gospel.

According to Jean Pierre de Caussade, the eighteenth-century Jesuit, "The Holy Spirit writes no more Gospels except in our hearts. All we do from moment to moment is live this new gospel of the Holy Spirit. We, if we are holy, are the paper; our sufferings and our actions are the ink. The workings of the Holy Spirit are his pen, and with it he writes a living gospel."

The holiness of the church is not a guarantee against failure, weakness, or temptation. It is the mark of a community that continually repents of its flaws and brokenness, that grows in the love of Christ, and so by its witness in the world continues to write a living gospel.

CHAPTER 5

The Church Is Catholic

Cardinal Avery Dulles, SJ

Avery Dulles, SJ, an internationally known author and lecturer, was born in Auburn, New York, on August 24, 1918. He received his primary school education in New York City, and attended secondary schools in Switzerland and New England. After graduating from Harvard College in 1940, he spent a year and a half in Harvard Law School before serving in the United States Navy, emerging with the rank of lieutenant.

Upon his discharge from the Navy in 1946, Dulles entered the Society of Jesus, and was ordained to the priesthood in 1956. He received the licentiate in philosophy and the licentiate in sacred theology, both from Woodstock College in Maryland, and was awarded the doctorate in sacred theology from the Gregorian University in Rome.

During the time of Vatican Council II, Fr. Dulles was teaching at Woodstock College (1960–74). He was a professor at The Catholic University of America (1974–88). Since 1988, he has been the Laurence J. McGinley Professor of Religion and Theology at Fordham University. He has also been a visiting professor at universities and seminaries both in the United States and abroad. The author of over 650 articles on theological topics, Dulles has published twenty-one books including Models of the Church, Models of Revelation, The Catholicity of the Church, The Craft of Theology, The Assurance of Things Hoped For: A Theology of Christian Faith, *and his latest book,* The New World of Faith.

Past president of both the Catholic Theological Society of America and the American Theological Society, Dulles has served on the International Theological Commission and as a member of the United States Lutheran/ Roman Catholic Dialogue. He serves as a consultor to the Committee on

Doctrine of the United States Conference of Catholic Bishops and an Associate Fellow of the Woodstock Theological Center in Washington, DC. His awards include Phi Beta Kappa, the Croix de Guerre, the Cardinal Spellman Award for distinguished achievement in theology, the Boston College Presidential Bicentennial Award, the Religious Education Forum Award from the National Catholic Educational Association, America magazine's Campion Award, the F. Sadlier Dinger Award for contributions to the cate- chetical ministry of the church, and twenty-one honorary doctorates. In February 2001 he was appointed cardinal.

The church is catholic.[60] Since the Reformation it had become common in Roman Catholic apologetics to assert that the church of Christ, with its four marks of unity, holiness, catholicity, and apostolicity, was simply identical with the Roman Catholic communion, and that catholicity, consequently, belonged to it alone. In opposition to the Anglo-Catholics, the Holy Office declared in 1864: "No other church is catholic except that which is built on the one individual Peter, and which grows up into one body closely joined and knit together [see Eph 4:16] in the unity of faith and love."

Vatican Council II, without directly contradicting this doctrine, nuanced it in a remarkable way. In its Dogmatic Constitution on the Church it predicated catholicity not directly of the Roman Catholic Church but rather of the church of Christ, which the council depicted as "subsisting" in the Catholic Church (*Lumen gentium* [LG] 8), so that the fullness of catholicity was not obtainable except in communion with Rome (*Unitatis redintegratio* [UR] 4). But the church of Christ was held to be present in some measure in other Christian communities, which could participate in catholicity to the extent that they continued to accept and live by the authentic Christian heritage. The Decree on Ecumenism could therefore teach that the "entire heritage of spirituality and liturgy, of disci- pline and theology" in the various traditions of the Orthodox churches "belongs to the full catholic and apostolic character of the Church" (UR 17), and that "some Catholic traditions and institutions continue to exist in certain Western communities, such as the Anglican Communion" (UR 13). Vatican II's concept of catholicity may therefore be called cautiously ecumenical rather than narrowly confessional.

The council's vision of the church, moreover, was not limited to the Christian arena. While acknowledging that the church may at times appear as a "little flock," the council asserted that Christ, the universal Savior, continues to use it as an instrument for the redemption of all (LG

9). "All are called to be part of this catholic unity of the People of God" (LG 13). The Dogmatic Constitution on the Church goes on to assert that all human beings, even those to whom the gospel has not as yet been preached, are related to the church of Christ (LG 16). This general statement is then specified with respect to four groups: Jews, Muslims, adherents of other religions, and atheists. None of these groups is excluded from the redemptive influence of Christ, which impels its recipients toward the catholic unity of the church. The grace of Christ thus operates in a secret way in all persons of good will, ordering them toward salvation and disposing them to accept the gospel if and when they hear it credibly proclaimed (LG 16–17).

The church, according to Vatican II, achieves its catholicity in a historically palpable way by evangelizing all peoples. Missionary activity is therefore seen both as an expression and as an intensification of the church's catholicity. By evangelizing the world the church can become in manifest actuality what in principle it has been from its origins—the universal communion of all men and women with God in Christ. "It is plain, then," we read in the Decree on Missionary Activity, "that missionary activity wells up from the Church's innermost nature and spreads abroad her saving faith. It perfects her Catholic unity by expanding it" (*Ad gentes* [AG] 6). The New Covenant, according to the same decree, calls for a church that speaks all tongues and "thus overcomes the divisiveness of Babel" (AG 4). Inspired by this vision, the church "prays and labors in order that the entire world may become the People of God, the Body of the Lord, and the Temple of the Holy Spirit" (LG 17).

At various points in its documents, Vatican II acknowledged that the catholicity of the church is in fact limited. One reason has already been indicated: the failure of Christian missionary activity to have effectively reached all peoples and all individuals with the good news of Jesus Christ. A second reason, chiefly treated in the Decree on Ecumenism, is the inner dividedness of Christianity itself. To overcome this, the church is under grave obligation to pursue the apostolate of Christian unity. "The divisions among Christians," says the Decree, "prevent the Church from effecting the fullness of catholicity proper to her in those of her children who, though joined to her by baptism, are yet separated from full communion with her" (UR 4). This renders it "difficult for the Church to express in actual life her full catholicity in all its aspects" (*ibid*). In other words, the Catholic Church is a less splendid expression than it ought to be of Christ's universal redemptive power.

A third obstacle to catholicity is the failure of Catholics themselves to realize in their own household the kind of unity God wills for the church. In this connection the Decree on Ecumenism insists on the importance of preserving a healthy freedom and diversity in styles of spirituality, discipline, and liturgy, and in the formulation of revealed truth (UR 16–17). The council at this point echoes the axiom popularized by Pope John XXIII: unity in necessary matters, freedom in others, and charity in all.

A new development in Vatican II, in comparison with previous official Catholic teaching, is the doctrine that the whole Catholic Church is present and operative in the local church. This dynamic presence is variously attributed to the bishop, the gospel, and especially to the Eucharist, as the sacrament of unity in which Christ himself is truly present with his grace (LG 26, *Christus Dominus* [CD] 11).

In summary, Vatican II presents catholicity not as a monotonous repetition of identical elements but rather as reconciled diversity. It is a unity among individuals and groups who retain their distinctive characteristics, who enjoy different spiritual gifts, and are by that very diversity better equipped to serve one another and thus advance the common good. Individual Christians and local churches are bound to one another in mutual service and mutual receptivity. This relationship is founded not upon domination but on a free exchange of trust and respect.

Thanks to Christ's faithfulness to his promise to be with his people, catholicity is never lacking to the church. But it is dynamic and expansive; it continually presses forward to a fullness and inclusiveness not yet attained. It is a ferment at work in the Catholic Church and in every authentic Christian community. Even beyond the borders of explicit Christianity, the grace of Christ, working in the hearts of all who are open to it, brings individuals and groups into a saving relationship with the Church catholic, the God-given sign and sacrament of the ultimate unity to which the entire human race is called. Thus the Catholic Church is, according to the teaching of Vatican II, "a lasting and sure seed of unity, hope, and salvation for the whole human race" (LG 9).

Vatican II's doctrine of catholicity is not, to be sure, a totally new invention. It is for the most part a selection and recombination of elements taken from the tradition. It draws heavily on the New Testament and on ancient theologians such as Irenaeus and Eusebius, Augustine and Aquinas. Here and there one can perhaps detect the influence of a Johann Adam Möhler, a John Henry Newman, an Henri de Lubac, and especially an Yves Congar. Although securely rooted in the tradition, the council's teaching on catholicity is attuned to the new situation that became evident after World War II. It takes cognizance of the plurality of cultures, the other Christian churches, the non-Christian religions, and atheism. Optimistic without being overweening, modest without being abject, this treatment of catholicity is serene and attractive. In comparison with papal teaching of the nineteenth century, Vatican II shows a remarkable respect for freedom and diversity, both within the church and in the larger sphere of human relations.

CHAPTER 6

The Church Is Catholic

Michael Novak

Michael Novak currently holds the George Frederick Jewett Chair in Religion and Public Policy at the American Enterprise Institute in Washington, DC, where he also serves as Director of Social and Political Studies. Mr. Novak has served as Ambassador of the U.S. Delegation to the U.N. Human Rights Commission (1981–82), as head of the U.S. Delegation to the Conference on Security and Cooperation in Europe (1986), and as a member of the Presidential Task Force on Project Economic Justice (1985).

Mr. Novak has authored more than twenty books, including The Spirit of Democratic Capitalism, Will It Liberate? Questions About Liberation Theology, *and* The Catholic Ethic and the Spirit of Capitalism. *He was co-founder of the publications* This World, Crisis, *and* First Things. *He was also the publisher and editor of* Crisis *until 1996. Mr. Novak has published regular columns in* National Review *and* Forbes Magazine, *and he has published essays in* The New Republic, Commentary, The Atlantic, *and many other journals here and overseas.*

Mr. Novak was born in Johnstown, Pennsylvania. He studied at The Catholic University of America and Harvard University, where he earned a master's degree in history and philosophy of religion. He has taught at Stanford University, SUNY Old Westbury, Syracuse University, and Notre Dame. In 1978 he joined the American Enterprise Institute as a resident scholar.

Mr. Novak has received more than a dozen honorary degrees and numerous awards, including the George Washington Honor Medal from the Freedom Foundation (1984), the International Award from the Institution for World Capitalism (1994), and the Templeton Prize for Progress in Religion, which was awarded in 1994 at Buckingham Palace in London.

The Church Is Catholic[61]

The prophet motive leads easily to the sectarian impulse, which is quite the opposite to the Catholic impulse. The sectarian impulse seeks a church of the like-minded, the saved, the saintly, the small homogeneous community. Its normal temptation is to see all others as less than holy and all worldly tasks as somehow corrupt. The sectarian normally sees the outside world as depraved, while trying to nourish a small band of the saved against surrounding darkness....

By contrast, we believe in the Catholic Church. The first meaning of this commitment is that we are *not sectarian*; we resist the sectarian impulse. The Catholic spirit does not believe that the church is a church of the saved, the saints, the true believers. It is, rather, a gathering of the struggling, the voyaging, the weak, those in whom there remains much unbelief, and sinners. *Lamb of God, you take away the sins of the world: have mercy on us.* Further, the Catholic spirit does not hold that this world or its institutions are depraved. In Greek culture, in Roman law, in Gothic vitalities, in democratic institutions, in economic progress it sees signs of grace. Such things are of this world, surely, and are not the full and proper locus of human salvation. On the other hand, it is the vocation of Catholics to labor in and to build up such institutions, shaping them by degrees ever more closely according to the spirit of the gospels. For grace normally works not all at once but gradually, as yeast in dough, as a mustard seed buried from sight. The sectarian spirit sees the church as far more pure than does the Catholic spirit and the world as far more depraved. To believe in a Catholic Church is to accept a church of sinners and a world in which grace gradually, not without setback, manifests itself in humble institutions which are never more than sinful and imperfect.

The Catholic spirit contrasts, as well, with the ethnic spirit. To believe in a Catholic Church is to believe in a church composed of all ethnic groups, all peoples, and all nations. Such belief does not deny a proper role to ethnicity, for Christianity is a religion of incarnation, of flesh and time and place and history. It respects the incarnate nature of human life. The human family is not universalist but particular; human peoples are differentiated by cultures, languages, traditions, customs, and habits. Christianity does not (should not) ride roughshod over these, for to wipe out such things would be to treat humans as though they were angels, rational spirits disembodied from the particularities of history. To be human is to be ethnic. The Catholic spirit, then, is compatible with the ethnic spirit but is not identical to it. The Catholic spirit respects ethnic identity, but opposes ethnocentrism....

Third, then, to believe in a Catholic Church is to believe in an inclusive church, seeking to discern in all cultures and all particular histories the workings of grace from the beginning. All peoples spring from the Creator, have been made in the image of the Word, and have felt the workings of the Spirit. It remains true that the message of Jesus comes filtered through history, implanted in history at one time and in one place, not everywhere at once. Centuries were required before this message was, in fact, carried to all nations, until now there remain few spots in the world to which the news of Jesus has not been carried. In the nature of things, many distortions have also arisen. As we each come to understand the message more clearly for ourselves, so also the nations are also led to ever fuller understanding.

The British layman Donald Nicholl has brilliantly written about the Catholic spirit in this context as a spirit of *pleroma*, the spirit of fullness. In a sense, the Catholic spirit grows ever larger through its contact with the nations. The gospels meditated upon and lived out in various circumstances reveal new angles of vision. Buddhism and Hinduism, Tao and Islam, and all the other world religions—above all, Judaism—have spiritual riches to teach. They are not merely to be conceived as passive recipients of the Christian message. On the contrary, in the Christian view, Creator, Word, and Spirit have been active everywhere from the beginning, and it is the task of Christians to learn and to discern as well as to preach. Without in the least denying what is distinctive in the Christian word and historical experience, indeed in giving witness to it as clearly and fairly and wisely as they can, Christians are nonetheless well instructed to recognize that the Catholic spirit has not yet reached its appointed fullness.

The Catholic spirit is, therefore, an open spirit. It is open, not in the empty-headed way of being without content and learned convictions of its own, but in the commonsense way of humble charity. Graced as Christian history has undoubtedly been, daily God's grace is yet more abundant still. The Catholic spirit recognizes the obligation, century by century, generation by generation, culture by culture, of becoming larger than it has been, of expanding to its ultimate vocation. Its aim is to incorporate into itself all signs of God's light, beauty, love, liberty, and communion among the world's peoples. Its aim is not to rest self-enclosed, parochial, shut tight, but to remain alert and docile to the teaching of God in history. God's grace, Georges Bernanos writes, is everywhere. It speaks from the grain of sand, from rocket ships that reach the moon, and from every historical experience of the human race. To be Catholic is to try to include within one's faith all God's actions among peoples everywhere. The Catholic spirit is a spirit less of limits than of fullness.

The danger, here, of course, is sentimentality. There are ways of being "all things to all people" that are fraudulent. A premature and merely enthusiastic syncretism can dilute Christianity to nothing more than vacuous good will. The danger of mere eclecticism is great. The danger of gnosticism is still greater.

Thus one may under the abiding power of gnosticism in particular—the single most persistent and potent threat against Christianity—so "spiritualize" Christianity as to deprive it of its actual roots in flesh and history. Christianity is not, cannot be, everything. It denies as well as it affirms. It is falsifiable. Unless it stands for specific interpretations of what is true and false about human experience, it is conceptually empty. The danger of the open spirit is that it may become both intellectually and spiritually otiose. To hold, for example, that the narrative form for human experience embodied in each of the world's religions is equally true is not to honor all but to demean each. Each must be taken seriously in its particular claims. And decisions about each particular truth and particular falsehood must be reached. It is wise to be tentative and respectful. It is not wise to be as open-minded as a sieve. To do so is to abandon every claim to honesty, conscience, and integrity.

Not all faiths, for example, are compatible with the Christian Creed. To hold as part of one's creed a belief in an open church cannot be construed as simply abandoning a creed. That would be absurd.

For it is the lot of humans to proceed to fullness, not as God or angels do, in a glance, all at once. It is to proceed by the ways of embodied spirit, step by painful step, seeking concrete insight and exact verification as one goes, never leaping beyond the evidence, although not hesitating, either, to test new paradigms and new approaches. We proceed in an incarnate way.

Thus, the fourth meaning of Catholic is to love the method of concretion. The Catholic spirit respects the flesh as the Catholic sacraments respect the flesh. Baptism is not solely a spiritual act, although it is that. It is the sensation of cool water flowing on one's brow, a taste of salt upon one's tongue. Receiving the Lord in the Eucharist, one tastes flour and water in a wafer that clings to the roof of one's mouth, melts on one's tongue, and is swallowed, and one tastes wines that differ from occasion to occasion. The Catholic spirit is a spirit of incarnation. Gifts of the spirit seldom come to us apart from the flesh. Faith comes by hearing. Against materialism, the Catholic spirit wishes to say, "Not by bread alone." Against gnosticism, the Catholic spirit wishes to say, "Not by pure spirit alone." The Catholic way is humbly appropriate to our embodied spirits, our slow and plodding ways, our bodies and flesh....

The Catholic view of the faith is quite fleshly. It takes the incarnation so far that it sees grace in everything—in bureaucrats, corporations, public officials, bishops, and even in theologians.

CHAPTER 7

The Church Is
Apostolic

Mary Ann Donovan, SC

Mary Ann Donovan was born in Cincinnati, Ohio. She grew up in a strong German-Irish family in a vibrant parish. Her vocation as a Sister of Charity grew out of her home and upbringing. Like many of her peers, she entered at age eighteen. Not much later came Vatican II. The church of the council, with the accompanying ecumenical movement, shaped the climate in which she went off to Toronto to do doctoral studies in theology. She received the doctorate in 1977. Since then she has been on the faculty of the Jesuit School of Theology at Berkeley, teaching students from around the world, including candidates for the priesthood, other religious, and increasing numbers of lay people.

Her book One Right Reading? A Guide to Irenaeus *was honored with the annual Book Award of the College Theology Society in 1998. Her service to the field of theology has included a term as president of the Catholic Theological Society of America (1997–98). Sister Donovan's current research and teaching interests include the history and women of the early church, patristic and medieval spirituality, feminist questions, and ecumenism. Despite the sometimes depressing news in the daily papers, she reports that she is a happy woman. Over the years she has learned that joy is more an internal state than an external situation. (After all, it is a fruit of the Holy Spirit.)*

Fruitful Apostolicity

More than once I have been asked: "Why in the present state of things do you remain a Catholic?" My reply is simple: "Because the church is my home." It may be bruised, broken, sinful, but it remains central to who I am.

The church—one, holy, catholic, and apostolic—is my home. As my home, I think of the church fundamentally as people. Vatican II piled up metaphors for the church, but it took as a central theme the church as the people of God. (*Lumen gentium* #9; see 1 Pet 2:9–10) As a people, we who are the church are marked by the presence of the Spirit from our baptism. Our law is love. Our destiny is the fullness of the kingdom of God, incorporating all of creation. We are meant to be a seed of hope for the whole human race.

The people in whom we are incorporated through baptism gathers weekly at Eucharist. Eucharist, like all the sacraments, nests within the word. The Scripture readings, and the homily interpreting them, are integral to the eucharistic celebration. While the separate elements—word, sacraments, and teaching of the church—are quite distinguishable, they are typically encountered together. It is through such encounters that we are in contact with the apostolicity of the church in the form of the apostolic tradition. Apostolic is what comes from the witnesses who knew Jesus, in his earthly and/or his risen life among us. Tradition is the way a family or a people remembers its past for the sake of continuity. The "object" of the tradition of the church, that is, the "thing" passed on, is the teaching, "the truth" the apostles received from Christ or from God and passed on to the church. At a minimum, tradition so understood includes word (or Scripture) and sacraments.

When we consider who does the passing on, we turn to the "subject" of tradition. The church, as the living people of God, vivified by the Holy Spirit, is the subject of tradition, that is, the "one" who continues the "traditioning" or passing on. How does this happen? Consider the example of the Eucharist. The oldest narrative of the institution of the Eucharist comes to us from Paul in the formal language of tradition: "For I *received* from the Lord what I also *handed* on to you, that the Lord Jesus on the night when he was betrayed, took a loaf of bread…" (1 Cor 11:23). Paul is making clear that his knowledge of the institution was directly from the Lord. The continuity is through the apostolic witnesses to the deeds and words of Christ in his earthly and risen life. In that sense the apostles are irreplaceable, what the Book of Revelation calls the foundation stones of the new Jerusalem (Rev 21:14). But as the group of witnesses died out, various leaders, including bishops, deacons, prophets, and teachers, came to exercise pastoral care for the church.

During the second century the responsibility to assure continuity of the apostolic tradition was identified as one role of the bishop. In that century teachers who claimed to have secret traditions from the apostles proliferated. The question of the day became: "Who carries the apostolic tradition?" Irenaeus, bishop of Lyons, described how the church's tradition descended from the Lord through the apostles to the bishops, whom the apostles established as their successors. He buttressed this description with reference to the succession lists of the churches (see his *Adversus haereses* III. 1–5). His point is that succession of teaching is not hidden. There are no secret traditions in the church, only the public tradition. This tradition, which he also calls the teaching and the truth, has been deposited in the church just like money in a bank.

Often overlooked is that Irenaeus balanced his presentation of the church as place of authoritative teaching with a presentation of the church as place of the Spirit:

> Where there is the church, there is the Spirit of God; and where the Spirit of God, there is the church and all grace: for the Spirit is Truth. That is why those who do not participate in it are not nourished for life from the breasts of the Mother nor do they lay hold of the most brilliant stream flowing from the body of Christ, but they dig for themselves broken cisterns, and they drink water putrid with filth, fleeing the faith of the church lest they be exposed, rejecting the Spirit lest they be taught. (*Adversus haereses* III.24.1)

In this text he completes his presentation by describing the church as the place of the Spirit, and so as the place of living truth. The actions of the church even in teaching are presented as the activity of a nursing mother. Her milk should be like (or perhaps should be) the limpid stream flowing from Christ's body. It is by contrast with this vision of the church that false teaching can be seen as putrid water flowing from broken cisterns.

Thus, when we affirm that we believe in "one, holy, catholic, and *apostolic* church," *apostolic* denotes that we believe in a church which, though battered, bruised, and sinful, is in continuity with the teaching received through the apostles and handed on (traditioned) by the bishops. Christ did not promise to keep the church free from sin. He promised to remain with it. He also asked the Father, who sent another Advocate, the Holy Spirit, to be with it.

Bear in mind that the apostles themselves were not unbattered. It is helpful to remember that, of those whom Jesus chose, two betrayed him. Judas died a traitor. Peter died a martyr. Peter's story may help us here. Jesus had been arrested and was before Annas. Meanwhile, outside in the courtyard the maid who was the gatekeeper questioned Peter: "You are not also one of this man's disciples, are you?" And Peter said, "I am not" (Jn

18:17). Yet, earlier that very evening Peter had said to Jesus, "Lord, why can I not follow you now? I will lay down my life for you" (Jn 13:37). This is the man whom Jesus had called "the Rock" (Jn 1:42). He, together with James and John, had been invited by Jesus to accompany him in Gethsemane, just as some time before these three had been privileged to witness the transfiguration. Yet Peter betrayed Jesus. Then came Easter. Risen, the Lord asked of a repentant Peter only a pledge of love. Receiving it, Jesus did two things: he charged Peter to care for his lambs and sheep, and he prophesied a martyr's death for Peter.

As an apostolic people, what might we learn in our present situation from the writings of Peter, James, and John, the three favored apostles? If we asked Peter, he might say: "Once you were not a people, but now you are God's people; once you had not received mercy, but now you have received mercy." And he would urge: "All of you, have unity of spirit, sympathy, love for one another, a tender heart, and a humble mind. Do not repay evil for evil or abuse for abuse; but, on the contrary, repay with a blessing. It is for this that you were called—that you might inherit a blessing" (1 Pet 2:10; 3:8–9). Bitter experience taught him the meaning of repentance and forgiveness. His words call us to remember the mercy we in turn have received so as to be compassionate ourselves. Rather than prescribing a given penance for a specific deed, what the Rock recommends here is an attitude of heart.

The epistle written under the name of "James" also carries the weight of apostolicity as part of Scripture. Listen to this advice to our chattering world: "How great a forest is set ablaze by a small fire! And the tongue is a fire. The tongue is placed among our members as a world of iniquity; it stains the whole body, sets on fire the cycle of nature, and is itself set on fire by hell. For every species of beast and bird, of reptile and sea creature, can be tamed and has been tamed by the human species, but no one can tame the tongue—a restless evil, full of deadly poison. With it we bless the Lord and Father, and with it we curse those who are made in the likeness of God" (Jas 3:5–9). In a wordy environment, where talk is constant and communication instant, control of speech is rarely considered an apostolic virtue. Yet disciplined speech nurtured by periods of reflective silence can be a balm to the spirit, and offers room to grow to the attitude of compassion recommended by Peter.

That attitude is a seed. It comes to fruition in charity. Charity, love, is one of the great themes of the Johannine literature. In the First Letter of John we read: "In this is love, not that we have loved God but that he loved us and sent his Son to be the atoning sacrifice for our sins. Beloved, since God loved us so much, we also ought to love one another. No one has ever seen God; if we love one another, God lives in us, and his love is perfected in us" (1 Jn 4:10–12). Jesus has redeemed us. Our task is to love as he has loved. So we render God present in our world. This is the fruit of apostolicity in the church. The witness of word and sacrament, preserved through the apostolic tradition, nourishes the lives of the faithful. Our task is to love as God has loved. In so doing we become the face of God, the only face God shows in this life.

CHAPTER 8

The Church Is Apostolic

Francis A. Sullivan, SJ

Francis Sullivan was born on May 21, 1922, in Boston. After graduating from Boston College High School, he entered the novitiate of the New England Province of the Society of Jesus, and was ordained to the priesthood in 1951. During his course of studies, he obtained the master of arts degree in philosophy at Boston College, the master of arts degree in classics at Fordham University, and the licentiate in sacred theology at Weston College. After ordination he was sent to Rome for further study of theology at the Pontifical Gregorian University, where he obtained the doctorate in sacred theology in 1956. Although he had expected to return to his province to teach at Weston College, he was then assigned to teach ecclesiology at the Gregorian Univerisity. He continued to do this for the next thirty-six years, serving also as dean of the faculty of theology from 1964 to 1970. After being declared emeritus in 1992, he returned to New England, where he continues to teach in the the department of theology at Boston College.

He has published seven books and numerous articles. His more recent works include Magisterium: Teaching Authority in the Catholic Church, Salvation Outside the Church? Tracing the History of the Catholic Response, *and* Creative Fidelity: Weighing and Interpreting Documents of the Magisterium.

For his outstanding contributions to theology, he was awarded the John Courtney Murray Award of the Catholic Theological Society of America in 1994.

When Mike Daley asked me to contribute to this volume, one reason he gave for suggesting that I write about the church as "apostolic" was the fact that for so many years I had "lived in the apostolic city." I'm sure no one needs to be told that by "apostolic city" he meant Rome, where, in fact, I spent thirty-nine years: three as a doctoral candidate, and thirty-six teaching at the Gregorian University.

My first reflection on this mark of the church is suggested by the way that we are accustomed to identify Rome as the apostolic city—as though Rome were the only city with a right to that title. Back in the third century, Tertullian would not have allowed such an exclusive claim. His advice to those who wanted to know the true Christian doctrine was:

> Go to visit the apostolic churches, those places, where the chairs of the apostles even now preside in their places. Where the authentic letters are still read, bringing to us how they sounded and how they looked. If Achaea is close by, you have Corinth. If you are not far from Macedonia, you have Philippi. If you can go to Asia, there is Ephesus. If you are in the vicinity of Italy, you have Rome, whence [apostolic] authority came also to us. Blessed is that church upon which the apostles poured out their entire teaching along with their blood.

While Tertullian recognized that the church of Rome, where the two greatest apostles had confirmed their teaching by martyrdom, had a special claim to be called apostolic, he knew that it was not the only church with a right to that title. Tertullian might well have objected if in his day Rome was calling itself "the Apostolic See," naming important documents issued by its bishops "Apostolic Constitutions," calling its legates "Apostolic Nuncios," and publishing the record of its activities as *Acta Apostolicae Sedis*. He would hardly have approved of Rome's use of terms that so clearly implied its claim to being the one and only apostolic church.

In our own day, a great many Christians would object if the Catholic Church were still claiming to be the only church with the right to call itself apostolic. However, it is not so long ago that such a claim was part of a standard proof that the Catholic Church alone was the true church of Christ. The argument went this way. The true church of Christ must possess the four "marks" that in the creed we confess the church to have. But only the Catholic Church possesses these four marks. Therefore it alone is the true church of Christ. In that argument, the crowning proof that the Catholic Church alone is truly "apostolic" was that it alone is in communion with the Apostolic See, and with its bishop, who is the successor to Peter, the "Prince of the Apostles."

The ecclesiology of the Second Vatican Council has made us realize that we can no longer simply identify the Catholic Church with the one, holy, catholic, and apostolic church of the creed. On the one hand, the council recognized that the Catholic Church does not realize these attributes in their fullness. While it is holy, still it is "always in need of purification" (*Lumen gentium* [LG] 8), and hence its holiness is "imperfect" (LG 48). Similarly, the divisions among Christians "prevent the Catholic Church from realizing the fullness of catholicity proper to her" (*Unitatis redintegratio* 4). On the other hand, we have come to recognize the presence of these attributes in other Christian churches and communities, where likewise they are imperfectly realized.

In this essay I am specifically concerned with the progress that has been made in ecumenical dialogues regarding the church's apostolicity. To begin with, there was no Christian church that did not claim to be apostolic both in its faith and in its ministry. But deeply divisive questions arose when each church set out to explain how it substantiated its claim to profess apostolic faith and to continue apostolic ministry. For instance, some insisted that the sole norm of apostolicity in faith is the written record of the apostles' teaching that we have in the New Testament. For these churches, only what is set down in these apostolic writings had any claim to be normative for apostolic faith. Other churches, while maintaining the primary importance of the New Testament, also insisted on the normative role of tradition as a vehicle by which the church has handed on its understanding and its practice of the apostolic faith. These churches have seen the apostolicity of their faith also shown in their adherence to the teaching of the Fathers of the church, and to the doctrinal decisions of the great ecumenical councils.

Likewise churches have employed different criteria as the basis of their claim to have maintained apostolic ministry. For some, the apostolic mandate was transmitted to the whole Christian community, so that each Christian congregation can impart a share in its apostolic mandate to the person whom it chooses as its minister. Other churches found in the New Testament a pattern of ministry which the apostles and their co-workers established by choosing certain men in each community and ordaining them with the laying on of their hands. Some churches hold that only those so ordained can in turn ordain others, but since the New Testament does not clearly distinguish between presbyters and bishops, they maintain that presbyters have the fullness of apostolic ministry and can share this by ordaining others. Finally, there are churches that consider bishops to be the successors of the apostles in the ministry of pastoral leadership and authoritative teaching, in a sense that is not true of presbyters. These churches have taken as permanently normative the ancient tradition that limits to bishops the power to share the apostolic mandate by ordination.

It is not difficult to see the correlation between the various understandings of apostolicity in faith, on the one hand, and the various patterns of ministry, on the other. Those churches that insisted that the New Testament writings constitute the sole criterion of apostolicity in faith will find in the New Testament the basis of the apostolicity of their pattern of ministry, whether it be congregational or presbyterian. The churches that recognize the normative character of apostolic tradition, along with Scripture, will insist that apostolicity of ministry requires ordination by bishops who share the apostolic mandate through their membership in the episcopal college.

These two ways of understanding how the church is apostolic justify the common practice of dividing the Christian churches into two broad categories: those with a protestant view of apostolicity, and those with a catholic view. Among the latter are listed the Anglican, Old Catholic, Orthodox and other Eastern churches, and the Roman Catholic; the first category would include all other churches. For centuries the separation between these two groups of churches had seemed an impassible chasm. However, ecumenical dialogue has given rise to hope that it can be bridged, and that one day unity can be restored.

One fruit of this dialogue is that it has resulted, on both sides, in a more balanced notion of apostolicity. Whereas previously, those of the protestant tradition had tended to identify apostolicity with fidelity to apostolic doctrine, and those of the catholic tradition had tended to identify it with apostolic succession in ministry, the concept of apostolicity that is being expressed in ecumenical statements today is generally a well-balanced one. There is now a broad agreement that apostolic faith and apostolic ministry are equally essential to the church's apostolicity.

Second, through the shared effort to achieve a deeper understanding of the doctrines on which the churches have been divided, a great deal of progress has been made to arrive at the realization that doctrinal convictions that had seemed irreconcilable are really compatible after all. This has resulted in the mutual recognition that both of the churches involved in a dialogue have in fact remained apostolic in their faith. A striking example of such a recognition is seen in the "Joint Declaration on the Doctrine of Justification" that was affirmed by the Lutheran World

Federation and the Roman Catholic Church in 1998. More recently, the USA Lutheran-Roman Catholic Dialogue has published a Common Statement entitled: "The Church as Koinonia of Salvation: Its Structures and Ministries." After five years of study and conversation, the Lutherans and Catholics in this dialogue were convinced that their churches have maintained both apostolic faith and apostolic ministry. On the basis of this shared conviction they have made the following recommendations to their respective churches.

> We recommend that each church recognize that the other realizes, even if perhaps imperfectly, the one church of Christ and shares in the apostolic tradition.

> We recommend that each church recognize that the ordained ministry of the other effectively carries on, even if perhaps imperfectly, the apostolic ministry instituted by God in the church.

If the two churches follow these recommendations, we will have further proof of how far we have come from the idea that only the church that is in full communion with the "Apostolic See" has the right to call itself apostolic.

PART TWO

The Church's Other Marks

CHAPTER 9

The Church Is
Active in Ministry

Thomas F. O'Meara, OP

Thomas O'Meara was born in May 1935, in Des Moines, Iowa. He first met members of the Dominican Order in elementary school. When he was a sophomore in high school, his family moved to Madison, Wisconsin, where he attended a high school run by the Sinsinawa Dominican sisters. After two years at Loras College he entered the Dominican novitiate in Winona, Minnesota.

After three years of philosophical study and four years of theological study, O'Meara was ordained to the priesthood in 1962—just three months before Vatican II began. At that time the three seminaries in Dubuque, Iowa (Presbyterian, Lutheran, Dominican) were having their first ecumenical contacts with each other and began what was to become an early and extensive program of ecumenical cooperation. In order to have a faculty member who knew something about Protestant theologies, O'Meara's superiors sent him to Munich, Germany, for doctoral studies. His time there coincided with the years of Vatican II and with the arrival of Karl Rahner at the Bavarian university.

Father O'Meara returned to the United States in 1967 and taught in Dubuque and elsewhere until his appointment at the University of Notre Dame in 1981, where he held numerous positions, including director of the master of divinity program and co-director of the undergraduate program. At Notre Dame, Fr. O'Meara wrote books on fundamentalism, theology and art, Catholic theology in Germany at the end of the nineteenth century, Thomas Aquinas, and the Jesuit theologian Erich Przywara.

In recent years he wrote a memoir about his theological career, A Theologian's Journey. He had come to see that by being sent to Europe for his

65

studies he had become a witness of the great change inaugurated by the Second Vatican Council. He had come to see that his generation of Catholic theologians had lived on both sides of Vatican II and had done their education twice, in the neoscholasticism of the former theology manuals and in one of several contemporary approaches. Father O'Meara had experienced both a church that was solely European, automatic, and constrained, and a church that accepted the challenge of adapting liturgy and theology to the culture of the world. In the midst of rapid and numerous changes, he felt blessed living with members of a large community of gifted and generous people—students of the great theologians at Vatican II who had spent their energies in the service of the church in the United States.

The four marks of the church holding such prominence during the centuries reaching from the counter-Reformation to the end of Baroque and Modern apologetics are static characteristics. One and holy became aspects of the church existing apart from time and development, while catholicity and apostolicity, although realities of history and culture, were presented as facets of a reality timeless and ancient.

This stands in contrast to the dynamic ethos that distinguishes Christians and their communities as they appear in the letters of the New Testament. Paul cannot speak enough of the movement, liberation, and empowerment which life in the *Pneuma* brings to a baptized woman or man. His ecclesiology is a theology of active service, of the *diakonia* we call by its Latin form, ministry. One of the striking aspects of ecclesial life is that the baptized are neither passive observers of a temple priesthood nor attendants on the end of time but people called to some activity. The early Christians, avoiding words associated with Jewish or Gentile temple cults, named their religious enterprises with action words, with ordinary verbs. Apart from "elder" every ministry mentioned in the New Testament is a verb: to announce the good news, to teach, to oversee, and to be sent. Activity flowing from the Spirit within a follower of Christ is evidently a basic aspect of being-the-church.

Very rapidly, in the years after the Second Vatican Council, ministry changed: it changed by expanding into ministries of education, liturgy, and social justice, and changed by a dramatic increase in the numbers of people at work in parishes and dioceses. The very model of community in ministry changed, as it came to involve staffs of full-time ministers, in a larger community of ministers led by the pastor; each group had its own education, expertise, natural gifts, charisms, and commissionings.

I was ordained a priest in the Dominican Order in June 1962, three months before the opening sessions of Vatican II, and in those times a parish offered Masses and sacraments, and little more, in Latin. Converts were occasional and quickly instructed; marriages needed brief, legal preparations; baptisms, except for the gingerly pouring of water, were not engaging. No one not ordained entered the sanctuary and little ministry formally and publicly connected to the church's life took place outside of the sanctuary. The parish today does not resemble the forms and style of a parish in 1962. From the council came new impetuses for the life of the church: the theology of the people of God, baptism as entrance to service, liturgy as the nourishing of ministry, charism flowing into ministry. This translation, this inculturation, occurring rapidly and enthusiastically in the United States, drew on American characteristics: a delight in belonging to groups, a tradition of helping and service, a natural activism.

The mark of activity in the church is the mark of ministry. The source, milieu, and goal of each service lies in what Jesus calls the kingdom of God, and the life of the Spirit of the Risen Christ in each Christian. Activity in and for the church is not the possession of a small clique. Ministry presupposes but goes beyond the basic life of the believer (which is important in itself); ministry aims at sustaining, enriching, and expanding the church, although it may serve the presence of the Spirit outside of the church; ministry is not directly concerned with being a better political leader or artist. The active mark of ministry touches the entire community—Paul's theology of the body of Christ implies that Christians will be active—and stimulates the spiritual organism to live in different ways.

In fact, the mark of activity is at the source of the four traditional marks. The church's unity comes not from monoformity but from a unity of people and activities: diversity in ministry encourages and challenges growth in unity. Holiness is not an ontic status but the result of life in the Spirit, and such life includes ministry. The catholicity of the church comes not from imitating some Hellenistic or Roman template but from a diversity of churches around the world whose liturgical, theological, and social ministries have their proper color and form. Apostolicity is the active life of the church in continuity with the apostles and Jesus through a long history of diversity.

The Catholic world recently celebrated the anniversaries of Yves Congar and Karl Rahner, both born in 1904. In one of Congar's last writings in 1972, he noted the change in ministry.

I have gradually corrected my vision which at first was principally and spontaneously clerical....The church of God is not built up solely by the actions of the official presbyteral ministry but by a multitude of diverse modes of service, more or less stable or occasional, more or less spontaneous or recognized, and, when the occasion arises consecrated, while falling short of sacramental ordination. These modes of service do exist...mothers at home, the person who coordinates liturgical celebrations or reads the sacred text, the woman visiting the sick or prisoners, adult catechists. These are good examples of church *diakonia.* Such modes of service proceed from gifts of nature or grace, from those callings which Saint Paul names "charisms" since they are given "for the common good" (1 Cor 12:7, 11). They exist right now, but up to now were not called by their true name, ministries, nor were their place and status in ecclesiology recognized.[62]

One could find a similar ecclesiology in the writings of Karl Rahner. It begins with the dialogue of each human person with divine grace. The world of grace assumes in the world of the church, under the impetus of varied charisms, the activities of a collective person. Here too there is a pattern of concentric circles of ministries arranged around the Spirit but concretely around human leadership. The parish and diocese today can, from the point of view of ministry, be best understood as a community which has circles of ministries arranged around the pastor or bishop, although all the ministers have their own ecclesial and graced identities.

Activity marks life. Healthy parishes and dioceses inevitably involve activity, and the fulfillment of the ministerial potential of baptism draws adults today to a church. The baptized look for what is being done in a local church, and for what is being done well. They ask not for entertainment or mystery but for preaching and liturgy and community.

The ecclesial mark of activity implies an encounter between the Spirit of the Risen Jesus and the people of God. This meeting, filled with renewal, was prepared for and furthered by studies of the Bible and the early church, and by theologies re-emphasizing the ministerial mission of baptism. Apparently the Holy Spirit wanted to alter, that is, to restore, the church. A theology of baptism calls people to a life whose ministries and charisms await direction. A local church is one where there are increasing opportunities for ministry all around. A true mark of the church is realistic and significant: activity points to the ground and to the goal of the church as servant and sacrament of the kingdom of God. As Jesus, Paul, and Thomas Aquinas state, we are the Spirit's friends and co-workers.

CHAPTER 10

The Church Is Beautiful and Holy

Alex Garcia-Rivera

Born June 4, 1951, Garcia-Rivera is a former Lutheran pastor now turned Catholic and is associate professor of systematic theology at the Jesuit School of Theology at Berkeley. He did his doctoral work on the semiotics of culture under the direction of Robert Schreiter (Catholic Theological Union) and received his doctorate in theology from the Lutheran School of Theology. He holds degrees in physics from Ohio State University and Miami University. His current research and teaching focus on aesthetics and liturgical theology, theology and the arts, suffering and the human person, and the intersection between science and theology.

Garcia-Rivera is an award-winning author. His publications include St. Martin of Porres: The "Little Stories" and the Semiotics of Culture, *which was nominated for the American Academy of Religion's Award for Excellence in the Study of Religion in the analytical-descriptive studies category;* The Community of the Beautiful, *which won the 2000 Catholic Press Award for academic theology; and* A Wounded Innocence: Sketches for a Theology of Art. *His work regularly appears in* U.S. Catholic, Nuestra Parroquia, *and* Momento Católico.

Garcia-Rivera is active in various academic communities such as the Catholic Theological Society of America, the American Academy of Religion, and the Society for the Arts in Religion and Society. He was president of the Academy of Catholic Hispanic Theologians in the United States, and received the Virgilio Elizondo Award for distinguished contribution in theology in 2003.

I had come to Allentown, Pennsylvania, to begin a ministry with Hispanics. It was the result of a long spiritual journey that began as a Roman Catholic in Havana, Cuba. An angry adolescence in Ohio followed. The anger, occasioned by the blindness and prejudice of a church very different from the one I had known in Cuba, resulted in my consciously leaving the church of my baptism and devoting myself to a new religion, the rational and scientific world. But, then, love happened. I fell in love and married a lovely Lutheran woman while working on a doctorate in physics. Such bliss would not last long. I was plunged into a crisis of conscience while working on a project of the Boeing company in Seattle—the air-launched cruise missile. How could I live with myself knowing that the first fruit of my scientific knowledge was a weapon that could kill thousands, even millions of human beings?

This crisis of conscience was actually God calling me back home to the Roman Catholic Church but in an unexpected way. Since our marriage, my wife through the grace of the Holy Spirit had managed to get me to go back to church except this time it was the Lutheran Church. Having become active in the Lutheran Church, I now felt a call to leave my science career, my "fishing boat," and follow Christ to another shore. That shore was Allentown, Pennsylvania. I left Seattle and spent the next four years at the Lutheran seminary in Chicago. I was ordained a Lutheran pastor and was given my first assignment. I was to begin a new ministry with Hispanics in Allentown. It did not take long for God to point me in the direction my ministry was to follow.

My first pastoral act was to bury a two-month-old infant, Estefanía. She was born of an impoverished Puerto Rican couple. She had died from SIDS in a shabby housing project. The funeral home called me. "Would I perform a funeral service *pro bono*?" The couple had no way of paying for the expenses of a funeral so the funeral home could not pay for my services. I arrived at the gravesite but was puzzled. I stood on a barren lot overrun with weeds framed by two busy roads. Was this the gravesite? Yes, it must be. I could see the family standing by what was obviously a freshly dug grave. But what sort of gravesite was this? There were no tombstones or marks to indicate that it was anything but an undeveloped lot. As I stood by the grave of little Estefanía, her father pointed to a spot not too far away and said, "Pastor, my father is buried over there." And, then, it came to me. This was a pauper's grave. It also became the seed of a new church in Allentown.

From that small beginning, my ministry grew and in four years I had a fairly active and vital congregation. We were a very poor congregation, but we made up for it in spirit and, also, art. We had, among our poor, very talented folk artists. They took our host church by surprise by making a life-size papier-mâché nativity scene in the Latin American style. They also held liturgical dramas, processions, and a variety of other activities that dealt with the only freedom possible under their circumstances—the freedom of the arts. What really scandalized our host church, however, was not the nativity scene but the life-size statue of St. Martin de Porres that arrived in a big truck in front of the very Protestant and statue-less St. Paul Lutheran Church. St. Martin de Porres was the great, mulatto Dominican saint of Peru. He is second in the popular devotion of Hispanics all over the Americas. Only Our Lady of Guadalupe commands greater devotion.

The statue had been given by an anonymous donor to our little congregation and now our host church was caught in a dilemma. What sort of a Lutheran church is it that has statues of saints? Worse, this saint was not in the Bible. Even worse, he was a Dominican, and mulatto, and Latin American! This was too much for our host church, and anxiety and conflict followed. As a young adult Lutheran, I experienced anew the prejudices and lack of kindness that I had known as a young Roman Catholic. Eventually, the senior pastor of the host church asked us to leave.

To make a long story short, the bishop stepped in and asked our congregation to start a new church. "What name do you want to give it," he asked. All responded, "St. Martin de Porres!" To my surprise, he took it calmly. He shook his head at this profound joke God had played on him and now there exists a "St. Martin de Porres Lutheran Church" in Allentown, Pennsylvania.

From an unmarked gravesite to a church with a mark, that is, a name, I saw in this experience God calling me back to my Roman Catholic roots. Eventually, I did return and am now a Roman Catholic lay professor of theology at the Jesuit School of Theology at Berkeley. I have written several books including one on St. Martin as well as several on the theology of the beautiful such as, *The Community of the Beautiful* and *A Wounded Innocence.* I wrote these books out of this experience. I had learned something profound about the reality of the church: it has marks. More important, these marks are often unrecognized by academic theology, but are seen quite easily by the poor. There is one special mark, however, that by its very visibility truly defines the church. It is *kalokagathia,* the union of the beautiful and the holy.

Kalokagathia is a Greek word for which we have no modern counterpart. It is a word that grasps an intrinsic connection between the good (*agathos*) and the beautiful (*kallos*). I see that mark in that statue of St.

Martin de Porres. As such, *kalokagathia*, as represented by this simple statue, calls to question what the world has come to know as either beautiful or holy. It also recovers one of the lost marks of the church.

We used to see them, after all, in every church. I mean statues. Now, they are often found in dark corners, or church basements, or attics. When the church made its peace with the modern world, it also became embarrassed by its devotional art. Placed in the light of modern tastes and scholarship, much of the church's art fell out of favor. A modern church, for example, puts much store in the historical study of the Bible. It would allow artistic depictions of Biblical stories. Unfortunately, much of the church's art dealt with non-biblical, or more accurately, non-canonical stories. By this, I am speaking of the legends surrounding the apostles, Mary, and Jesus that are known by Bible scholars as the Apocrypha.

When you see a statue of St. Joseph holding a staff with lilies growing out of it, what you see is an artistic depiction of a story found in what is known as the *Proto-gospel of James*. This gospel never made it into the Bible but it did make it, physically, into the church. As such, it has formed the imagination of innumerable Christians who saw this statue and wondered about the mystery of Joseph's election to be the husband of Mary by having his dead, wooden staff suddenly flower forth with lilies! Such stories and the art that depicted them were an embarrassment to a church that thought it had come of age by developing a critical consciousness of the historical origins of its sources. Perish the thought that the life of the church could be marked by childlike imagination rather than responsible scholarly critical thought!

There was, however, another reason accounting for the church's embarrassment. As the church entered the modern age, the notion of holiness began to change. The modern world increasingly identified holiness with morality. Holiness has to do with setting apart and it is God who sets apart. With the new emphasis on human freedom that came out of the eighteenth century, this setting apart became associated more with those who had achieved moral purity than with those whom God had set apart. Christians, however, have resisted seeing this setting apart in terms of moral purity. Did Mary Magdalene, for example, become holy in spite of her sins or because of her sins? Indeed, Magdalene's holiness is measured less by her moral purity, but by her ability to become innocent again. And such innocence is beautiful. It is beautiful because it is a work of art, God's art. God fashions Magdalene's soul out of her former sins into a new innocence that is beautiful. If I were to translate the word *kalokagathia*, it would be wounded innocence.

The church has marks. I saw this as I stood in front of the unmarked gravesite of little Estefanía. I sensed then that God would not leave that place unmarked. In the ecumenical miracle of a St. Martin de Porres Lutheran Church, I saw that a very special mark of the church transcends the sins of the human church. It is the innocence of those who stand at an unmarked gravesite yet hope for things unseen. Such hopes then become marks, marks that have filled the church with music, color, tapestries, statues, paintings, dance, drama, and a thousand other forms since its beginning. It is the mark of a wounded innocence. It is the mark of *kalokagathia*. It is a mark of the church.

CHAPTER 11

The Church Is Biblical

Dianne Bergant, CSA

Dianne Bergant was born in 1936 in Milwaukee, Wisconsin. There she attended a grade school staffed by the Sisters of St. Agnes, a congregation that she eventually joined. After teaching grade school for several years, she entered a doctoral program in sacred scripture at St. Louis University. She returned to Wisconsin to teach in a liberal arts college owned and operated by her congregation; she was also elected to a four-year term on the congregation's general council. She finished her dissertation in 1975, while also teaching part-time at the college. When a full-time position opened in Old Testament Studies at Catholic Theological Union in Chicago (CTU), she was encouraged to apply and was offered the position. Sister Bergant has been teaching there for more than a quarter century, and has also served as director of CTU's joint Doctor of Ministry Program.

She is the author or editor of more than twenty books, including Israel's Wisdom Literature: A Liberationist-Critical Approach *and the three-volume* Preaching the New Lectionary, Cycles A, B, C, *an exegetical aid for liturgical ministers. Dr. Bergant has also published more than a hundred articles dealing with biblical interpretation and many critical reviews and essays in a wide variety of academic journals as well as in publications for general readers. In addition, she has served on the editorial board of* The Bible Today *for more than twenty years, including five as its general editor. She has continued on the board as Old Testament book reviewer. Dr. Bergant has also served on the editorial boards of such publications as* The Catholic Biblical Quarterly *and* Biblical Theology Bulletin. *Currently she writes the weekly column "The Word" in* America *magazine.*

Sister Bergant says that over the years she has received more from Catholic Theological Union than she has contributed. The horizons of her theological world have been expanded by remarkable colleagues, many of whom are world-renowned in their respective fields. Students from every inhabited continent and diverse racial and cultural backgrounds, she reports, have sharpened her multicultural sensitivities. This richness in faculty and student body serves the mission of the school, which is the formation of future ministers of the church.

The Second Vatican Council brought to new light the importance of our biblical tradition. Readings from the Bible were always a part of the Mass, but the Latin language in which they were read was understood by very few, if any, ordinary parishioners. The council's decision to change to vernacular languages and the openness to new approaches to the study of the Bible significantly altered this. Bible prayer groups sprang up everywhere. Serious Bible study became a fundamental component of most adult and youth catechetical classes. The Bible itself (if a family even possessed one) ceased to be merely a family heirloom showcased on the coffee table and became a well-worn, dog-eared, frequently-consulted best-seller.

Painstaking examination of the artifacts and manuscript fragments uncovered by archaeology, and new interpretation of the biblical texts themselves, greatly assisted scholars. They were now able to reconstruct, though in a manner that is sketchy and tentative, the historical situations that produced what we today call the Bible. Something extraordinary was discovered: Just as it is correct to say that the early church fashioned its Scriptures, one can also say that these scriptural traditions in a significant way fashioned a church.

The Bible Yesterday

The gospels do more than tell the story of the life, death, and resurrection of Jesus. The point of view from which these stories were told reveals the struggles of the early church and the way it came to understand itself. Their constant reference to ancient Israelite traditions shows that the early believers considered themselves the heirs of that rich religious heritage. In this way, they sought to demonstrate how the promises God made to their ancestors were now being fulfilled in their midst. They did this by showing that Jesus was the long-awaited Messiah. Examples of this approach can be found throughout the gospels, from the infancy narratives: "Look, the virgin shall conceive and bear a son, and they shall name him Emmanuel" (Mt 1:23; see Isa 7:14), to the account of Jesus' death on the cross: "They divided my clothes among themselves, and for my clothing they cast lots" (Jn 19:24; see Ps 22:18). Again and again the gospel writers appealed to earlier Scriptures as they shaped this new community. They explained present reality in terms of the past: "As it is written..." (Mt 4:6–7, 10; 11:10; 21:13; 26:24, 31; Mk 1:2; 7:6; 9:13; 14:21, 27; Lk 2:23; 3:4; 4:4, 8, 10; 7:27; 19:46; 24:46; Jn 6:31; 12:14).

At the heart of the teaching of Jesus, and of the followers who make up the church, we find the theme of the "reign of God." This notion of God's rule originated in ancient Israel at the time when the people were growing more deeply disappointed with the monarchy. They had hoped that the king, appointed by God, would be able to lead them to success and prosperity, but also to guide them in fidelity to the covenant made with God. When king after king failed, the people began to look to the future for an "anointed one" who would be able to accomplish this on their behalf. It was to this hope for future fulfillment that John the Baptist appealed when he announced: "The kingdom of heaven has come near" (Mt 3:2). As he launched his own public ministry, Jesus himself proclaimed: "The time is fulfilled, and the kingdom of God has come near" (Mk 1:15). Once again we see that Jesus' own ministry is rooted in the traditions of his religious past.

Paul of Tarsus, the great theologian of the early church, was steeped in the religion of Israel. Once converted, he came to believe that faith in Christ was the fulfillment of the promises made by God to his own ancestors. He situated his Christian theology squarely within the traditions of Israel. Probably more than any other writer, he appealed to earlier Scriptures, declaring, "As it is written...": Rom 1:17; 2:24; 3:4, 10; 4:17; 8:36; 9:13, 33; 10:15; 11:8, 26; 12:19; 14:11; 15:3, 9, 21; 1 Cor 1:19, 31; 2:9; 3:19; 9:9; 10:7; 14:21; 15:25; 2 Cor 8:15; 9:9; Gal 3:10, 13; 4:22, 27. The Christian faith is indeed rooted in the people's experience of the Risen Jesus. However, as Paul's writings show, reinterpretation of the Scriptures of the Jewish people is a significant dimension of the expression of this faith.

The Bible Today

In so many ways the biblical character of the church is evident today. Only three such ways will be mentioned here: biblical spirituality, the biblical basis of theological statements, and ecumenical partnership.

Today's church is similar to the church of the first centuries in the way its spirituality is grounded in biblical theology. The biblical character of the liturgy is evident. The prayers and music are often based on or include biblical themes, and the preaching generally flows from the readings of the day. Many people now belong to Bible prayer or study groups. *Lectio divina*, the prayerful reflection on Scripture once practiced almost exclusively by nuns and monks, is a common devotional practice of laywomen and laymen. It is clear that the people of God are turning to the Bible to satisfy their spiritual hungers.

Since the Second Vatican Council, one can see a noticeable difference in the relationship between church teaching and Scripture than had been the case in the past. Earlier, doctrinal statements were developed and then biblical passages were used to give biblical support to these statements. This was often referred to as "proof-texting." While some within the church still employ this method of theological development, the theological documents that have been published by the United States Conference of Catholic bishops since the council demonstrate a different approach. They normally begin with a careful explanation of biblical theology pertinent to the theme or themes of the statement. The theological position is then developed out of this explanation. This approach is similar to the practice of the church in the first centuries, when most theology was actually an interpretation of the Scriptures.

A third way that today's church is marked as biblical can be seen in one aspect of ecumenical dialogue. There is no longer a strictly Catholic way of reading the Bible, or a Lutheran way, or Presbyterian way, etc. Differences in understanding certainly continue, but these are usually the result of different methods of interpretation used rather than simply specific denominational loyalties. Very few passages are interpreted from the point of view of the denomination, but there are some, for example: "You are Peter, and on this rock I will build my church" (Mt 16:18). Because of the basic similarity of approach, a notable amount of collaboration is occurring in the field of biblical theology. Actually, denominational differences did not arise with the Scriptures, but in the way certain passages were interpreted to reenforce distinctive theological positions.

The Bible Tomorrow

What role will the Bible play tomorrow in the life of the church? It is hard to predict. However, some signs of the biblical character of the church today might be indicators of tomorrow. Before the Second Vatican Council, only the clergy and a very small group within the laity had any kind of formation in biblical methodology or interpretation. The situation is quite different today. As mentioned above, the liturgy itself is thoroughly biblical, and the most popular topics in adult education classes, workshops, or lectures are biblical ones. It is almost as if the people of God could not get enough of the Bible once they were enriched by its treasures. It seems most unlikely that this desire will diminish in the future. Furthermore, the decline in the number of clergy has not affected this desire. More and more laywomen and laymen are engaged in serious study of the Bible.

At different times in the history of the church one or other of its marks or characteristics shines brighter than at other times. We are living in the biblical period of the church. This is so primarily not because we have made known the importance of the Bible, but because the importance of the Bible has been made known to us.

CHAPTER 12

The Church Is Catechetical

Thomas Groome

Thomas Groome was born September 30, 1945, in County Kildare, Ireland, the youngest of ten children—nine who lived. His father, Terence, was a local politician with a keen commitment to social justice—though he wouldn't have called it that. His mother, Margaret, was a devout Catholic with a deep spirituality—though, he says, she wouldn't have called it that either.

In his time, St. Patrick's Seminary, Carlow did not confer degrees, so Groome never received a bachelor of arts degree at the end of his college course or a master of divinity degree after four years of theology, though he had the equivalent of both. Groome's first earned degree was a master of arts degree in religious education from Fordham University, followed by a doctorate in theology and education from the joint program of Union Theological Seminary and Columbia Teacher's College.

Since 1976, Groome has taught theology and religious education at Boston College, rising through the ranks to full professor in 1992. He is also director of Boston College's Institute of Religious Education and Pastoral Ministry.

His first book was Christian Religious Education: Sharing Our Story and Vision. *With it he introduced a "shared Christian praxis approach" to religious education; essentially this is a participative pedagogy of bringing "life to Faith, and Faith to life." Though he has written a number of books since then,* Christian Religious Education *continues to receive new translations—now in many languages—and to be used widely throughout the world. His most recent publication is entitled* What Makes Us Catholic: Eight Gifts for Life.

Much of Groome's writing over the years has been of children's religion curricula. He is the primary author of William H. Sadlier's God With Us *curriculum, grades K to 8, and of Sadlier's* Coming to Faith, *grades K to 8; the latter has had two major revisions. For almost twenty years, literally millions of Catholic children in parish programs and parochial schools in the United States have received their formal catechesis through these texts—all in the spirit of Vatican II. They are likely Groome's most significant contribution.*

From Catechism to Community

I won the prize in first grade for catechism—the *Maynooth Catechism* in my Irish context. Old Miss Geraghty told me I was "a great boy" and gave me a holy picture of an obscure saint I'd never heard of, but no baseball card has been more cherished. My mother glowed with pride at my great success and told me, "Keep yer prize safe, Tom," that it could be the first of many. A portent, surely! I still have it, some fifty years later.

Though I didn't hear words like "catechetical" or "catechesis" back then, I assumed from early childhood that the church uses an easy-to-memorize question/answer catechism to teach its faith. Later I'd learn all those cognate terms, their root being *katechein*, to echo or hand on, and that an integral aspect of the church's mission is to hand on its faith. But first impressions are lasting. I continued to associate the church being catechetical with some kind of textbook, long after we moved beyond the question/answer format.

I even wrote such modern curricula and they have a vital place in the church's catechetical mission. A good and easy-to-use curriculum series, with sound theology and engaging pedagogy, is a powerful tool of catechesis. To implement such curriculum within a school or parish program fulfills one aspect of the church as catechetical.

Of late, however, I've reclaimed a more ancient tradition of catechesis that reaches before and beyond formal instruction through a textbook—without leaving it behind. Before the "schooling paradigm" came to dominate Western education (circa seventeenth century), family and community had a far more central role, and especially in catechesis. It was the family, community, and culture that forged people's Christian identity. In practice these are now largely overlooked because modernity equates education with schooling. Though Vatican II tried to reclaim the notion that formation in Christian identity requires the socializing influences of a witnessing parish and family, the school paradigm—a teacher with a textbook—has continued to dominate catechesis. We must break beyond this stranglehold and mount what I'm calling *total community catechesis*.

This requires a deeper realization that the church is catechetical—in its whole life—more than simply thinking that the church *does* catechesis as one thing among many. Everything about the church and everything it does in the world should be effected in ways that nurture people in faith. The whole life of a parish is its curriculum; it should do every ministry in ways likely to inform, form, and transform the community and each member in lived Christian faith. The Risen Christ gave the mandate to evangelize and teach to the whole Christian community assembled on that hillside in Galilee (see Mt 28:16–20). Catechesis cannot be delegated to a select few; by baptism, it is the responsibility of every Christian person and community.

Likewise for the Christian family; rather than delegating this responsibility to a parochial school or parish program, parents must become the primary religious educators of their children. The church must give parents the confidence, the resources, the opportunities, the guilt—whatever it takes—to empower them to be proactive in catechizing their children. And our formal programs of catechetical education, whether in parish or parochial school, must move beyond being informative in Christian faith to be formative and transformative as well.

This shift toward total community catechesis—or the whole church as catechetical—requires us to continue doing catechesis well as a ministry of the word, but also to recognize and harness the catechetical potential of all other ministries. And this must be effected in every parish, family, and school/program. Since the early days, the church has described its core ministries as *koinonia* or witness, *leitourgia* or worship, *diakonia* or welfare, and *kerygma* or word. Let's imagine every parish, family, and school/program as fulfilling each of these—as appropriate to their context—and doing so *with a catechetical consciousness.*

The Whole Parish as Catechetical

Parish as Community of Witness. The more a parish realizes itself as a Christian community of faith, hope, and love, the more likely it is be catechetically effective. There is nothing more formative than a Christian community that lives its faith. By the same token, the faith life of a parish will be enhanced if it constantly asks of every aspect, "What are we teaching?" and, "How might we witness to our faith more effectively?" To say that the church itself is a sacrament means that it must be an "effective" witness to what it teaches. If it does as much, it will indeed catechize well.

Parish as Worshiping Community. Every parish must assemble for the "public work" of worshiping God. And this is always the primary function of liturgy—to worship God; to use the liturgy to catechize in a didactic way would be an abuse of liturgy. On the other hand, because the sacraments "are signs they also belong in the realm of instruction. They not only presuppose faith…they also nourish, strengthen, and express it" (Constitution on the Sacred Liturgy, 59). The social sciences reiterate this insight of Vatican II. Every community shapes its people primarily through its symbols, and its sacred symbols are the most formative of all because they have "an aura of ultimacy" (Clifford Geertz). So, the quality of a parish's liturgy measures its effectiveness as an educator in faith; the better its liturgy, the more effective the parish as catechist.

Parish as Community of Human Welfare. Every parish must be a community that cares for human welfare—spiritual and physical, personal and social. It should offer people the inspiration and organization, the support and persuasion that prompts them to continue this social aspect of Jesus' ministry to the world. Diakonia is required of Christians by our faith. I add that it is also required of the parish as catechist. When a parish has outreach to the poor and marginalized, when its people participate in the social struggles for justice and peace, then it surely educates well.

Parish as Community of Word. Every parish must give its people ready access to the word of God that comes through Scripture and tradition. The parish achieves this most eminently through its preaching and formal programs of catechetical education. But beyond our current child-centered efforts, total community catechesis requires that explicit catechesis be "permanent…for the whole of life" (*General Directory for Catechesis*, 56). The whole community should be ever teaching and learning together, from cradle to grave.

The Whole Family as Catechetical

Beyond the two-parent ideal, "family" must include extended and blended families, single, double, and triple parent families; in fact, *any bonded network of domestic life* can function as a family for faith education. The Second Vatican Council in its Dogmatic Constitution on the Church reclaimed an ancient image of the family as "the domestic church." In its own way, the family should intentionally participate in all of the church's ministries, and, I highlight here, do so with a catechetical consciousness.

Family as Witness. The whole life of the home is to be suffused with the values and perspectives of Christian faith. The members must constantly review the family's environment and atmosphere, lifestyle and priorities, relationships and gender roles, language patterns and conversations, work and recreation—every aspect—to monitor how well it reflects the convictions and commitments of Christian faith. If still caught in the schooling paradigm, we hear that parents are the primary religious educators as requiring them to become more didactic. But more important is their attention to the whole ethos of the home and family life. Everything about the Christian family should bear witness to its faith; this is how it catechizes.

Family as Worshiping Community. The family is called to integrate shared prayer and sacred ritual into its patterns of daily life. As catechist, every Christian family needs its home liturgy to symbolize and celebrate its faith. I once asked a devout Jewish friend how she came by her strong Jewish identity; she immediately responded, "Oh, from the rituals in my home." Surely every Christian family can create or rediscover sacred rituals for the home that will nurture the Christian identity of its members. Without family prayer, rituals, and sacred symbols, the home simply cannot educate in faith.

Family as Promoter of Human Welfare. The family is required to care for the spiritual, physical, and emotional well-being of its own members, rippling outward toward others in need and serving the common good of society. Family life must reflect love and compassion toward all, promoting justice within and without. If children grow up and adults dwell within a family that tries to live the social values of God's reign, it will surely be catechetically effective.

Family as Community of Word. Family members are called to share their faith around Scripture and tradition, among themselves and in the broader community. Parishes must help parents—with resources, training, suggestions, support, encouragement, expectation—to integrate attention to God's word into the patterns and conversations of family life. Modern parents are admirably intent to teach even the youngest children their numbers, letters, and so on. Why not be equally attentive to handing on the faith?

The Whole School or Program as Catechetical

"School" here includes any church-sponsored school that has a catechetical curriculum. By "program" I mean any formal process of catechetical education, including the graded parish curriculum, intergenerational- and family-centered programs, all efforts at adult religious education, RCIA, youth ministry, faith sharing groups, and so on. Indeed, "school" and "program" epitomize the church's formal curriculum of faith education. However, total community catechesis requires that schools and programs integrate the other functions of ministry as well.

School or Program as Community of Witness. The whole environment of the school or program should reflect the communal values of Christian faith—respect and reverence for every person, hospitality and care toward all, and living witness to faith, hope, and love. Years ago, John Dewey argued that schools should reflect the values of a democratic society—if they intend to educate people for democracy. Surely a Christian school or parish program should be suffused with the values and commitments of Christian faith.

School or Program as Community of Worship. I'm not suggesting that the Catholic school or catechetical program replace the parish in its ministry of worship. Yet, opportunities for shared prayer and worship, for experiences like retreats and spiritual reflection should be integral to every catechetical curriculum. And the very pedagogy of a class or gathering can include moments of prayer and contemplation, of ritual and celebration. Likewise, the formal curriculum is enhanced by correlation with the liturgical year—making Advent wreaths, putting on Christmas plays, organizing lenten fasts, preparing Easter candles, and so on.

School or Program as Community of Welfare. In parishes and schools, service programs have come to be recognized as powerfully effective in faith education. This is as it should be. We can probably do a better job in the formal curriculum of giving students opportunity to name and reflect on their service experiences, and to correlate their reflections with Catholic social teachings. When corporate decisions are made, the catechetical program—within its limits—should offer students the opportunity to carry them out; for example, works of compassion, justice, and peace.

I doubt if I'd "win the prize" today for total community catechesis. Come to think of it, the church itself wouldn't win many prizes for making its whole life catechetical. Like the traditional four marks, becoming a catechetical church is as much our vision as our story. Let's get on with it!

CHAPTER 13

The Church Is Charismatic

Amos Yong

Of Chinese descent, Amos Yong was born in July 1965, in the small village-town of Taiping in West Malaysia. Growing up as an Assemblies of God pastor's kid in Malaysia for the first ten years and then as a missionary kid in northern California, where his father took a pastorate among first-generation Chinese immigrants to the United States, allowed him to experience two very different kinds of pluralistic environments: the Malay-Chinese-Indian ethos of Malaysia, and the American-Asian-Hispanic world of Stockton, California. Yet all of this was filtered through a fairly traditional Pentecostal worldview. Yong completed an undergraduate degree in Christian ministry at Bethany College (Assemblies of God) in Santa Cruz, California.

During his work on a master's degree in Christian history at Western Evangelical Seminary in Portland, Oregon, he came to see for the first time that Pentecostalism was one among many valid expressions of Christian faith, rather than either the only or the supreme incarnation of that faith. He says that he had to wrestle during these years with the question of why he remained a Pentecostal, especially given his sensing a transition vocationally from the pastorate to the academy and his firsthand knowledge of the pervasive anti-intellectualism among grassroots Pentecostalism.

He completed a second master's degree (in history) at Portland State University, and a doctorate (in religious and theological studies) at Boston University. His doctoral dissertation, which was published as Discerning the Spirit(s): A Pentecostal-Charismatic Contribution to Christian Theology of Religions, *summarized his own theological journey during much of the 1990s as he wrestled with his Pentecostal identity in a religiously plural world.*

Dr. Yong began teaching in the Fall of 1999 at Bethel College in St. Paul, Minnesota, an institution affiliated with the Baptist General Conference, an Evangelical denomination. As a theologian, he continues to wrestle with the issues at the crossroads of Pentecostalism, Evangelicalism, religious pluralism, and theological method. Among the books he has written, two of the most important are Spirit-Word-Community: Theological Hermeneutics in Trinitarian Perspective, *and* The Spirit Poured Out on All Flesh: World Pentecostalism and the Reconstruction of Christian Theology in the 21st Century.

From a Pentecostal perspective, the church is the body of Christ and a charismatic fellowship of (constituted by) the Holy Spirit. But what does this mean? Allow me to identify seven interrelated elements in order to elaborate on this more general claim.

First, the church is a spiritual organism vivified by the Spirit poured out on the day of Pentecost. As a spiritual organism, the church is made present whenever and wherever there is a gathering (even of only two or three) in Jesus' name by the power of the Spirit. This presence may be manifest variously, insofar as the Spirit imparts life through the preaching of the gospel, water baptism, the eucharistic enactment of the Lord's Supper, the proclamation of the forgiveness of sins, and congregational worship, among other sign-events. Institutionally, the church is manifest whenever and wherever the Spirit imparts life through its offices (ministries), officials (ministers), and teachings (doctrines). In every case, what is decisive is not the mere presence of any specific activity or institutional element, but the workings of the Spirit in and through that activity or actuality.

Second, the church is a community of worship joined to God in Christ by the Spirit. The newly established people of God on the day of Pentecost gathered together daily to praise God (Acts 2:47a). The Pauline injunction to "be filled with the Spirit, as you sing psalms and hymns and spiritual songs among yourselves, singing and making melody to the Lord in your hearts, giving thanks to God the Father at all times and for everything in the name of our Lord Jesus Christ" (Eph 5:18b–20), calls attention both to the centrality of worship for the Spirit-filled community and to the possibility of the manifestation of this community at any and every moment that the Spirit inspires such songs of praise. What is decisive is not mere liturgical enactment, but the workings of the Spirit in and through a variety of liturgies. In authentic worship, the Spirit unites the believing community with the triune God as we enact and realize on earth the heavenly choir that hallows the divine name eternally.

Third, the church is a community of the word of God made alive by the Spirit. The newly established people of God on the day of Pentecost "devoted themselves to the apostles' teaching" (Acts 2:42a). This concerns the word of God given to instruct us in the salvation available through Jesus Christ. Yet, "the letter kills, but the Spirit gives life" (2 Cor 3:6b). This means that the words of Scripture do not function magically, as if their recantation possesses a power innate to certain syllables being articulated in certain ways at certain times and places. As the seven sons of Sceva discovered, there is nothing magical even about the name of Jesus (Acts 19:13–16). Rather, the name of Jesus is powerful on the lips of those filled with the Spirit of Jesus. Similarly, the Scriptures are God-breathed (2 Tim 3:16) both in their origination and in their application. The teachings (doctrines) derived from Scripture, however, are life-giving only when vivified by the Spirit. What is decisive is not the mere articulation of the "right" words (see Mt 7:22–23), but the workings of the Spirit in and through those words. When the Spirit is active in the community gathered around the Word, the people are instructed, corrected, trained in righteousness, sanctified to participate in the divine life, and transformed into the image of Jesus.

Fourth, the church is a community of fellowship gathered by the Spirit. The earliest disciples devoted themselves also to fellowship, "to the breaking of bread and the prayers. All who believed were together and had all things in common; they would sell their possessions and goods and distribute the proceeds to all, as any had need. Day by day, as they spent much time together in the temple, they broke bread at home and ate their food with glad and generous hearts" (Acts 2:42b and 44–46). Here, we see the work of the Spirit involves the building of community, the fostering of generosity, and the establishing of mutuality. In addition, there is the eating together, both in the communal sense of daily meal-sharing, but also in the sacramental sense of celebrating the Lord's Supper. It is not the mere enactment of the Eucharist or mere communal life that is important, but the sanctifying work of the Spirit in and through the feast and the edifying and relational life of the Spirit in and through the members of the community. So, whether represented by the *epiclesis* (the formal invocation of the Spirit's presence) with regard to the eucharistic supper, or whether represented by communal hospitality and reception of each meal with thanksgiving and prayer, the community is enabled to have fellowship with each other and with God in Jesus Christ only by "the communion of the Holy Spirit" (2 Cor 13:13b).

Fifth, the church is a community empowered by the Holy Spirit to bear witness to the gospel. The first Christians lived in such a way so that "day by day the Lord added to their number those who were being saved" (Acts 2:47). This bearing witness includes proclaiming the *kerygma*, doing works of service, and manifesting communal hospitality as those upon whom the love of God has been poured out through the Holy Spirit (see Rom 5:5). In each of these cases, the Spirit bears witness to the reconciling work of God in Jesus Christ and transforms the believing community and its surrounding environment through their reciprocal interactivity. Here it is not just the mere presence of "good works" that is at issue (without impugning the importance of works as the fruit of the Spirit), but the witness empowered by the Spirit in and through the community of faith.

Sixth, the church is a charismatic community, a community vivified by the charisms or gifts of the Spirit poured out on the day of Pentecost. The predominant manifestation of the charismatic Spirit on that day was the gift of speaking and hearing various and strange tongues (Acts 2:11b). Paul later explains that the varieties of gifts and services are of the same Spirit "for the common good" (1 Cor 12:7b). Using the analogy of one body having many members, each of which serves particular functions, so also does the one body of Christ have many members, each serving indispensable functions through the charisms of the Spirit. Again, it is not the mere presence of charisms that marks the church as the fellowship of the Spirit, but their serving to edify the body as a whole. As the various languages at Pentecost were blended together symphonically by the Spirit for the glory of God, so too are the diverse gifts harmonized by the Spirit for the building up of the church. The result is not uniformity or homogeneity, but a unity-in-plurality orchestrated by the Spirit of God.

Last but not least, the church is an eschatological community of the Spirit, living between the ascension and parousia of Christ. The gift of the Spirit marked the beginning of the last days, as Peter understood Joel to prophesy (Acts 2:17), and the Spirit groans for and is the down payment of the full redemption to come (Rom 8:22–23; 2 Cor 1:22; Eph 1:13–14). The church, as the charismatic fellowship of the Spirit, both marks the presence of the reign of God (Lk 17:21) and heralds its imminent arrival. Insofar as the fruits of the Spirit (Gal 5:22–23) are manifest, so is the reign of God. Insofar as the full reign of God includes those from every tribe, tongue, and nation, so too is the present charismatic people of God hospitable and open to all. In a dynamic way, the church's relation to the world involves both giving and receiving. The church not only shapes, but is also shaped by its environment. There is no intention here of blurring the identity of the church with that of the world. Rather there is the humble acknowledgment that the economy of the Spirit is not circumscribed by the institutional church, but points us toward the *eschaton* when the gifts of the Spirit bestowed upon all peoples will be redeemed for the full manifestation of the reign of God and the full unveiling of the glory of God. At the same time, like the pointing finger that is no longer needed once the object pointed to is seen, so the church itself will have completed its purpose once God's reign is fully manifest.

A couple of final comments need to be made. First, these seven elements are not intended to be an exhaustive explication of what it means to say that the church is a charismatic fellowship of (constituted by) the Holy Spirit. Much more can and should be said, including the important work of critiquing this pneumatological understanding of the idea of the church from other New Testament perspectives.

Second, although some readers may want a more concrete understanding of the Spirit than what I have offered, I cannot oblige them. For how can such a concrete understanding be provided of the Spirit whose comings and going are untraceable (see Jn 3:8)? On the other hand, I am also tempted to say that if we have caught a glimpse of the church from the foregoing comments, then we've also caught a glimpse of the ever-mysterious Holy Spirit! And if that is the case, perhaps this is one of the gifts of the Pentecostal churches to the Church catholic.

CHAPTER 14

The Church Is Conciliar

Michael J. Himes

Michael J. Himes was ordained to the priesthood for the diocese of Brooklyn in 1972. He was awarded with distinction a doctorate in the History of Christianity from the University of Chicago. From 1977 until 1987, he served as dean of the Seminary of the Immaculate Conception in Huntington, New York, and from 1987 until 1993 was associate professor and director of the collegiate program in theology at the University of Notre Dame. Currently he is professor of theology at Boston College.

He has been awarded four honorary doctorates and is a recipient of the Social Concerns Medal of the University of Notre Dame, the Washington Theological Union's Sophia Award for Excellence in Theology, and was recently voted the Phi Beta Kappa Award for Outstanding Undergraduate Teaching by the students of Boston College. For several years he was a member of ARC-USA, the Anglican-Roman Catholic Dialogue in the United States. His books include Fullness of Faith: The Public Significance of Theology, *which he co-authored with his brother and which was awarded the Catholic Press Association Book Award in 1994,* Doing the Truth in Love: Conversations about God, Relationships, and Service, *and* Ongoing Incarnation: Johann Adam Möhler and the Beginnings of Modern Ecclesiology, *which received the Catholic Press Association Book Award in 1998. He is the co-editor of* Finding God in All Things *and* The Legacy of the Tübingen School, *an associate editor of the* HarperCollins Encyclopedia of Catholicism, *and the translator of a nineteenth-century classic, J.S. Drey's* Introduction to the Study of Theology. *His articles have appeared in many books and numerous journals here and in England. He has lectured widely in the United States, Canada, Europe, and Australia.*

The Acts of the Apostles provides a report of a gathering of Christians in Jerusalem that included the leaders of the community there—James and Peter and the other major figures—as well as delegates from the community in Antioch, including Barnabas and Paul. The question under discussion was whether Gentiles could be baptized into full membership in the church without having to observe the whole Jewish law. The leaders reached a compromise that seemed good "to the Holy Spirit and to us" (Acts 15:28) as they wrote to the Christians in Antioch. This gathering has been called "the council of Jerusalem," and it set a pattern which long continued in the church. Between the middle of the second century and the end of the sixth, it is estimated that over four hundred synods and local councils of bishops took place. They met for various reasons: to discuss doctrinal questions, decide disciplinary issues, and settle disputes within and among local communities. Some were harmonious, and some extremely contentious, even violent. The point to be noted, however, is not their success or their influence (although they were frequently remarkably successful, and in many cases their influence is felt to the present day), but the fact that they happened and so frequently.

I grew up in the 1950s, a time when, to many Catholics, councils seemed to be only a historical memory, an outmoded practice of the church that was no longer needed. There had been no general council of the church for four hundred years since the Council of Trent (1545–63) with the exception of the First Vatican Council (1869–70), which, by its decree on papal primacy and infallibility, seemed to render councils unnecessary. After all, if the bishop of Rome can speak authoritatively for the whole church on matters of faith and morals, why should the bishops of all the other local churches go through the time and trouble of meeting to decide issues that could be handled by Rome? In the United States the bishops of the country had not met in council since the Third Plenary Council of Baltimore in 1884, and there seemed no likelihood of any national or even local synods in the foreseeable future. And then came Vatican II.

Vatican II was a council with a very different purpose from Trent and Vatican I. They had been convened to deal with doctrinal issues of the day. From the outset, however, John XXIII made it clear that the council he called was pastoral in purpose. Vatican II was to be a gathering of the world's bishops more like many of the synods of the early centuries and Middles Ages, that is, an opportunity for discussion of the state of the church in the world of the time. Perhaps what was most striking for many Catholics during and just after the council was that the world's bishops had come together not to approve some action of the bishop of Rome but to consider together the nature of the church and its mission in the modern world. The authority of the council's statements did not have to be established by appeals to the canonical status of ecumenical councils; it was apparent from the extraordinary sight of the nave of Saint Peter's basilica filled with bishops from every continent. The weight of the council was self-evident.

To claim that a quality is a mark that characterizes the church, however, more is needed than simply to show that it has been manifested frequently in the community's history. It is perfectly possible to state that there have been many councils, general and local, in the life of the church from its inception to the present and still to regard this as accidental and in no way necessary to the church as church. To claim that a conciliar dimension is an intrinsic mark of the church and characterizes its very nature is a much stronger statement. That is, however, what I suggest. Fully exploring this claim would require a great deal more space than I have, so I will confine myself to what I think is its most fundamental ground.

If the church is one, it not only ought to be seen as one, it *must* be seen as one. The unity of the church is not a utopian goal—something devoutly to be wished but never experienced in fact. The church's oneness must be manifested if it is to be real. This is intrinsic to the sacramental nature of the church's life. Long ago Augustine wrote that "a sacrament effects what it signifies," a statement often repeated by theologians, including Thomas Aquinas. One way to paraphrase that rich statement is that a sacrament makes something real ("effects" it) by signifying it, by demonstrating or embodying it. If the church is a sacrament of unity—the unity of Christ with his disciples, of believers with one another, and ultimately of the whole world with God—then it must make that unity real by demonstrating it. The coming together of the bishops of a region and even more of the whole world to discuss and decide what the church should say and do is a demonstration and therefore a realization of the church's unity far more striking and effective than an exercise of authority by the bishop of Rome alone. The sacramental oneness of the church is more fully and fruitfully manifested by a council than by the actions of any one bishop or local church, and according to the sacramental principle, what is more fully manifested is by that fact made more fully real and true. Thus the coming together of the church in council is not simply a historical fact or a useful tool or a happy event. It is a necessary structure of the church's existence for the carrying out of its mission.

I mentioned that Vatican I's definition of papal infallibility is sometimes seen as rendering the meeting of the church in council unnecessary. There is, however, a very important statement in that definition which, in my opinion, has not been sufficiently noticed. According to Vatican I, when the bishop of Rome teaches under certain specific conditions, he possesses "that infallibility which the divine Redeemer willed his church to enjoy in defining doctrine concerning faith and morals" (*Pastor aeternus* 4). Clearly, according to its definition of papal infallibility, Vatican I states that the primary recipient of the gift of infallibility is the church at large and that, under certain circumstances, the bishop of Rome exercises that infallibility that belongs to the whole community. If this is so, then without in any way diminishing the papal role, the coming together of the church in united assembly can certainly exercise the charism that its Lord willed that it possess.

This is especially important to remember today when the church's authority is more highly centralized than at any time in its history. In the nineteenth century, distinguished and influential theologians such as Johann Adam Möhler and John Henry Newman insisted that the church's nature and structure were badly distorted if the church is thought of as pyramidal. Rather, in different ways, they described the church as a tension between necessary balancing principles. One way of understanding this is to consider the church as a healthy tension between a centripetal or papal principle drawing authority and decision-making toward one point of focus of the community and a centrifugal or episcopal principle drawing them toward the multiple local churches. The church's well-being and fulfillment of its mission requires that both these principles be honored and maintained. If, at present, the former principle tends to overbalance the latter— and I think it surely does—a righting of the balance and restoration of healthy tension between the two is very much needed. When the church comes together in universal council—when the bishops of the world assemble together with the bishop of Rome—both principles are manifested. A council more clearly embodies and demonstrates the full and essential structure of the church than does the exercise of authority by any one bishop.

Councils are not always general or ecumenical, bringing together all or most of the world's bishops. Indeed, some local councils have had more impact on the church's life than some general councils. For example, the Council of Carthage in 411 at which the north African bishops condemned Pelagianism, or the Council of Orange in 529 where a small group of Gallic bishops did so much to determine our theology of grace, have had a far greater influence on the church than the Second Lateran Council (1139) or the Council of Vienne (1311–12), even though both the latter are officially remembered as ecumenical. When I speak of the church as conciliar in character, I mean that it is marked on every level of its life by the coming together of those charged with leadership in the community. Obviously this is clearest in a general council of the bishops (although there is no necessary reason that membership in a general council must be limited to bishops; often in the church's history general councils included many other people, clergy and lay), but meetings of national hierarchies, diocesan synods, meetings of priests' senates and parish councils are all instances of the conciliar nature of the church. When, on any level of the church's life, the people of God assemble to consider the welfare of the community and how to better fulfill its mission, the true character of the church is displayed and the conclusions they reach may well seem good to the Holy Spirit and to us.

CHAPTER 15

The Church Is Courageous

Donal Dorr

Donal Dorr was born in a very poor part of the west of Ireland in 1935. He was one of the fortunate few in his school who did not have to emigrate at the age of fourteen to find work. He received a scholarship that enabled him to go to high school. After joining St. Patrick's Missionary Society in 1953, he earned a bachelor of arts degree at Cork University. He was ordained in 1961 and obtained a doctorate in theology from Maynooth College with a dissertation about the concept of salvation in the writings of John Wesley. Father Dorr then taught philosophy and theology in Irish colleges.

In 1973 Fr. Dorr went to Africa, where he taught for a couple of years in an interchurch and Christian-Muslim institute attached to the University of Ibadan. He returned to Ireland in 1979 and held a research fellowship in the theology of development in St. Patrick's College, Maynooth. In 1983 he returned to work in Africa for some years.

At the age of forty he had a conversion experience which involved adopting the Paulo Freire model of education. He has worked mainly through participatory workshops rather than by lecturing within the formal educational system ever since. For twenty years (1975–95) he organized empowerment programs for poor people in several African countries and in Ireland.

Since 1995 he has focused on specialized workshops in spirituality. In these workshops the participants (Christians and other spiritual searchers) get in touch with their intuitive and creative powers and seek guidance from the Spirit. Some of the workshops are designed to enable people to integrate spirituality with management skills.

For some years Fr. Dorr was a consultor to the Pontifical Council for Justice and Peace. He is the author of numerous articles about spirituality, justice, and mission and of eight books, of which the following are still in print: Option for the Poor: A Hundred Years of Catholic Social Teaching, *and* Mission in Today's World. *His latest book,* Time for a Change: A Fresh Look at Spirituality, Sexuality, Globalization, and the Church, *was published by Columba Press in Ireland in 2004.*

January 2027

Dear Friend,

You asked me to explain why the church deserves to be called "courageous." So I look back twenty years to the time in 2007 when the big change occurred. The breakthrough can be dated to the announcement that year of a new ecumenical council.

The decision to hold the council in India was courageous and significant. It showed that our church was acknowledging the fact that most of the world's population are Asian; and it suggested that we were at last willing to engage in a really serious dialogue with the religions of Asia. It also indicated that the pope and his new advisory council were determined to break free of the notion that the universality of the Catholic Church depended on strict conformity to Roman thinking and on the imposition of the Western code of canon law. All this called for exceptional courage, since the pope had been surrounded up to that time by people who spoke and acted as though caution and fearfulness were the most important marks of the church.

The announcement of the new council brought about an upsurge of new energy and new thinking. In some ways it was similar to what happened when Pope John XXIII announced Vatican II. But this time the emphasis was not just on new ideas but mainly on a deepening of our spirituality. The church authorities had the courage to trust that the Holy Spirit is guiding and inspiring the whole church, and not just its top leaders. They set up those marvelous listening sessions in every local community where people prayed together and then listened for inspired words to be spoken by the most unexpected people.

Bishops, priests, and theologians sat and listened as patiently as they could while ten-year-old children and eighty-year-old grandparents shared what the Spirit was saying to them. They listened to people with disabilities, to divorced people, to men who had left the priestly ministry, to gays and lesbians, as well as to the mainstream Catholics who were the backbone of the Christian community. They listened with special attention to what was said in the gatherings of women, for they had come at last to recognize that the Spirit works not just powerfully but also at times differently through the religious experience of women. And they had the courage to invite Christians from other churches and key members of other religions to take part in these meetings, and in special meetings devoted to hearing what non-Catholics had to say.

The courageousness of the church became evident in many of these meetings. It was not just that people spoke up, sharing the truth that was in their hearts. Even before that, the participants courageously let go of their fears and pet ideas to open their hearts and minds for the inspiration of the Holy Spirit. It took courage, too, for the church leaders to abandon their busy schedules and give priority to these endless meetings, believing that this was a *kairos* time for themselves and for the church.

The appointment of the central organizing committee for the council and its panel of advisers was an act of the highest courage. The skeptics had expected that these tasks would be given to "safe" people who would sift the material from the listening sessions in accordance with their own preconceived ideas. So there was great surprise and delight when Christians from all over the world were invited to be involved in working out the membership of the organizing committee and of the panel of advisors. At that point a few of the more cautious bishops began to wonder out loud where it would all end. But most of them were won over by that lovely prayer of the pope where he reminded the doubters of the words of Jesus, to "have courage and fear not" and where the pope invited the Spirit to enlighten and guide the church not just through the wise and the prudent but also—and especially—through those who are "low and despised," "the weak in the world" (1 Cor 1:26–7).

The atmosphere at the council was very different from that of Vatican II. Those who took part felt themselves floating on an ocean of prayer generated by Christians and non-Christians all over the world. This infused the sessions with a spirit of respect, sensitivity, and reverence. In this atmosphere it was easy for the bishops taking part to make space for lay women and lay men to play an active role in the deliberations of the council.

The procedures used in this council were very different from those of the Vatican Council of the 1960s. Instead of having an endless series of monologue speeches, the participants took the risk of working for much of the time in what were called "discernment groups," under the guidance of skilled facilitators. In these groups they used the model of Ignatian communal discernment (and other discernment processes) to address contentious issues. In this way they largely avoided the polarization which had characterized the first and second Vatican Councils. Of course there was an occasional clash of views. But these differences were resolved not so much by argument or majority voting but by creative processes of discernment.

A definite high-point of the council was when those taking part replaced the phrase "the voice of the Spirit" with the phrase "the many voices of the Spirit." This was an act of great courage because many had feared that it would appear to be an adoption of a post-modernist or relativist position.

In fact, however, this was a moment of special enlightenment and inspiration. It removed the pressure that many of the participants had felt to convert others to their viewpoint and to have full agreement on all issues. It was a recognition that our faith puts us in touch with a God who remains mysterious, one who cannot be fully tied down in our neat sentences. From that point on, the council and the whole church began to understand the unity of the church not just in terms of acceptance of carefully worded doctrines, but more especially in terms of love, concern, and commitment.

The prayerful and Spirit-led atmosphere in the council encouraged church leaders to be very courageous. They took the risk of looking with fresh eyes at the issues of women's ordination, contraception, homosexuality, and compulsory celibacy for priests—and of undoing mistakes of the past. The more cautious among them were pleasantly surprised to find that the acknowledgment of past mistakes did not undermine the standing of church authorities but rather gave them greater credibility.

This credibility was put to the test when church leaders took the risk of taking a very strong and practical stand against the exploitative model of globalization that was current at the time. To give credibility to this stance they disinvested their resources from companies that were locked into that unjust model of globalization; they instead invested in cooperative ventures that were pioneering a more humane and ecological style of economic development.

At this time, too, the church authorities began to relinquish their ownership of most of the treasures of art inherited from the past. They did this in a way that did not suggest any playing down of the importance of good art in the life of the human and Christian community. They invited philanthropic individuals and foundations to buy out the church museums and art galleries and to open them to the public. The vast amounts of money generated by these sales were devoted to care for poor people affected by HIV/AIDS and to various training and educational programs for people left on the margins of society.

Perhaps the most courageous act of all came at the end of the council when the whole leadership of the Catholic Church publicly asked forgiveness for the church's part in the divisions between Christians. They then went on to make that dramatic gesture of inviting Christians of the Orthodox, Anglican, and Protestant Churches to share with them in a service of mutual recognition of ministries, culminating in a joint Eucharist and communion.

These many courageous actions, begun twenty years ago in 2007, have opened up new horizons for us as Christians, and for the world. Of course there have been ups and downs since then. But we are not likely to forget the lesson we learned at that time: that courage is not just a human virtue but is also a precious gift of the Holy Spirit and a crucial mark of the church. The gift of courage enables us to entrust ourselves and our church into the loving hands of God, to be led by the Spirit into a future that is beyond all that we could ask or imagine.

CHAPTER 16

The Church Is Creedal

Luke Timothy Johnson

Luke Timothy Johnson was born in Wisconsin in 1943, the youngest child of a widow who herself died when he was eleven. His Catholic life spans the church of Pius XII, the church of John XXIII, the church of John Paul II, and the church of Benedict XVI. He went to seminary at age thirteen, and became a Benedictine monk at nineteen. He loved the monastic life, but at age twenty-nine he left the monastery and at thirty married Joy Barnett (the mother of six children). He and Joy had a child together—bringing the total number of children in the family to seven—and they have been married thirty years, adding thirteen grandchildren and three great-grandchildren in the process. Along the way he picked up a bachelor of arts degree in philosophy at Notre Dame Seminary, a master of divinity degree from St. Meinrad School of Theology, a master's in religious studies from Indiana University, and a doctorate in New Testament Studies from Yale University. Dr. Johnson taught New Testament at Yale from 1976 to 1982, then at Indiana University from 1982 to 1992, before becoming the Robert W. Woodruff Distinguished Professor of New Testament and Christian Origins at the Candler School of Theology, Emory University.

Dr. Johnson devotes much energy to teaching, and is proud of the recognition given his efforts by students whom he has taught. Even after thirty years at this demanding craft, he admits that he has much to learn, but has never swerved from the conviction that the classroom is potentially the most powerful arena for human transformation ever devised. He has extended his teaching into public lectures and the writing of many books. His personal favorite is Faith's Freedom: A Classic Spirituality for Contemporary Christians. *Two of his most popular books are* The Real Jesus: The Misguided Quest for the Historical Jesus and the Truth of the Traditional Gospels, *and* The

Writings of the New Testament: An Interpretation. *Dr. Johnson's most recent book is* The Creed: What Christians Believe and Why it Matters, *which brings him to the following topic.*

What Christians Believe Matters

When I was a young theologian, I subscribed to the fashion of the 1960s, which was to diminish the significance of belief in favor of a more robust understanding of faith as a deeply personal response to the living God. Belief was easily caricatured as "belief alone" (see Jas 2:19), a matter of content rather than commitment. I still hold with that rich sense of faith as a response of the whole person to the living God. But I have changed my mind about belief. Two experiences have led me to revise my view.

The first experience was a simple matter of education. A combination of exposure to cognitive psychology and to ancient moral philosophy persuaded me that what people think about reality shapes their responses to it. To put it as simply as Scripture does, "without faith it is impossible to please God, for whoever would approach him must believe that he exists and that he rewards those who seek him" (Heb 11:6). It struck me that if Christians were in the least consistent, the practices that followed from their profession would be startling.

The second experience was pastoral, deriving from my work in the ecumenical church. As a professor in a Protestant school of theology, I grew increasingly aware of the erosion of the sense of church in the United States. Christianity in the U.S. is intensely individualistic, not simply in the sense that people are concerned about themselves, but in the sense that they make up their own version of Christianity to suit themselves. Belief, it seems, is a matter of consumer-choice. Christians think in terms of "my theology" or "my spirituality," not in terms of "the faith of the church." Indeed, it can be questioned whether it is meaningful in any sense to speak of the church in the contemporary United States. The question, then, is how to recover some real sense of church that is firmly grounded in Scripture yet enables a common vision even of the meaning of Scripture. The answer, I think, is renewing a commitment to the creed. Like the notion of a canon of Scripture, in fact, the notion of a creed is correlative to a strong sense of church.

Christianity, in fact, has never been without some sort of creed. It was not, as the popular view today has it, an imposition by fourth-century bishops. Statements of belief are found already in the New Testament, simply because of the complexity of the experience of a crucified and raised Messiah within the symbolic world of Torah. If the crucified Jesus is now raised to God's own life so that we can, and must, call him "Lord" (1 Cor 12:3), we are faced immediately with the problem of what that designation means within a strict monotheism. From that basic struggle arose a variety of creeds, leading eventually to the set formulation called the Apostles' Creed and in the fourth century—in response to heresy—the longer and more complex Nicene-Constantinopolitan Creed. These are the creeds that most Christians recite in worship, with the Apostles' Creed favored by Protestants—while used by Catholics in private devotion—and the Nicene-Constantinopolitan Creed favored by Catholic and Orthodox believers.

Such "creedal Christians" who recite the creed out loud together at worship are engaged in activity more provocative than they might suppose. I quote my book: "In a world that celebrates individuality, they are actually doing something together. In an age that avoids commitment, they pledge themselves to a set of convictions and thereby to each other. In a culture that rewards novelty and creativity, they use words written by others long ago. In a society where accepted wisdom changes by the minute, they claim that some truths are so critical that they must be repeated over and over again. In a throwaway, consumerist world, they accept, preserve, and continue tradition. Reciting the creed at worship is thus a counter-cultural act" (*The Creed*, 40–41).

The creed is a mark of the church as church because it is a public profession of faith. Each person who recites the creed understands its propositions individually and diversely, but the church as such believes more and better than any individual believer. I am aware each week that I fall short of true belief in all that the creed states—and I suspect there is a similar disbeliever within us all, whose practice does not match profession—but when I recite the creed with my fellow parishioners at Sacred Heart Church in Atlanta, I commit myself again to the fullness of the church's faith. From the beginning, then, the creed has been an instrument of Christian self-definition by which the church as such not only expresses its faith, but through that expression, comes into being as a believing people.

The creed does five things to shape the church as church. First, it narrates the Christian myth. It does not state a philosophy of life, but a story of God's profound and mysterious involvement with humanity, a story in which God came among us so that we might be brought into God's own life. Second, the creed interprets Scripture. It does not exhaust the significance of Scripture, but it provides readers with a rule for reading rightly: Christians find in Scripture the one God who creates the world and who is the Father of the Lord Jesus Christ. The creed points readers to what is essential in the story. Third, the creed constructs a world. The church is a people with a definite understanding of reality, one that often stands in tension with the understandings offered by this age (or any age). When the creed declares that God creates everything, both visible and invisible, it makes a definite—and not trivial—statement about the origin, nature, and destiny of the world, and of us. Christians who recite the creed dare to state as truth a vision of the world not based in science, technology, or sociological surveys, but on God's own self-revelation.

Fourth, the creed guides Christian practices. This is a dimension few of us think about: what would happen if we actually lived out what we profess in the creed? What attitudes toward other creatures, what ecological practices, what uses of material possessions might follow from the proposition that God is the creator of all things visible and invisible, and therefore, all creatures are equally gifts from God? What practices might follow from taking seriously the creed's proposition that the church is, at once, "one, holy, catholic, apostolic"? Not only would we be required to understand what these terms might mean, we would also need to struggle with a vision of holiness that included unity, an understanding of catholic that embraced apostolic.

Fifth, the creed prepares a worshiping people. How fortunate that the creed ended up in its present place in the Mass, between the Liturgy of the Word and the Liturgy of the Eucharist! In antiquity, the creed was used to mark the transition (at baptism-chrismation-first eucharist) from catechumen—one involved in an apprenticeship in the Christian life—to fully-initiated member of the people of God and participant in the apostolate. Now it mimics that same transition every week at Mass. We listen during the liturgy of the word and hear the readings and the homily, and sing our psalms and our acclamations. Then the creed summons us to gather in an explicit and powerful expression of our shared faith, the faith that embraces and exceeds the small belief of each one of us. Together, we recite, each with our own limited understanding, these ancient and noble truths. And by professing our shared faith together, we grow strong as church, ready to make intercessions and pray our eucharistic prayer together, and ready to bear into our daily lives the reality of a world created, saved, and sanctified by the living God.

It is difficult to know how seriously to take a claim to be church by Christians who neglect the creed. Certainly they may be Christians, and very fine ones. But are they church? Do they share some common history, hear some of the same Scriptures, engage in some of the same practices? It is equally difficult to understand why Christians who are creedal have not taken more seriously the implications of this precious mark of the church.

CHAPTER 17

The Church as Democratic and Constitutional

Leonard Swidler

Leonard Swidler has been a professor of Catholic thought and interreligious dialogue at Temple University since 1966. With his wife, Arlene Anderson Swidler, he co-founded in 1964 the Journal of Ecumenical Studies. *He is also the founder/director of the Institute for Interreligious, Intercultural Dialogue.*

Swidler was born January 6, 1929, to an Irish-American mother and a Ukrainian-Jewish father (who became a committed Catholic when he was sixteen). He grew up during the Great Depression in Green Bay, Wisconsin—leading naturally to a passion for football, which he played on teams from primary school through college. He graduated from high school just after World War II and earned his bachelor of arts degree from St. Norbert's College. During those years he decided that he had two goals in life: to be an intellectual and a saint. Hence, he joined the Norbertine order. After four years of theological study, he decided not to go on to ordination. He then studied at Marquette University (where he earned a master's degree), the University of Wisconsin (where he earned his doctorate), the University of Munich, and the University of Tübingen (where he earned a licentiate in sacred theology).

After a brief teaching stint at Duquesne University, Dr. Swidler accepted in 1966 a professorship in the newly-formed religion department at Temple University, which quickly developed a strong doctoral program.

Dr. Swidler has published more than 180 articles and sixty books, including: Jewish-Christian-Muslim Dialogue, Religious Liberty and Human

Rights, A Bridge to Buddhist-Christian Dialogue, Human Rights: Christians, Marxists, and Others in Dialogue, Toward a Catholic Constitution, For All Life: Toward a Universal Declaration of a Global Ethic—An Interreligious Dialogue, The Study of Religion in the Age of Global Dialogue, *and* Dialogue in Malaysia and the Globe.

Mandate for a Democratic Constitution in the Catholic Church

Set up a constitution not just for civil states, but for the whole Catholic Church! Those were the instructions of Pope Paul VI during Vatican II, and he set up an international commission to begin that process. The commission worked for fourteen years and produced several drafts of what is called the *Lex Fundamentalis Ecclesiae*, the "Fundamental Law of the Church" or constitution. Unfortunately, Pope John Paul II decided in 1980 not to pursue its completion and implementation.

We Catholics need to take up the papal mandate to draft and put into practice the dream and wish of Pope Paul VI, to make it also *our* dream and *our* wish: to create and put into practice, at every level, a whole series of constitutions for the Catholic Church.

Constitutions and democratic structures are not something new or strange to the Catholic Church. Throughout its history the Catholic Church has been a kind of "limited democracy." We learned in primary school that the Greek word for "people" is *demos* and the Greek word for "rule" is *kratia*, and from those two words we derive the term "democracy," rule by the people. After more than two centuries of civil experience we are comfortable with the idea that the people should rule in civil society. But, how do we know that the people should rule in the Catholic Church?

We know first from Scripture: *all* people are made in "God's image" (Gen 1:26), "knowing good and evil" (Gen 3:25). Second, from tradition: at the Second Vatican Council, in the Decree on Ecumenism, the pope and all the bishops insisted that Catholics' primary duty is to make an honest and careful appraisal of whatever needs to be renewed and achieved in the Catholic household itself. This was a continuation of the tradition from the very beginning of the church when all the faithful gathered together to choose a successor to the Apostle Judas (Acts 1:15–26). Two other first-century documents confirm this approach: "You [the faithful] must, then, elect for yourselves bishops and deacons" (Didache 15:1–2); bishops should be chosen "with the consent of the whole church" (1 Clement 44, 5).

This practice passed into the post-apostolic period, as evidenced by one of the oldest known synods (already in the second century). "For this reason believers in Asia often assembled in many Asian localities, examined the new doctrines, and condemned the heresy" (Eusebius, *Ecclesiastical History* [PG 20, 468]). St. Cyprian, in the third century, bore witness to the custom of the people having the right not only to elect, but also to reject and even recall bishops: "The people themselves most especially have the power to choose worthy bishops or to reject unworthy ones" (Epistle, 67, 3, CSEL, 3.2.737). Following the old Roman principle, "Whatever affects everyone must be decided upon by everyone," Cyprian often convoked synods and wrote to his priests and deacons: "From the beginning of my episcopate I have been determined to undertake nothing on my own private judgment without consulting you and gaining the assent of the people" (PL 4, 234).

Every Catholic schoolgirl and schoolboy knows the stories of the elections of Ambrose as bishop of Milan and Augustine as bishop of Hippo (fourth and fifth centuries) by the acclamation of the people: "Nos elegimus eum! We elect him!" A little later Pope Celestine said: "No one is given the episcopate uninvited. The consent and desire of the clerics, the people, and leadership are required" (Epistle, iv, 5; PL, 50, 431). That redoubtable Pope Leo the Great, who faced down Attila the Hun and saved Rome from the sack, wrote: "Let him who will stand before all be elected by all" (Epistle, x, 4; PL, 54, 634).

These principles from the early centuries of Christian practice were reiterated in various synods until as late as the Council of Paris in 829. Basically the election of bishops by the clergy and people remained until the twelfth century—over half the present span of Christianity. In addition, the first seven ecumenical councils, which set all the basic Christian doctrines, were all convoked, presided over, and promulgated, not by popes or bishops, but by laymen and—shocking—a lay woman! Further, every religious order of priests, sisters, or brothers has from its beginnings, starting with Benedict in the sixth century, governed itself by *constitutions*, which include the election of leaders, limited term of office, due process of law—all democratic structures appearing centuries before the United States Constitution.

Even at the beginning of the United States, our first bishop, John Carroll (1735–1815), and his two coadjutor bishops were, with the full approval of Rome, elected at least by all of the priests of the U.S. Carroll's greatest successor, John England, bishop of the Carolinas from1820 to 1840, governed his diocese with a constitution, which the entire diocese approved before it took effect. Following his constitution, he held an annual diocesan convention, at which he gave a full accounting of all activities, including the finances.[63]

The Contemporary Magisterium Supports Democracy

Pope Paul VI not only called for a Catholic constitution (*Lex Fundamentalis Ecclesiae*), but also called for the laity to take the initiative as appropriate. In 1967 he declared: "It belongs to the laity, without waiting passively for orders and directives, to take the initiative freely and to infuse a Christian spirit into the mentality, customs, laws, and structures of the community in which they live" (*Populorum progressio* 81). One of the most important communities we live in is the Catholic Church. And in 1971 he stated: "Let each one examine himself, to see what he has done up to now, and what he ought to do. It is not enough to recall principles, state intentions, point to crying injustices and utter prophetic denunciations; these words will lack real weight unless they are accompanied for each individual by a livelier awareness of personal responsibility and by effective action" (*Octogesima adveniens* 48). Here is a call to action to all of us by the pope himself.

More recently, Pope John Paul II noted that "Democracy…represents a most important topic for the new millennium….[The church] values the democratic system inasmuch as it ensures the participation of citizens in making political choices, guarantees to the governed the possibility both of electing and holding accountable those who govern them, and of replacing them" (to the Participants in the Sixth Plenary Session of the Pontifical Academy of Social Sciences, February 23, 2000).

In brief, then: what the church needs in the twenty-first century is a return to the tradition of shared rights and responsibilities for all the people of God, spelled out in written form for *all* to see—a constitution!

Such a constitution will be in the spirit of Jesus' gospel of liberation and love and adaptive of the most mature governance principles available at the start of the third millennium. Spearheading this international movement is the Association for the Rights of Catholics in the Church (http://arcc-catholic-rights.org), which with world-wide collaboration has drawn up a proposed Catholic constitution. It has been carefully researched and re-drafted numerous times, but nevertheless is intended as a proposed draft to launch a discussion that must range long, wide, and deep before the constitution will begin to be accepted as an effective instrument to undergird the governance of the whole Catholic Church.

A Needed Change of Catholic Consciousness

Perhaps the most important change needed, however, is a change in the consciousness and mentality of Catholics—laity and clergy. Our Catholic tradition and community must be a living source of something liberating for which we mature Christians feel a sense of responsibility. This includes an adult sharing in claiming rights and shouldering responsibilities, in short, a sharing in democracy—in a constitution. If the seemingly endless sexual abuse scandal has taught us anything, it is that we cannot allow secrecy, closed-door decisions about where our money goes, about who gets appointed to what positions, about who appoints them. We need the governance of law, and that means the laws have to be written down for all to see and know, and there have to be procedures to make certain that the laws are followed. In other words, we are talking about a constitution.

Thus, all Catholics need to work together for increasing responsible democratic structures in the church, and most of all for the creation and ratification of the greatest single advance in Catholicism in centuries—a *Catholic constitution* for all levels of the church.

A constitution for the church, called for by Pope Paul VI, revised by the people of God, and established in our communities, will indeed lead to a church *of* the people of God, *by* the people of God, and *for* the people of God.

CHAPTER 18

The Church Is Dialogical

Paul F. Knitter

Born in Chicago, Illinois on February 25, 1939, Paul Knitter entered the minor seminary of the Divine Word Missionaries out of eighth grade. That explains his early, and abiding, interest in other religions. That interest deepened throughout his theological studies and teaching: his years in Rome for the licentiate at the Gregorian University (while the Second Vatican Council was in session), his doctoral studies at the University of Marburg in Germany (1969–72), his teaching at Catholic Theological Union in Chicago (1972–75), and his long tenure at Xavier University, Cincinnati (1975–2000) where he is now a professor emeritus.

In his teaching and writing, Dr. Knitter has tried to combine a strong commitment to Christ and to social justice with a genuine openness to what God may be revealing in other religions. Among the books he is proudest of are: No Other Name? A Critical Survey of Christian Attitudes toward the World Religions; One Earth Many Religions: Multifaith Dialogue and Global Responsibility; *and* Introducing Theologies of Religions.

Throughout his career Dr. Knitter has tried to balance academics with activism. He has been a member of Christians for Peace in El Salvador since 1986 and on the Board of Trustees of the Interreligious Peace Council since 1996. He has also served since 1987 as general editor of Orbis Books' series, Faith Meets Faith. He says that his wife, Cathy, and children, John and Moira, have supported him and kept him honest in all that he does.

"Catholic" Means "Dialogical"

As I struggle, like many in my church-community, with what it means today to be Catholic, I've found myself in recent years taking many of my cues, and drawing much of my hope, from my fellow Catholics in Asia. Those cues and that hope are summarized in a relatively recent book titled *Pentecost in Asia: A New Way of Being Church* (Orbis Books, 2002). In it, author Tom Fox describes how the many facets of this "new way" boil down to one word: dialogue. The Asian bishops, listening to their people and assisted by their theologians, have clearly and powerfully insisted that the church can be a church-in-Asia only if it is in authentic dialogue with other Asian religions *and* with the many Asian poor and marginalized.

In my life as a Catholic believer and in my labors as a Catholic theologian, I have come to realize that what is true of the local churches in Asia is just as true of the universal church. Pentecost, which might be called "the big bang" that launched the *ecclesia*, will continue rippling through the ecclesial universe of the third millennium mainly through the energy of dialogue. In order for the community of Jesus' followers to be faithful disciples in our present world it needs to understand "catholic" to mean "dialogical." To be the "Roman Catholic Church" of old, we need to be the "Roman Dialogical Church" of the twenty-first century. Let me try to explain why and how I believe that to be true.

A World in Need of Dialogue

The world that the church is called to serve, challenge, and transform is a world in dire need of dialogue for two reasons: it is a pluralistic world, and it is a violent world.

Pluralism—the vast variety of peoples, cultures, religions—has, of course, always colored the fabric of human history. But today, mainly because of the push-button speed of communication and travel, those differing colors have become all the more evident. In fact, for many people, they have become bewildering or blinding. This is especially true of the multiple colors of religions. *Religious pluralism*—the abundant, persistent, exuberant diversity of religions—is confronting, often perplexing, Christians as never before. The shapes and colors and even smells of other religions are no longer on the other side of the world. They often emerge from the house next door! In a recent, highly-regarded book, Diana L. Eck gives convincing data that there is *A New Religious America* (the title), and she describes *How a "Christian Country" Has Become the World's Most Religiously Diverse Nation* (the subtitle) (HarperSanFrancisco, 2001).

The many-ness of religions, therefore, isn't going to go away. It seems that religious pluralism is "as it was it in the beginning, is now, and ever shall be." If that's the case, the simple, immediate conclusion is that

Christians have to learn to *co-exist*, to live with and be good neighbors to people who are Buddhist, Hindu, Muslim, etc. But being good neighbors to each other means more than tolerance, more than just accepting the pluralistic state of affairs. Rather, it means learning about each other, appreciating and valuing each other. Pluralistic co-existence—that is, really living and thriving together as different religions—requires dialogue.

But co-existence is not enough. Because our world is not just a pluralistic world but also a violent world, we have to do more together. I'm talking mainly (but not only) about the violence that erupts from the barrel of a gun, the impact of a missile, the explosion of an airplane crashing into a building. I'm talking about military or terroristic violence. The dreams of a new age of peace after the fall of the Soviet Union have turned, it seems, into nightmares. Besides the multiple, rampaging conflicts of ethnic and/or religious groups, the world is witnessing what some call the "clash of civilizations"—a clash fueled by the terrorism of scattered movements pitted against the military might of world powers. All too often, religion is used to fuel such violence.

But if such "use" of religion for violence is, as is generally said, a "misuse," then the religions of the world are going to have to do something to prevent that misuse. And they're going to have to do it *together*. So, besides co-existence, we also need *cooperation* among the religious traditions of the world. Speaking as a Catholic Christian, I feel the need to cooperate, as a Catholic, with persons of other religions in order to prove that religions are a much more powerful tool of peace than they are a weapon of war. But such cooperation can be realized only through dialogue. The well-known dictum of Hans Küng, therefore, rings true: "There will be no peace among nations without peace among religions. And there will be no peace among religions without dialogue among them."

What Is Dialogue?

But just what do we mean by dialogue? That's an important question, since dialogue nowadays is a term that gets thrown around facilely and sloppily. As it is generally understood in interreligious encounters, dialogue can be described as follows: a relationship between differing parties in which all parties speak their minds and open their minds to each other, in the hope that through this engagement all parties will grow in truth and well-being. Dialogue therefore is always a *two-way street* which can lead all who travel it to greater understanding and cooperation. All participants in a dialogical encounter have to be ready both to listen and to speak, to teach and be taught. A true dialogue is always both a "give and take"—one gives witness to what one holds to be true and at the same time accepts the witness of what the other holds true and dear. Everyone seeks to convince and is ready to be convinced. And if in the dialogue I come to see and feel the truth of your position, then I must also be ready to clarify, correct, even change my views. Dialogue is always exciting; it can also be threatening.

And it is just this kind of dialogue that the Catholic Church, since Vatican II, has been holding up as an ideal—one might even say, an obligation—for all Catholics. With humble pride, Catholics can recognize that their church has been on the forefront of all Christian denominations in calling its members to respect and dialogue with followers of other religions. And over the years since Vatican II, this call has become clearer and louder.

In 1965, the bishops at Vatican II called on all Catholics to "enter with prudence and charity into discussion and collaboration with members of other religions" (*Nostra aetate* 2). In 1984, this gentle invitation became a requirement when the Vatican Secretariate for Non-Christian Religions (later called the Pontifical Council for Dialogue) announced that dialogue is an essential part of the Church's mission (in *The Attitude of the Church toward Followers of Other Religions*). Then in 1991, the meaning of dialogue was boldly clarified in Pope John Paul II's encyclical *Redemptoris missio* (RM) and in the Declaration *Dialogue and Proclamation* (DP) from the Pontifical Council for Dialogue. These official statements expressly acknowledged that the intended fruits of dialogue are in the "mutual enrichment" of *all* sides (RM 55, DP 9), that in the dialogue Catholics should allow themselves to be questioned, perhaps purified, (DP 32), maybe even transformed (DP 47). Surprisingly, the Vatican document even goes so far as to recognize that in a true dialogue, all the participants (including Catholics) must be open to being converted, that is, open "to leave one's previous spiritual or religious situation in order to direct oneself to another" (DP 41). Clearly, this official teaching of the Catholic Church recognizes dialogue as a two-way street.

A New Way of Being Church

So as the sun of the new millennium rises over the church and the world, this understanding and challenge of dialogue can help Catholics to grasp and practice what it really means to be catholic. As we learned in catechism class, "catholic" means "universal"—embracing of, open to, sent into the whole world with its many peoples and cultures and religions. But for most of church history, this universal quality of our community has been viewed as a one-way street. We bring the saving message to them; we give, they receive.

But "catholic" understood as "dialogue"—and "dialogue" understood as Pope John Paul II and the Pontifical Council for Dialogue understand it—means that the relationship between the church and other cultures and religions must be two-way. If the church is to grow and be faithful to the gospel of Jesus, it must not only deliver the good news but also be open to whatever good news God may be providing through other religious traditions. Not only by teaching all nations but also by learning from all nations can the church cooperate with other religions in the work of overcoming violence and bringing justice to the poor of our planet—and to our poor planet suffering from environmental devastation. To call itself Catholic means that the community of Jesus' followers needs others—people and religions who are really different. Only through a dialogical relationship with *others* can the church understand and be faithful to the message of Jesus.

Dialogue *is* indeed a meaningful, challenging new way of being church. If this is what it means to be Catholic, I'm happy and proud to be one.

CHAPTER 19

The Church Is Discerning

Jeannine Gramick, SL

Jeannine Gramick joined the School Sisters of Notre Dame in 1960. She taught in junior and senior high schools for several years in Baltimore.

In 1971 she became involved in pastoral outreach to the lesbian and gay community. She continued this pastoral ministry while teaching mathematics at the College of Notre Dame of Maryland. She is co-founder and chaplain of the Baltimore and Washington, DC chapters of Dignity, a national organization for Catholic lesbian, gay, bisexual, and transgender people, their families, and friends.

In 1977, along with Father Robert Nugent, Sister Gramick co-founded New Ways Ministry, a national Catholic social justice center working through education for the reconciliation of lesbian and gay people and the church. Since that time she has engaged in writing, research, speaking, retreats, and consultation on lesbian and gay issues and Catholicism.

Sister Gramick has written and edited numerous articles and several books. Two books, Building Bridges: Gay and Lesbian Reality and the Catholic Church *and* Voices of Hope: A Collection of Positive Catholic Writings on Lesbian/Gay Issues, *were the subject of a Vatican investigation. Building Bridges was translated into Italian in 2003 and published as* Anime Gay: Gli omosessuali e la Chiesa cattolica.

For approximately twenty years, the School Sisters of Notre Dame assigned her to lesbian and gay ministry. In 1999 the Vatican's Congregation for the Doctrine of the Faith permanently prohibited her from any pastoral work with lesbian or gay persons. In 2000 the School Sisters of Notre Dame ordered her to cease speaking about the Vatican investigation and about homosexual-

ity in general. In 2001 she transferred to the Sisters of Loretto where she continues to engage in lesbian and gay ministry.

Many Catholic groups, as well as lesbian and gay groups, have recognized her work in this pioneer ministry. She is the subject of a documentary film, In Good Conscience: Sister Jeannine Gramick's Journey of Faith.

Sister Gramick holds a doctorate in mathematics education from the University of Pennsylvania. She is vitally interested in religious life, in promoting the recognition of women's ministries, and in reform and renewal in the Catholic Church. She has served on the national boards of numerous women's organizations and is strongly committed to a justice agenda.

Moral Discernment

As a young girl growing up in Philadelphia in the 1940s and 1950s, I believed implicitly in what I was taught by the church. The sisters in the Catholic schools I attended trained me well to respect and follow authority. Indoctrinated in the *Baltimore Catechism*, I could recite questions and answers on demand. While love might have been the supreme virtue in name, obedience was the ultimate value in fact. And obedient I was. I did whatever "sister said," preaching the instructions of the black-robed women to my parents at home.

In many ways, I cherish the religious education I received, imparted by women who were kind and loving. I was grounded in a value system of family, honesty, self-discipline, perfection, work, and finding pleasure in the world of mind and spirit. I sense that my teachers *believed* in these values and I imbibed their beliefs.

The Catholic culture I experienced did not exist throughout all the centuries of Christianity because religious culture of beliefs and rituals change over time. As individuals engage in moral reflection, they may challenge some doctrines or practices held by the group. When sufficiently large numbers of individuals share moral discernment, a new thought emerges for communal discernment. New meanings and understandings may replace past traditions. This transformation most often happens gradually so that it is almost imperceptible at any one moment. While the conversion of the group may take centuries, it begins at a certain point in time with the moral discernment of an individual.

Unfortunately, my generation was not trained in moral discernment or encouraged to question, probe, or analyze. We were to memorize facts and teachings and to conform to authorities. The problem was not assuaged by my entrance into religious life, which emphasized the vow of obedience.

A cataclysmic awakening in my moral development came after twenty years of assigned ministry to lesbian and gay Catholics. In 1999, the Congregation for the Doctrine of the Faith notified the Catholic community that I was permanently prohibited from any pastoral work with lesbian or gay persons. If I chose to continue this ministry, there was the possibility of dismissal from my community. I faced an enormous moral dilemma. Should I obey a Vatican directive, signed by the Pope, to cease this ministry to which I felt called by God since 1971?

During one of many retreats at this time, I pondered what God was asking of me. One afternoon as I jogged around the monastery grounds, I looked down at my sneakers and realized how well they fit my feet. I thought of my floppy Birkenstocks, and knew I might trip with those sandals on my feet. The smart-looking shoes I wear for more formal occasions would hurt my feet after a few jogs around the convent grounds. I certainly *could* walk in shoes that were too big, too small, too loose, or too tight for a limited time; but if I walked long enough in shoes that didn't fit, I would ruin my feet, my back, my posture, and my health.

That meditation on shoes became an allegory for me. The shoes that fit just right are the shoes that God asks us to walk in during life. They may or may not fit others, and they probably won't fit everyone! But each one of us needs to walk in the designer shoes that sport God's label.

Finding our God-shoes is a poetic way of describing the process of making an informed conscience decision. The *Pastoral Constitution on the Church in the Modern World* describes conscience.

> Deep within their consciences men and women discover a law which they have not laid upon themselves and which they must obey. Its voice, ever calling them to love and to do what is good and to avoid evil, tells them inwardly at the right moment: do this, shun that. For they have in their hearts a law inscribed by God. Their dignity rests in observing this law, and by it they will be judged. (16)

This moral discernment is vital for our faith life and our love relationship with God. If we are to grow in faith and not remain as children who blindly follow without question, then we must begin to make our own moral decisions. The extensive process of finding our God-shoes by wrestling with an issue and hashing it out with God will inevitably draw us closer to our divine maker and best friend.

Sometimes our moral discernment results in a choice to set aside a church teaching or a directive from religious authorities. This act of good conscience requires great courage because it does not feel comfortable to discount the accumulated wisdom of the community or to oppose respected spiritual leaders.

How do we know the God-shoes that are right for us? Christians are blessed to be part of a community that often has guidelines on deciding moral problems. Therefore, we need to know those guidelines or teachings and why the community has come to a particular judgment. We need to be familiar with contemporary theology, scripture, scientific findings, and even world events dealing with the moral problem. Furthermore, we need to examine our own personal experiences, our likes or dislikes, our instincts or feelings, and our common sense about the matter because God often uses these natural predispositions as indicators of a direction. Speaking with a wise or upright person is often helpful.

We take all this study and advice to prayer. We talk at great length with our loving God in some quiet space or sanctuary of our soul. Eventually we make a conscience decision that feels right and brings peace within. Even though there may be upheaval without, we are walking in God-shoes.

Making conscience decisions is not only indispensable for the individual's adult faith life, but also critical for the entire church. Development in the church can come about only when individuals, whose moral discernment differs from that of the past, make their positions public and create a public debate. Vatican II supported public expressions of opinion. The *Pastoral Constitution on the Church in the Modern World* states, "Provided they respect the moral order and the common interest, people should be entitled to seek after truth, to express and make known their opinions" (59).

Communal discernment on dissenting views can lead to development of doctrine. In the church's history, there are myriad examples of development on theological issues such as the Trinity, Christ's nature, the Petrine office, and Marian dogma. Some changes have been outright contradictions. For example, the church's teaching that error had no rights, expressed by Pope Pius IX in the 1864 *Syllabus of Errors*, changed to the teaching of respect for religious differences, embodied in the *Declaration on Religious Freedom* of Vatican II. This and other reversals of doctrine have yet to be fully explained by theologians and, I might add, to be fully accepted by some within the church.

Unfortunately, since the 1980s, the church envisioned by Vatican II has been reconstructed so that a free expression of opinion has been discouraged. This hostile climate rewards conformity, punishes dissent, promotes fear and self-silencing, and has jeopardized the moral development of the whole community.

The suffocating effects of self-silencing were impressed on me in the course of the Vatican investigation through another image. Almost a year after the first attempted silencing, I was summoned to Rome and given a command not to speak about the investigation that led to the prohibition.

As I sat in my community's Generalate office, a vivid image came to mind. I saw a woman, whose spouse had physically abused her for years. I saw a battered woman, made old beyond her years, who remained silent because she feared further reprisals against her. I saw a weeping woman, who was concerned about the safety of her children if she spoke up.

Like that woman, I felt intimidated to remain silent about the psychological abuse I had experienced. During the investigation, I was afraid to speak publicly and terrified of standing alone. After the first silencing order, as I addressed audiences across the United States telling my story, I began to lose my fear of ecclesiastical authorities. After finding my voice and feeling the freedom of the Spirit, I could no longer be silent. Because I had engaged in much prayer during the past year, I quite naturally responded, "I choose not to collaborate in my own oppression by restricting my basic human right to speak about my experience. To me this is a matter of conscience."

I believe most Catholics have remained silent when they disagree with church authorities, locked away in a closet of fear, and unable to find a key to open the door. Perhaps that key is the realization that the faith development of the whole church in some way depends upon one's personal moral discernment and the courage to speak the truth as one perceives it. There is a freedom in speaking one's truth and a grace in knowing that one cannot do otherwise and maintain one's own integrity.

Authoritarian structures rely on self-censorship to maintain power and control. Sometimes I feel the Catholic community is in danger of imitating Obadiah Slope, a character in Anthony Trollope's *Barchester Towers*. Slope is the bishop's obsequious and hypocritical chaplain, who "kissed the rod that scourged him."

The locus of all authority resides in the Holy Spirit, who has been given to the whole church. The people of God have an enormous contribution to make to needed reforms in our church. These reforms will come only if individuals grow into spiritually mature adults by making their own conscience decisions. These reforms will come only if individuals do not silence themselves, but speak their truth, and contribute to a vigorous, communal discernment in the church.

CHAPTER 20

The Church as Domestic

Richard Gaillardetz

Richard Gaillardetz was born on May 11, 1958, and was raised in a military family, traveling frequently. He earned a bachelor of arts degree in humanities from the University of Texas in 1981. He then devoted the next two years of his life to full-time volunteer work for the Roman Catholic Church in campus ministry, working in Denton, Texas, in exchange for room and board.

After this volunteer work, he returned to school to get a master of arts degree in theology at St. Mary's University in San Antonio and then was hired by the Catholic Diocese of Ft. Worth to work in adult religious education. Several years later he began doctoral studies in theology at the University of Notre Dame, receiving a doctorate in systematic theology.

Immediately upon graduation he accepted a position at the University of St. Thomas in Houston. After ten years teaching both seminarians and lay students preparing for ministry, Dr. Gaillardetz accepted his current position as the Thomas and Margaret Murray and James J. Bacik Professor of Catholic Studies at the University of Toledo. He has published numerous articles and authored or edited six books, including By What Authority? A Primer on Scripture, the Magisterium, and the Sense of the Faithful, *and* A Daring Promise: A Spirituality of Christian Marriage. *Dr. Gaillardetz is currently an official delegate on the U.S. Catholic-Methodist Ecumenical Dialogue. In 2000 he received the Sophia Award from the faculty of the Washington Theological Union in recognition of "theological excellence in service to ministry."*

At the time of writing the following reflection, he and his wife were on the eve of celebrating fifteen years of marriage. He says that he could not have imagined the innumerable ways in which those vows, uttered fifteen years ago, would create the space in which their family of six would, in fear and trembling, work out their salvation. Their marriage vows were ecclesial vows, both in the sense that they were made before the gathered assembly in which they worshiped weekly, and in the sense that in their vows they were constituting themselves as a new ecclesial reality, the most basic among the community of disciples, the domestic church.

The Family or Household as Domestic Church

The view of the family or Christian household as an *ecclesia domestica* goes back to the origins of Christianity, but it has only been explored within the Catholic tradition in the last four decades. In his apostolic exhortation on evangelization, *Evangelii nuntiandi*, Pope Paul VI highlighted the evangelical and missionary character of the Christian family:

> The family, like the church, ought to be a place where the Gospel is transmitted and from which the Gospel radiates. In a family which is conscious of this mission, all the members evangelize and are evangelized. The parents not only communicate the Gospel to their children, but from their children they can themselves receive the same Gospel as deeply lived by them. (71)[64]

A notable feature of this text is the reciprocal character of evangelization within the family. Indeed, the very substance of the daily life of the family has an evangelical and catechetical dimension. In a similar vein Pope John Paul II wrote on the deliberations of the episcopal synod on the family in his apostolic exhortation, *Familiaris consortio*:

> The synod too, taking up and developing the indications of the council, presented the educational mission of the Christian family as a true ministry through which the Gospel is transmitted and radiated, so that family life itself becomes an itinerary of faith and in some way a Christian initiation and *a school of following Christ*. (39, emphasis mine)[65]

This image of the family as a "school of following Christ" is rich in possibility for a theological vision of the family.

The family household, as a true ecclesial community, cannot be isolated from the larger fabric of human society. Again, Pope John Paul II writes: "the family is by nature and vocation open to other families and to society and undertakes its social role" (FC 42). These texts help demonstrate how the Catholic Church in the last forty years has come to recognize the ecclesial character of the Christian household.

Some Dangers in the Notion of the Domestic Church

There are some dangers with this approach, however. One of them is the tendency to view the Christian family as ecclesial only to the extent that it mirrors some larger ecclesial entity, for example, the parish (because we have religious statuary in the home, just like at the parish, or because we have family liturgies, just like in the parish). In fact, the Christian household is ecclesial not because it is "church-like" but because in the self-conscious patterning of household relationships on the paschal mystery and the demands of the gospel, we become church. In our home we pray regularly. We have religious art prominently displayed and each Advent we break out the Advent wreath, which becomes the focus of our family prayer for four weeks. But the ecclesiality of our household is determined as much by the mundane interactions that occupy us, for example, that hectic first hour before the kids go off to school, when chores are done and morning squabbles emerge or fester or are subject to reconciliation.

A second danger in speaking of a domestic church concerns the use of the word "family." First, the teaching of Jesus virtually exploded the category of the family in the ancient world. Jesus taught that under God's rule, kinship relations were to be subordinated to the spiritual bonds of discipleship (see Mark 3:31–35).

The gospel of Jesus Christ stresses the creation of a new family, a new household—the household of believers. Our truest identity is discovered in the recognition that God is our Father/Mother and that we are children of God. All other relations are subordinated to this one. This teaching of Jesus need not be understood as the renunciation of the family (though Jesus apparently envisioned that some might do so for the sake of the kingdom). However, it does suggest that the family must now be reinterpreted in the light of the call to discipleship. That means that the life of discipleship—and not blood relations—defines the family as domestic church.

Consequently, I prefer the language of household to that of family. Like the family, a household *may* be multi-generational and *may* be constituted by marriage and kinship relations. However, unlike the family, the defining feature is not necessarily blood, marriage, or adoption but a common domicile or home. Thus, Christian households might include not only traditional families like my own, but the L'Arche communities founded by Jean Vanier.[66]

It is in the household that we eat, sleep, bathe, get dressed, relax, and converse with others. In the context of the home we learn basic social conventions, from table manners to the demands of hospitality toward guests. In the household we learn how to be accountable for our lives; we learn when we are expected for dinner (or to prepare dinner); we learn what chores and other miscellaneous responsibilities are assigned to us and how the smooth functioning of the household depends on the fulfillment of those chores and responsibilities. More importantly, in the household we learn about the possibilities for committed intimate relationship with others and the privileges and responsibilities that those relationships bring with them.

The ecclesial character of the Christian household is grounded in this unique and complex set of relations realized within a common domicile. Because in that complex set of relations we are engaged in the most basic of human relationships, the impact of the household on us is all the greater. Even the most active parishioner is at the parish church only a few times a week, a couple of hours at a time. We all live a far greater percentage of our lives in the household.

It is in this nexus of patterned relationships which constitutes the household that we can better understand the image of the Christian household as a "school of discipleship." To be a disciple of Jesus is to be shaped and formed in the ways and values of the kingdom with which Jesus was preoccupied. Jesus taught in parables and modeled in his actions the prodigal love of God, the scandalously inclusive and generous justice which typified God's reign. Jesus' teaching on the reign of God was much more than a set of precepts to be memorized; it was nothing less than an alternative way in living, a new mode of existence. Initiation into this new mode of existence cannot be done in a private manner, and no social institution has a greater potential for mediating religious conversion and formation than the household.

Aristotle held that if you wish to become virtuous, you should surround yourself with virtuous people. We do not become virtuous by memorizing rules or church teachings. We become virtuous by being engaged with other people who live the life of virtue. Gospel values are not passed on so much by explicit moral catechesis as by the way in which a set of values has shaped basic human interactions. And so it is with the household. We pass on gospel values to our children when those values infuse our most mundane interactions within the family. When our children see how decisions are made, how conflicts are resolved, how work gives way to healthy play, how household tasks are undertaken out of a sense of commitment to the welfare of others, how affection and encouragement dominate all family interactions, how challenges, corrections, and even discipline are engaged in ways that never demean but rather affirm the dignity of all—those children are being schooled in the life of discipleship.

Conclusion: Domesticity as a Mark of the Church

There is a certain irony in speaking of domesticity as a mark of the church. The word "domestic," when used in its verbal form, "to domesticate," has the sense of taming something, as when we domesticate a new puppy. Obviously, when I suggest that domesticity is a mark of the church, I do not mean that the church is to be tamed of its gospel wildness. Rather the church is domestic because, at its foundation, it is built on the call to discipleship, and discipleship is nurtured in a particularly profound way in the mundane patterns of living that characterize one's domicile, one's household, one's family.

The Christian domicile or household is evangelical in passing on the Christian faith primarily by the transformation of its most basic patterns of living, as the Catholic bishops of the United States acknowledged in "Follow the Way of Love."[67] The Christian household offers most of us our first experience of Christian community and socializes us in ways unlike any other social unit. As a school of discipleship, the Christian household is at the same time, as *Gaudium et spes* puts it, "a school for a richer humanity" (52). By presenting the most basic and mundane of household interactions as the locus for the life of grace and the work of our salvation, the church of the home participates in the church universal's mission to be a sign and instrument of God's saving love before the world.

CHAPTER 21

The Church Is
Ecological

Sallie McFague

Sallie McFague was born in Boston in 1934 to parents of Scottish-Irish descent. As an undergraduate at Smith College in the early 1950s, McFague was taught by first-wave feminists from the 1920s. This educational influence, together with the encouragement of her parents, was critical in her decision to enter the field of theology, which had few women at the time. After graduating from Smith College, she earned a bachelor of divinity degree from Yale Divinity School, followed by a master of arts degree from Yale University. She received her doctorate from Yale in 1964. After teaching at Smith and Yale Divinity School, Dr. McFague began her distinguished career at Vanderbilt University, where she served as dean of the Divinity School and as the E. Rhodes and Leona B. Carpenter Professor of Theology.

In her major published works, Dr. McFague has been concerned to identify the metaphorical nature of language about God and to imagine new models for conceiving God and God's relation to the world. In 1988, the American Academy of Religion recognized her book Models of God: Theology for an Ecological, Nuclear Age *with its Award for Excellence. During the past fifteen years, her major books have all dealt with different aspects of the interface between theology and ecology. These books include* The Body of God: An Ecological Theology, *and* Super, Natural Christians: How We Should Love Nature. *Her most recent book is* Life Abundant: Rethinking Theology and Economy for a Planet in Peril.

Dr. McFague has been a member of numerous academic societies, including the editorial advisory board of Theology and Science, *and has served on committees dedicated to the welfare of the environment, including Americans for Wilderness. Among her awards is the Yale Divinity School Alumna Award for Distinction (1995). After her retirement from Vanderbilt University, Dr. McFague served as distinguished theologian in residence at the Vancouver School of Theology in Canada.*

Simone Weil, a French theologian, asked how Christianity could call itself catholic if creation itself is left out.[68] One of the classic marks of the church—its catholicity or universality—calls for the inclusion of *the world*. Another theologian, Pierre Teilhard de Chardin, put it this way: "Jesus must be loved as a world."[69] The catholicity of the church has meant several things over the ages, from "widespread" and "orthodoxy of belief" to "communion of the saints."[70] However, in spite of its Oxford English Dictionary meaning of "as a whole" or "entire, without exception," the mark of catholicity when applied to the church has excluded the world. It has only referred to human beings, or in the words of the OED, what "touches the needs, interests, and sympathies of all men." The latent anthropocentrism of Christianity's central institution, the church, is thus evident in one of its classic marks.

Weil and Teilhard de Chardin suggest a broader definition of catholic: it must include the world. God's household is the whole planet: it is composed of all human beings living in interdependent relations with all other life-forms and earth processes. The Greek word for house, *oikos*, is the source of our words for ecology, ecumenical, and economics. If salvation is seen as the flourishing of God's household, then we must see these three words together. In order for the whole planet to flourish, the earth's resources must be distributed justly among all its inhabitants, human and otherwise, on a sustainable basis. If salvation means the well-being of all creation—and not just of some human beings who are saved for life in another world—then the catholicity of the church demands that creation itself not be left out and that "Jesus be loved as a world."

This means returning to the oldest and deepest Christian theology: cosmological theology. Theologian George Hendry has suggested that there are three major contexts for doing Christian theology: the cosmological, the political, and the psychological.[71] All three are necessary—the integrity of creation, the well-being of *all* humanity, and peace for the human spirit. However, during the modern era, the psychological context has predominated; in both evangelical Christianity and New Age religions, the sin and/or serenity of individuals has been central. The political context has resurfaced in the twentieth century in the insistence of the liberation theologies on "the preferential option for the poor." Finally, ecological theologies have returned Christianity to its roots in the cosmological context. From this context, the redeemer is understood to be the creator, whose theater of operation includes all that is, the universe. As dwellers of planet earth, we understand God's household specifically to be our earth. As with Adam and Eve, whose vocation was to care for the garden, our primary vocation is to work as God's partners to help creation flourish.

The catholicity of the church understood as its mission to help bring about a just, sustainable planet, is not the view central to Christianity for the last several hundred years. Rather, God is imagined as occupying another world while we human beings are sojourners on earth, hoping to return eventually to our true home in heaven. God is seen as spirit; the earth as flesh; and our task is to leave the flesh and attain life in the spirit. This is a strange understanding of an *incarnational* religion. One of the most distinctive characteristics of Christianity is its insistence that God is *with us* in the flesh, here and now, on our earth. Jesus Christ is the paradigm, the explicit good news, that we are not alone on the earth and that we do not belong somewhere else. God is not anti-flesh or anti-world; in fact, just the opposite: the incarnation says that God is the One in whom we live and move and have our being as fleshly, earthly creatures. God does not despise the world; God loves the world and expects us to as well.

Given permission by the incarnation of God in the world to love it, our assignment becomes figuring out what loving the world means. We have been given some hints in the contemporary, evolutionary, ecological world-view of our time which has replaced the three-story universe of heaven, earth, and hell. This new world-view says that all human beings and all other life-forms are interrelated and interdependent. We all share the resources of our finite house, planet earth, and we need each other to survive and flourish. Perhaps most importantly, this mark of the church— its ecological catholicity—suggests a new interpretation of *who we are in the scheme of things*. In the old picture, human beings were seen as God's darlings, as the special ones who merited salvation in heaven with God. In the new picture, human beings are seen as caretakers of God's household, the earth, just as Adam and Even were told to tend the garden.

Ecological catholicity is not a minor addition to the marks of the church: it is central to its mission to preach the good news to *all* of creation. It is sometimes the case in churches today that the gospel preached is principally to needy, anxious human beings seeking a one-on-one relationship with

God. Ecological matters are seldom seen as part of the church's central message. That message is only for people and especially people in their personal joys and sorrows. But if Jesus is to be loved *as a world*, if the church is not catholic if the world is left out, then how can we say that such a narrow, individualistic, human-centered gospel is Christian? Do not all three contexts—the cosmological, the political, and the psychological—need to be included since God the redeemer is also the creator of all that is? If we are interdependent and interrelated with all other human beings and all other life-forms, then the good news must include *all* of us.

This does not mean merely a St. Francis of Assisi feastday blessing of the animals, and even less does it mean privileging our pets—the poster animals of the ecological movement. For the whole earth to be included in the good news involves hard economic thinking and decisions. A just, sustainable planet is not possible unless all of its parts have access to resources. The whole cannot be healthy if parts are sick. In other words, ecological catholicity means radical changes in the lifestyle of some parts of the whole—specifically, the twenty percent of human beings who control eighty percent of the world's resources. This lifestyle is making the majority of human beings poor and it is destroying many other life-forms and earth processes upon which all depend. If ecological catholicity is a mark of the church, it is—or should be—one of the distinctive characteristics by which the church is known. Then Christians, especially those well-off, *must live differently*. We must live a life of limitation, of sacrifice. Discipleship for well-off contemporary Christians means cruciform living: living in solidarity with those who are oppressed and suffering. In our time, such oppression is epitomized by the billion or so human beings who exist on a dollar a day, by animals that are losing their habitats, and by a deteriorating planet that is dying from our excessive energy use. As Charles Birch puts it in a pithy phrase, "The rich must live more simply, so that the poor may simply live."[72]

Thus, *including the world* as a mark of the church is a necessity. Christianity is not a "world religion" if it does not do so. Neither is it faithful to its own gospel: God is with us, all of us, here and now, in this earth, in our world.

CHAPTER 22

The Church Is Faithful

Mary E. Hines

Mary Hines is professor of theology at Emmanuel College in Boston, Massachusetts. Prior to her current position she taught for a number of years at the Washington Theological Union. She received a doctorate in systematic theology from the University of St. Michael's College in Toronto. Her doctoral work was on the understanding of dogma in the works of Karl Rahner. Her theological interests concern theologies of church, theology of Mary, feminist theology, and the theology of Karl Rahner. She is the author of The Transformation of Dogma: An Introduction to Karl Rahner on Doctrine, *and* What Ever Happened to Mary? *Other publications on Mary include "Mary and the Prophetic Mission of the Church," in* Journal of Ecumenical Studies; *"What Ever Happened to Mary?" in* New Theology Review; *"Mary," in* The New Dictionary of Catholic Spirituality; *"The Changing Image of Mary in United States Culture," in* The Theological Image of Mary Today: Faith and Culture; *"New Perspectives on Mary: Voices of Women," in* Toronto Journal of Theology; *"She's Back! Themes in Recent Writing on Mary," in* New Theology Review; *"Mary at the Millennium: Recent Developments in Marian Studies" in* Carmel and Mary: Theology and History of a Devotion. *She is also the author of a number of articles on ecclesiology, feminist theology, and Karl Rahner.*

Mary and the Church

Once upon a time the church was Marian. In keeping with the theme of this book, the editors first suggested I contribute an essay entitled "The Church as Marian." Since then I have been reflecting on the reasons for my unease with that title. Perhaps it is because the church I grew up in truly was Marian—sometimes to the detriment of other more central truths of

Christian faith. Devotions such as May processions and May altars and the rosary played a central role in the religious life of Catholics in the immediate pre-Vatican II church. In fact, many suggest that the period between the definition of the Immaculate Conception in 1854 and the definition of the Assumption in 1950 represents a high point in the church's attention to Mary. In that pre-ecumenical period Mary was indeed a mark of the church, setting Catholics apart from their Protestant neighbors who not only did not share this devotion but were deeply suspicious of it. Mary had come to be a sign of the sad divisions in the Christian community. What follows reflects my own journey with Mary in the church and some of the influences on my present thinking. It is not a universal story. Many women and men with different background and experience have their own stories to tell.

The theme of Mary and the church is not a new one in Christian history. In the first chapter of Acts, Mary is associated with the Pentecostal origins of the church through her presence in the upper room. Ambrose saw Mary as a type of church and model for all Christians. Gradually, however, this understanding of Mary as within and in some sense exemplifying the Christian community was eclipsed by an increasing tendency to view Mary as above and apart from the church. Instead of model and exemplar, she became viewed as the great exception, the one uniquely loved and honored by God with privileges beyond the grasp of other human beings, and particularly beyond the grasp of women. Virgin and mother, Mary became an unreachable ideal for real women, who became more closely identified with Eve, who was viewed as a dangerous seductress.

The reasons, both theological and psychological, for the development of this traditional Mariology of privilege and exception are too numerous and complex to detail here, but by the time it reached its apogee in the mid-twentieth century many women were beginning to feel a certain discomfiture with this figure so often proposed to them for their emulation. For them Mary had become a sign of contradiction; a woman who occupied such a central place in the church had become a symbol of the restricted roles for women in that tradition. The great German theologian Karl Rahner suggested that the image of Mary in every generation reflected dominant expectations of women by society during that period. A brief survey not only of theology, but also of literature and artistic works (almost all, until recently, written and painted by men) would confirm this diagnosis. Rahner goes on to suggest that women should be in the forefront of developing new theologies of Mary that reflect the changed situation of women in society.

The confluence of the emergence of the second stage of the feminist movement with the reform movement of the Second Vatican Council set the stage for a reevaluation of Mary's role in the church. Ecumenism was also a driving force in this process.

Vatican II set theology of Mary in a new direction, a direction more in continuity with the biblical picture of Mary and with early church themes of Mary and the church. In a climate of Marian devotion that was calling for a new Marian dogmatic definition, such as Mary as mediatrix of all graces or Mary as co-redemptrix, and which expected a whole document of the council to be devoted to Mary, the council fathers chose to situate Mary clearly within the community of church. The final chapter of the Dogmatic Constitution on the Church (*Lumen gentium*) is devoted to Mary as the exemplar of the faithful disciple who has finished the course and kept the faith. It is no theological accident that the chapter on Mary follows the chapter on the communion of saints. She is held up not as the great exception but as one like us who can offer us insight on our human journey to God. Vatican II also clears the way for a Protestant reappropriation of Mary by making clear that there is one mediator with God and that is Jesus and by encouraging Catholics to avoid the exaggerated Marian piety of the recent past.

Though Vatican II concerns itself mostly with a purification of Marian piety, the apostolic exhortation *Marialis cultus* of Paul VI offers more positive directions for a renewed devotion to Mary in the church. It suggests that devotion to Mary should be in continuity with the biblical picture of a young Jewish woman; it should be ecumenically sensitive; it should be closely related to the eucharistic life of the church. Finally, it should recognize the changed situation of women in the modern world and avoid portraying Mary as "timidly submissive." Mary should be seen as an exemplar of strong and faithful discipleship for all Christians, women and men.

Upon reflection I have come to the conclusion that to be Marian is still a mark of the church but in quite a different key. To be Marian today implies walking in the footsteps of Mary of Nazareth in her journey of faithful discipleship. Her journey, as we gather from her portrayal in gospel vignettes, was not an easy one. Like us, she struggled to understand the meaning of her son's life and the claim it would have on her. Mary encountered the vicissitudes of a life lived in difficult times, a life which culminated, in her case, with the execution of her son and the emergence of post-resurrection faith that led to the gradual development of the community called church. Mary can serve as a model and a challenge for all who attempt the courageous task of Christian discipleship in today's world—also a period of difficult times.

To be Marian has in the past symbolized religious division and divisions between men and women. I have hope for the future that this Jewish woman who is honored in the Muslim Koran and, though not a goddess, has affinities with Hindu goddesses in the insight that divinity is inadequately imaged as male alone, can become a symbol of a new period of unity and understanding between women and men as co-equal disciples and a sign of reconciliation both within Christianity and among the religions of the world.

CHAPTER 23

The Church Is Humorous

Tim Unsworth

Tim Unsworth has been a columnist for the National Catholic Reporter *since 1982. His essays and reports have also appeared in* America, Commonweal, U.S. Catholic, Salt, Salt of the Earth, Catholic Digest, Christian Century, Chicago Tribune *and a number of other publications. He was editor of* U.S. Parish *and* U.S. Church, *two monthly newsletters published by Claretian Publications. His writings have won three awards from the Catholic Press Association. He is the author of five books, including award-winning* Last Priests in America, *and* I Am Your Brother Joseph, *a life of the late Cardinal Joseph Bernardin of Chicago.*

Unsworth spent over twenty years as a teacher and administrator in Catholic secondary education before going to Chicago's DePaul University as its alumni director. He also worked in development at the University of Chicago and as an alumni director and development director at Northwestern University's dental school. In 1986 he withdrew from higher education in order to devote his time to freelance writing. In addition to his books, he has written over 500 articles and over fifty encyclopedia essays. He resides in Chicago with his wife, Jean, an author and former professor of fine arts at Loyola University of Chicago.

Few things in my life were as important to me as my old, blue-covered paperback of the *Baltimore Catechism* (Official Revised Edition). It was right up there with my mint condition collection of Philadelphia Playball Cards, the holy cards of baseball that honored such greats as Van Lingle Mungo, Heinie Manush, and Mel Ott—just to mention a few for whom I sacrificed my teeth on the pink bubble gum that came with each pair of cards.

Catholics owe their catechism format to former Catholic Martin Luther, who introduced the question-and-answer handbook over 400 years ago. It was designed with concise answers and became the model for many that followed, such as those of Dutch Jesuit Peter Canisius and Italian Jesuit Robert Bellarmine.

The first American catechism appeared in 1785 and was christened the "Carroll Catechism" after Bishop John Carroll, America's first bishop. It introduced questions such as "Who made you?" and "Why did God make you?" It survived until about 1852. The first revision of the Carroll Catechism, circa 1852, was only seventy-two pages long and contained 421 questions and answers—ninety-one of them just a simple "yes" or "no." You could get your soul around it.

I wasn't a great student. In kindergarten, I flunked sandbox because I was too myopic. I wasn't a great reader, and the adventures of Dick and Jane often eluded me. But I had an elephantine memory. The *Catechism* was designed for my klunky mind.

Cardinal James Gibbons, archbishop of Baltimore, introduced the official Baltimore text in 1885 (although he didn't write it). That was the one I memorized. It stuck in my memory bank until the start of Vatican II. The first revised version, which appeared in 1941, had only 208 questions and answers divided into thirty-three chapters. (I was almost in eighth grade by that time and could recite yards of poetry and acres of essays as well as all the lists in the Catechism. But not so with the new *Catechism of the Catholic Church* [1994], which reads like a computer handbook, has 2,865 entries, and could test the memory of the Holy Spirit.)

The Revised Baltimore Three was flavored with gifts, fruits, virtues, attributes, etc. Buried among them were four important marks of the church that have survived decades of rewrites. The marks, according to the response to question 154, are "certain clear signs by which all men can recognize it as the true Church founded by Jesus Christ."

"One, holy, catholic, and apostolic" is a lot easier to swallow than "authority, infallibility, and indefectibility" (the third attribute I never fully understood; it means having the ability to resist decay). However, a wise, though somewhat bureaucratic church presents these four as "chief" marks. There are lots of others, many of them more concrete than the lofty quartet named in the little Blue Book (the *Baltimore Catechism*). Humorous is one of them.

Perhaps no other mark could save a church from the consequences of its own folly than humor. Clearly the Catholic Church has an iron grip on this expansive trait. Only the Jewish humor ethic comes close.

"I try to run my parish," the wise pastor said, "so that some day an idiot could run it. Because someday an idiot will." Earlier, English writer and critic Hilaire Belloc would posit that one proof of the divinity of the church was that it could have survived for nearly 2000 years with so many incompetents in charge.

Just think, from 1831 to 1846, Pope Gregory XVI, Peter's 252nd successor, banned railroads in his territories, calling them "instruments of the devil." He opposed Italian nationalism, and condemned freedom of conscience and of the press and separation of church and state. Gregory was a winner. To his credit, he condemned slavery (but not slave traders) although the American bishops in the South decided that his prohibition did not apply to "just" enslavement, a thin distinction that permitted them to tolerate slavery.

Such human folly permitted those possessed of the fullness of the priesthood to condemn some practices and then permit usury and anti-Semitism. It allowed them to place Galileo Galilei under house arrest until he died and it held to its own position until Pope John Paul II issued a qualified concession in 1984.

Not many years ago the church vigorously condemned the rhythm method of birth control. (It even condemned abstinence.) Now rhythm—or Vatican roulette—is the recommended procedure. There was a time when the church favored the election of bishops, a married clergy, and divorce and remarriage. Today, Catholics favoring such things would not pass "Go" or collect $200.

Some years ago, while visiting the Vatican for a synod on the laity, my friend Marty and I were short taken. We began our quest for a bathroom and soon discovered three of them, labeled "men," "women," and "clergy."

"Well, now we know where the indelible mark is," Marty observed without missing a beat.

When the crying kid in the pew drowned out the patient homilist, he looked down and addressed the bawling baby's mother: "That's all right, ma'am," he said. "He's not bothering me." Her response: "I know that, but you're bothering him."

And so it goes. No pastor is without a nickname. (Indeed, one cardinal has been christened "Alpine Ed," and another named "Colonel Klink.") Perhaps no other profession, other than the military or the police, has a larger deposit of humor to share at communion breakfasts, jubilees, parish picnics—even homilies.

The church is held together by stories that underscore its humanity. Ask any movie or TV series producer. If a church is involved in the narrative, the humor will be as Catholic as a bucket of holy water. Other faiths tend to be too fragile.

Or listen in on clerical conversations, at least those below the level of bishop. The chatter doesn't go three sentences without a joke or humorous anecdote. It is what keeps Catholics in the state of grace. It is the balm at funerals, the tranquilizer at weddings. And the stories have more lives than the rectory cat.

This is no joke. Humor is a mark of the true church.

CHAPTER 24

The Church as Immigrant

Peter C. Phan

Peter Phan was born on May 9, 1946. During the Vietnam War, he taught English and religion at the Salesian minor seminary in Thu Duc, a suburb north of Saigon. On Sundays, Father Phan would leave for his prison ministry in a nearby female penitentiary at about 6 AM. On Sunday, April 27, 1975, for some unknown reason, he was late in leaving. Meanwhile his parents, who were at church, learned that his eldest brother, an employee of the United States consulate, could get them out of the country. On the way home, one of Phan's sisters found him and told him that he too had to leave with them immediately. That evening a U.S. military plane took his family to Guam, and from there, the following Sunday, they were flown to the refugee camp in Pendleton, California. Two months later they were settled in Dallas, Texas.

Thus began Phan's odyssey in the United States as an unwitting immigrant and an accidental theologian. An unwitting, and even unwilling, immigrant because Phan never had wanted to live abroad, much less in the United States, which he had never seen. An accidental theologian because theology was not his academic preference. Although theology was part of his priestly training, Phan's intellectual propensities were for languages and philosophy. But the first job he got in the U.S. was a teaching position in theology at the University of Dallas. Ever since, he has continued to be active in the field of theology.

Phan earned three doctoral degrees: the Doctor of Sacred Theology from the Salesian Pontifical University, the Doctor of Philosophy from the University of London, and the Doctor of Divinity, also from the University of London. Dr. Phan has authored and edited two dozens books and has written hundreds of essays, several of which have received professional awards. In 1988, Dr. Phan joined The Catholic University of America where he held the Warren-Blanding Chair in Religion and Culture. In 2003 he moved to Georgetown University, where he holds the Ignacio Ellacuría Chair in Catholic Social Thought. Dr. Phan is also past president of the Catholic Theological Society of America, the first non-Caucasian to hold this position.[73]

At the beginning of my theological career I did not intentionally set out to carve a professional niche by developing a specific area of expertise. However, perhaps under the—albeit unconscious—impact of my experiences as a refugee/immigrant, I devoted my two first dissertations to the study of eschatology, the first in the Russian Orthodox theologian Paul Evdokimov and the second in the German Catholic Jesuit Karl Rahner, and have subsequently written extensively on this theme.

Because of both my life as an immigrant and my longstanding interest in eschatology, I find it theologically meaningful and spiritually fruitful to imagine the church as immigrant. Indeed, "immigrantness" (to coin a word) adds dynamism and vibrancy to the traditional four marks of the universal church—unity, holiness, catholicity, and apostolicity. Furthermore, this image of the church as immigrant is particularly and uniquely appropriate for the U.S. Catholic Church, which church historian Jay Dolan has aptly called an "institutional immigrant."

Being Immigrant:
The Essential Mark of the Church

While migration has been an ever-present world-wide fact of life, currently demographers are talking of it as a new global phenomenon, given the increasing large-scale number of people who leave their homeland, by force or by choice, because of economic poverty, violence, war, or political and/or religious persecution, in search of better living conditions and freedom elsewhere, legally or illegally. It is a common practice to distinguish between internal and external (or transnational) migrants, the former seeking safety and shelter within their own countries, and the latter in foreign lands. It is also common to single out among the latter the special category of refugees. Refugees are those whose emigration from their homeland is not motivated by economic reasons but caused by war or political and/or religious repression, and as a consequence are limited in their ability to set up transnational networks in their homeland until there is a change in the political situation there.[74]

The church is an immigrant primarily because the majority of its members are refugees and immigrants, both internal and external. This is true, paradoxically, of both the impoverished Third World and of the richest and most powerful country of the world, the United States of America. It is projected that by the middle of the twenty-first century two-thirds of Christians will live in Asia, Africa, and Latin America, and most of these Christians will have experienced displacement and migration due to economic poverty, war, political oppression, or religious persecution. It is also projected that by the same time the majority of the members of the U.S. Catholic Church will no longer be constituted by descendants of early immigrants from Europe but by Hispanics and immigrants from Asia and Africa. Thanks to the Hart-Celler Act of 1965 and recent amendments to it, near record numbers of immigrants from parts of the world other than Europe have come into the United States. Demographically, then, the church universal and the local church in the United States will have an immigrant/refugee face.

What are the implications of this mark of immigrantness for the church? First, the immigrant church is the church of the poor. The celebrated "option for the poor," which liberation theologians have espoused for the church's mission, is no longer an "option"—something optional—that a wealthy church makes in favor of some of its members who are poor, or for the poor who are outside the church. Rather, this option is a "necessity" for the church that will have to take care of the majority of its own members who are poor due to their status as immigrants and refugees. The poor are not outside the church; most of them live in its midst! *Liberation* then is a constitutive dimension of the church's mission, a task the church must perform, as it were, "selfishly," *pro domo sua*.

In addition to economic poverty, exploitation in terms of hard labor and low pay, and deprivation of health benefits and social security in the host country, refugees and immigrants are threatened with the loss of their language and culture. Pressured to learn their host's language and to conform to a new way of life, and often separated from their own families, immigrants and their children experience psychological uprootedness, loss of self-identity, dissolution of community support structures, and depreciation of their own language and culture. Culturally and socially, immigrants live betwixt and between: they are neither fully of their native country nor fully of the adopted land, even though they belong to both. The church as immigrant must help its members appreciate and promote their native language and customs and rituals, their cultural values and religious practices, while facilitating their necessary task of adapting to the new society and its mores. Thus, the church as immigrant will assume *inculturation* as one of the primary tasks of its evangelizing mission, incorporating what is true, good, and beautiful in all cultures, and purifying them, when necessary, with the values of the gospel.

Another feature of the church marked by immigrantness is that its members usually live in a multireligious context, especially in the Third World. Normally immigrants cannot choose to live with their fellow believers; they have to go to whatever country offers them refuge. This means that, often, they live cheek by jowl with followers of other religions. The church as immigrant then must undertake *interreligious dialogue* not simply as matter of convenience, in order to survive as a minority amidst the overwhelming non-Christian majority (Christians make up only three percent of four billion Asians), but as a way of discovering the many ways in which the Spirit of God is present in world religions—in their prayers and rituals, sacred writings and hymns, monastic traditions and ascetical practices.

In sum, the church as immigrant must be involved in a triple dialogue: dialogue and solidarity with the poor (liberation), dialogue with their cultures (inculturation), and dialogue with their religions (interreligious dialogue).[75]

The Church as Pilgrim People

In its Dogmatic Constitution on the Church (*Lumen gentium*), Vatican II describes the church not only as the people of God (chapter 2) but also as a pilgrim people (chapter 7). The council declares:

> until there shall be new heavens and a new earth in which justice dwells (see 2 Pet 3:13), the pilgrim Church in her sacraments and institutions, which pertain to this present time, has the appearance of this world which is passing and she herself dwells among creatures who groan and travail in pain until now and await the revelation of the sons of God (Rom 8:19–22). (48)

The council goes on to write about what is traditionally referred to as the "Last Things." Here the link between immigrantness and eschatology is made manifest. As immigrant, the church is a pilgrim people on the march toward the reign of God. Living between a partial though real realization and anticipation of the reign of God and its definitive and glorious coming at the end of time, the church lives in this world but is not *of* this world, like the immigrant living betwixt and between, still groaning and waiting for a real and true "home."

As immigrant, the church is *already* but not *yet* one, holy, catholic, and apostolic. These four marks are not ready-made and static possessions of the church. They are not attributes that one particular church can claim exclusively and with arrogance, much less ideological weapons to dismiss other Christian or religious communities as not the "true church" or the "true religion." They are rather *gifts* and tasks which all churches must receive in fear and trembling, with deep gratitude and profound humility. Immigrantness keeps the church honest when arrogating unity, holiness, catholicity, and apostolicity to itself. Like the immigrant forever hoping and striving for a fuller life and brighter future, the church must continuously repair its fractured unity and grow into oneness, overcome its sinfulness, and increase in holiness, lessen its sectarianism, and become more catholic, and bear greater witness to the faith transmitted by the apostles.

CHAPTER 25

The Church as Intellectual

Susan A. Ross

Susan Ross was born in 1950, a cradle Catholic, and so came of age with the Baby Boomer generation during the 1960s, when everything in the world seemed to be in flux, including the church. From eighth grade through high school, she was taught by an order of nuns that strongly emphasized academics and encouraged students to ask questions about their faith. One of her religion teachers introduced her to the thought of Teilhard de Chardin, a Jesuit priest who had been silenced in the years prior to Vatican II.

During sophomore year of college, Ross took a course in Old Testament, during which the professor discussed the use of the historical-critical method in interpreting the Bible. Ross reports that she asked whether this method might apply to theological doctrines as well as biblical texts. Receiving an affirmative answer, Ross began to consider the possibility of actually becoming a theologian. After completing her bachelor of arts degree at Manhattanville College, she earned her master of arts and doctorate degrees from the University of Chicago.

In college Dr. Ross was also a music major. She says that both then and now she finds that music and theology have a great deal in common: both try to express an encounter with something greater than ourselves. Music puts this experience in the language of rhythm, melody, harmony; theology puts it into metaphors, concepts, and commands. And for neither do notes or words on a page convey the depth of what it is they express. But without these notes, or words, we would be unable to give voice to our experiences of the transcendent.

Dr. Ross taught at St. Norbert College and Duquesne University before joining the faculty of Loyola University of Chicago. She is the author of Extravagant Affections: A Feminist Sacramental Theology, *the co-editor of* Broken and Whole: Essays on Religion and the Body, *and the author of numerous journal articles and book chapters on such topics as women and the Eucharist, embodiment, feminist theology, and feminist ethics. She finds that her vocation as a theologian is to continue to think with and about the church, sorting through the complexities of women's experience, the church's intellectual tradition, and the obligations of human life.*

The church has many characteristics, both positive and negative, and it may not seem that being intellectual would be one of the most important. Rather, one could say, being prophetic, being a servant, being loving, would rank higher than being intellectual, which today often means being "out of touch," or living in one's head (and not one's heart). But consider the difference that being intellectual makes when we look back at the church's long history.

In the first centuries of Christianity's existence, the church struggled to understand what it meant to say that Jesus Christ was "the Son of God." Surely he had a unique experience of God both in his life and in his glorious resurrection, yet he was also a human being who suffered and died a terrible death. How could this man be God's Son? Some early Christian thinkers, well-trained in the intellectual traditions of the day, thought that a term borrowed from Greek philosophy— *homoousios*—could help explain this mystery and also counter certain wrong ways of thinking about Jesus. *Homoousios* meant "of the same substance" and although its roots were not biblical, which is one reason why some opposed its use, it seemed to convey the basic belief that the church was trying to uphold: that Jesus and his *Abba* (the Aramaic word that Jesus used for God, meaning "Papa") were both divine, although also distinct. Some had argued that Jesus was simply a good human being and was "adopted" by God as his Son for his exemplary behavior. Others said that Jesus was really a divine figure who only appeared to be human. By turning to a Greek philosophical term, the church tried to preserve its basic understanding of who Jesus was while at the same time it pushed this understanding forward for greater clarity. Because only God can save us, a great deal was at stake in this seemingly "intellectual" debate.

This, I think, is what the church as intellectual means: that in its thinking, the church tries both to maintain its belief and to adapt its formulation to the needs and expressions of the present day. In the fourth century, there were so many competing ideas about Jesus, some of which were highly misleading, that the church needed to enter deeply into the thinking process to determine how to best express its belief in terms adequate to the time. Whether Jesus is *homoousios* with the Father may not be the subject of everyday conversation in the twenty-first century as it was in the fourth century. Then Gregory of Nyssa reported that "even the baker does not cease from discussing this, for if you ask the price of bread he will tell you that the Father is greater and the Son subject to him." Nowadays the subject you discuss with the baker may be more along the lines of the church's understanding of sexuality, or whether she has read *The DaVinci Code,* but the point is the same: what do the church's beliefs mean to us now? This is what the church as intellectual means: thinking through the meaning and the consequences of Christian belief in terms that make sense to the present day.

Another example can be seen in the church's understanding of what it means to say that Christ is present in the Eucharist. Christ's "real presence" had been assumed, but not really debated, until the Middle Ages. It was thought that Christ was present among us, as he had said, "where two or three are gathered together in my name." But then in the ninth century, two monks at a French monastery engaged in a debate about just how Christ was "really" present in the eucharistic elements. One of them, Ratramnus of Corbie, said that the bread and wine were *symbols* of Jesus' presence to us: that he is bread and wine to us, as bread is nourishing and wine brings gladness. His brother monk, Paschasius Radbertus, did not think that this understanding did sufficient justice to the idea of *real* presence, and proposed that the bread *really* becomes flesh and wine really becomes blood, so much so that the pious could even see the very body of Jesus himself in the mouths of communicants. The debates went on for over two centuries, and eventually resulted in the idea of *transubstantiation,* that the "substance" (the core identity) of the bread and wine changes into the body and blood of Christ, while their "accidents" (their outward appearance) remain the same.

Here again, the ideas of the time lent themselves to the church's thinking process. Aristotle's metaphysics (his understanding of how the universe is composed) was based on the idea that everything had a substance—a core identity, an "is-ness"—and accidents, such as skin color (for people) or leaf type (for trees). As with the idea of *homoousios,* the intellectual tradition of the church maintained its belief in Christ's presence and drew on the most advanced philosophical ideas of the time to bring greater clarity to this same belief. Yet in the twenty-first century, our metaphysical concepts are more likely to reflect the ideas of Einstein than Aristotle, and our scientific equipment tells us that everything in the world is not stable, but in process, in constant movement. As a consequence, some theologians question the adequacy of transubstantiation as the best way in the present to speak of the "real presence" of Christ in the Eucharist.

These two theological ideas represent both the efforts of the church to give greater clarity to belief and the tensions that result when these efforts borrow from the ideas of the time. Tertullian, an early Christian thinker, once asked, "What has Athens to do with Jerusalem?" By this he meant that Athens—the symbol of the academy, of intellectuals, of reason—was very far away from Jerusalem—the symbol of God's loving presence to us in Scripture, the person of Jesus, his scandalous death on a cross. Other theologians have echoed this concern. Thomas Aquinas, that great intellectual of the church, is said to have remarked at the end of his life that all his work was as good as straw. Martin Luther, a few centuries later, was contemptuous of theological intellectuals, and referred to them in terms that would be inappropriate for family consumption.

Yet we human beings are not only feeling beings, we are also thinking beings. Much as we may talk about a "leap of faith," our faith necessarily lends itself to intellectual reflection. Human beings are questioning beings, driven by "the pure desire to know," as one contemporary thinker put it. The mark of the church as intellectual means that we, the church, are always in the process of sorting out what our faith means and what its implications are for our lives. So the church will speak out on labor unions and on stem-cell research, as well as on the human and divine natures of Christ and the mystery of the Trinity.

To say that the church is intellectual in the present means that the church must continue to be open to the challenges that *thinking* poses. The church must avoid, on the one hand, the temptation to say that belief in a particular intellectual formulation equals faith. Surely faith is more than a cognitive act (although it includes it); rather, faith is that disposition of the whole person, mind and heart, that responds and assents to the graced presence of God in our lives. But on the other hand, the church must avoid an anti-intellectualism that regards *any* thinking about faith with suspicion, that thinks that *thinking* about faith is unfaithful.

It is a distinctive mark of the Christian church to be intellectual. Catholic theologians will often comment, quoting Thomas Aquinas, that "grace perfects, not destroys, nature," meaning that God builds on what

God has already given us: our minds as well as our hearts. In a very basic sense, then, theological statements *make intellectual sense*: they can be reasoned about, and people of good faith can disagree and propose alternatives. They are formulated in the experience, language, and ideas of the time, and so have a certain dependence on the time and culture from which they arise. This means that theologians from a culture less accustomed to "Western" ways of thinking may find a "traditional" way of phrasing theology to be less adequate for them than one drawn from their native culture. Feminist theologians have argued as well that some male theologians may not recognize that their own assumptions about human nature often arise out of their (male) experience.

Yet as much as theology is indebted to time, culture, and experience, the church's thinking ought never to be an intellectual "game." The church's thinking needs to be serious and responsible, arising from faith, but also open to the complex questions that each new age brings. The mark of intellectual is one essential dimension in the church's self-understanding, but it is located alongside all of the other marks of the church: one, holy, catholic, apostolic, but also dialogical, ecological, conciliar, domestic, humorous, etc. The words of Anselm can help to sum up the mark of the church as intellectual: "I believe so that I may understand."

CHAPTER 26

The Church Is the
Lay Faithful

Dolores R. Leckey

*Dolores Conklin was born April 12, 1933, in Queens, New York, the youngest of
five children of Joseph and Florence Conklin. The Second World War was at the
center of her childhood memories because her two brothers were combatants in
that war and her mother was in a constant state of worry about them. Her
parish, St. Mary Magdalene, was also a major influence in her early development. The pastor's Irish roots were close to those of her paternal grandparents,
helping to create bonds of trust and respect with him. Conklin grew up believing the church was reliable. Her continuing education at the Mary Louis
Academy and St. John's University confirmed that belief. Her first experience in
a non-Catholic environment was New York University, where she studied literature. In 1957 she married Thomas P. Leckey, with whom she had four children.*

*She reports that the civil rights movement, the election of John F. Kennedy,
and the Second Vatican Council all greatly influenced her family personally
and politically. She became involved in adult religious education and eventually returned to formal studies at George Washington University in the area
of adult education, receiving the master of arts degree.*

*In 1977 Leckey was asked to become the first director of the newly estab-
lished Secretariat for the Laity of the National Conference of Catholic
Bishops. At the bishops' conference she worked on a number of pastoral statements designed to empower the laity:* Called and Gifted, When I Call for
Help, Follow the Way of Love, Strengthening the Bonds of Peace, Called
and Gifted for the Third Millennium. *She was also the executive producer
for videos on the topics of laity and, in particular, women.*

Among her recent publications are: Seven Essentials for the Spiritual Journey, Facing Fear With Faith, *and* Spiritual Exercises for Church Leaders.

Leckey is the recipient of twelve honorary doctorates and a number of awards for her work in lay ministry and spirituality. The most recent is the Cardinal Joseph Bernardin Award presented by the Catholic Common Ground Initiative.

Who Are the Laity?

A nineteenth-century Vatican official is reputed to have asked a cynical and dismissive question in response to John Henry Newman's essay *On Consulting the Laity in Matters of Doctrine*: "The laity? Who are they? Aren't they the people who hunt and shoot and entertain?" And Newman reputedly answered, "The church would look rather silly without them."

The twentieth century, particularly in the deliberations of the Second Vatican Council and the synod on the vocation and mission of the laity, gives a more comprehensive and detailed answer to that question: the laity are *essential* to the church's life and mission. The twenty-first century is probing even more deeply into the theology and practice that places the laity at the center of the church in the modern world.

Learning to Share Responsibility

The first thing I noticed when I began work at the national headquarters of the U.S. Catholic bishops in 1977 was the statue of Christ, with one hand held high, in front of the building on Massachusetts Avenue. At the base of the statue were the words, "I am the light of the world." Once a visiting German bishop told me the scriptural citation was wrong. He insisted that Jesus said: "*You* are the light of the world," but I defended everything about the statue. Now I know the "light" shines both ways, but then I was happy with the inscription as it was.

The glow of the Second Vatican Council permeated the bishops' national headquarters in the 1970s, but so did the lingering confusion over the bishops' recently concluded national undertaking, popularly known as "The Call to Action." This major U.S. event had been conceived in the early 1970s as a celebration of the nation's bicentennial. The suggestion came from the National Advisory Council, a group comprised of bishops, priests, religious, and laity—the latter in the majority. Cardinal John Dearden of Detroit headed the overall program, which included historical and liturgical celebration and a major national consultation on justice. It was the latter that attracted attention from all quarters, civic as well as ecclesial. The consultation consisted of regional hearings and parish discussions over a period of a year and a half beginning in January 1975, and climaxing in a national convocation in the fall of 1976—the bicentennial year. The program invited American Catholics from all segments of the community to set forth their understanding of the major justice issues confronting church and society. This unprecedented process of consultation and shared responsibility with the laity was designed to produce a five-year pastoral plan for justice. The culmination of this ambitious venture occurred exactly one year before I walked past the statue of Christ on my way to the newly established Secretariat for the Laity.

A New Secretariat and Dialogue

This new secretariat (office), which had been approved in May 1977, was the result of dedicated effort on the part of Archbishop Edward McCarthy of Miami, who was committed to enlarging and strengthening the role of the laity in the mission of the church. The secretariat soon saw people on the margins seeking ways to be heard in the inner circles of pastoral care: divorced Catholics; homosexual men and women and their parents; women in violent domestic relationships; children, increasingly vulnerable and needy across the spectrum of our society. The call from deep within the church, as well as from the margins, was for dialogue.

Vatican II had given impetus to national dialogues between the Catholic Church and other Christian faith communities. Pope Paul VI's encyclical *Ecclesiam suam* further encouraged fruitful dialogue, which the pope described as "the art of spiritual conversation." Soon the principles of *Ecclesiam suam* were being applied to a number of different situations, from consultation with the laity to formal dialogues with the Women's Ordination Conference.

Still, no one was so naïve as to think dialogue would come easily. Experience brought everyone face-to-face with reality. In 1987, prior to the Roman synod on the "Laity in the Church and in the World," a national symposium for lay organizations and movements was sponsored by the secretariat to assist the bishop-delegates in their preparation for the international event. Groups from across the spectrum of church membership were present. The extremes—what Dr. Scott Appleby calls "the far edges"—objected, however, to the process of working in small groups. The "far right" objected to dialogue on principle, believing the only valid input was a repetition of official teaching or curial opinion on all subjects for which the bishops were seeking insight. On the other hand, the "far left" believed they had already worked through these issues and had the correct input for the bishops. Small groups were therefore unnecessary.

Difficult though it often is, dialogue remains an effective way to build consensus around a number of contemporary issues, including reception of magisterial teaching. It is also a way to enter into the dynamics of conversion, particularly intellectual conversion, so necessary if there is ever to be a shift of attitude in matters of change and development.

Women in the Church

Embedded in all of the secretariat's work on the enlarged and energized role of the laity was the role of women in the church. The bishops tried to produce an acceptable pastoral letter *to, for,* and *about* women, but finally could not pass such a document. In 1994, however, a pastoral statement *Strengthening the Bonds of Peace* was issued, in which positions deemed problematic a few years earlier were affirmed. The importance of women's leadership, the equality of men and women as an expression of Christ's will, the naming of sexism as sinful—all these found voice in the statement. Quietly but steadily women have been assuming positions of leadership in the church: in parishes, dioceses, at the national level, and within the learned societies. It is a story of progress.

Lay Ecclesial Ministry

Called and Gifted, the first official statement on the role of the laity since the conciliar *Decree on the Apostolate of Lay People,* created heated debate in 1980 over its use of the term "ministry." The document viewed ministry in two ways: as Christian service in the world (laity bringing their competencies to bear on contemporary challenges) and as ministry within the church. The latter was referred to as *ecclesial* ministry. A major part of the debate was whether or not that terminology could be used for non-ordained persons. Fifteen years later (1995) *Called and Gifted for the Third Millennium* updated the state of the question. By this time bishops had more experience of the competencies and commitment of the laity in ministry. And in recent years the Bishops' Committee on the Laity and its secretariat have studied in depth the theological foundations of lay ministry and the developing practice, and made these learnings widely known, especially among the bishops. Today there is more openness to and a deeper understanding of the new and relevant ways of the Spirit in matters of ministry. Lay ecclesial ministry, while not anticipated by the council, is one of the Spirit's gifts bestowed on the church of the third millennium.

The Present and the Future

The church in the United States in the early twenty-first century has been shaken by the clergy sex abuse scandals. The laity wonder if their official leaders are trustworthy, and they are voicing their misgivings. At the same time, a body of pastoral teaching regarding the laity's rights and responsibilities gives us a solid foundation for lay participation in decision-making. It is imperative, therefore, that church leaders review and remember their own pastoral pronouncements and pledges to the lay faithful, and the extensive teaching of Pope John Paul II on these matters. The current crisis can be the means of including lay voices in important aspects of church life. I suggest the following five steps be taken.

1. Pastoral councils that are truly inclusive need to be established in parishes and dioceses. (The impression is that where diocesan councils exist they are comprised of the bishop's golfing partners or private financial advisors.)

2. At the national level, competent laity should be included as consultants on all committees, not just those specifically focused on laity. In particular, committees working on priestly formation, priestly life and ministry, and bishops' life and ministry can benefit from lay input.

3. All members of the church, including the hierarchy, need to be genuinely committed (including financially) to the ongoing formation and education of the laity, including education in their rights according to canon law.

4. Communication between bishops and the laity must be ongoing and truthful. Obviously no one knows the whole truth; our perspectives and lack of understanding limit all of us. But each one can decide there will be no lies, no nimble politically appropriate sophisms, or conscious suppressions. Mistakes are inevitable; deception is not. And this applies to everyone, lay as well as ordained.

5. All members of the church should study papal and episcopal statements and pertinent canons about the rights of the laity to exercise initiatives. The U.S. bishops have stated: "Laity can and should exercise responsible participation both individually and in groups, not only at the invitation of church leadership but by their own initiative" (*Called and Gifted for the Third Millennium*). And *Christifideles laici*, the 1988 post-synodal apostolic exhortation of John Paul II, says that the liberty for such initiatives is not derived from any kind of "concession" by authority but flows from the sacrament of baptism (#29). This is an extremely important consideration for groups of laity who in their efforts to serve the mission of the church are at times misunderstood or mistrusted by the hierarchy and denied opportunities for dialogue within the church.

These five steps point to a door already open to the laity. An invitation to cross the threshold is all that's needed—along with the courage to stay with the project. The lay faithful need to make this step; for they are an essential mark of the church.

CHAPTER 27

The Church as Medieval and Free

Gary Macy

Gary Macy was born in Milwaukee on March 24, 1950. He received a bachelor of arts degree as well as a master of arts degree from Marquette University. Five years later he completed his doctorate at Cambridge University. For more than twenty-five years he has taught at the University of San Diego, where he specializes in the history of the Western medieval church. He has written about the Eucharist and ordination during this period, most recently collaborating with Bernard Cooke. Dr. Macy also works with Orlando Espín and María Pilar Aquino as associate director of the Center for the Study of Latino/a Catholicism. He says that he enjoys the warm sun of San Diego with his wife, Saralynn Ferrara. His hobbies include eating good food, drinking good wine, spending time in the company of good friends, and traveling to wherever the above are available.

A partial listing of his publications includes: Theologies of the Eucharist in the Early Scholastic Period; The Banquet's Wisdom: A Short History of the Theologies of the Lord's Supper; *editor with Bernard Cooke,* A History of Women and Ordination: Volumes 1 and 2; *"The Dogma of Transubstantiation in the Middle Ages,"* Journal of Ecclesiastical History; *"Demythologizing 'the Church' in the Middle Ages,"* Journal of Hispanic/Latino Theology; *and "The Ordination of Women in the Early Middle Ages,"* Theological Studies.

Freedom, a Medieval Mark

It seems odd to talk about a period of history providing a "mark" of the church. Yet throughout history, each time the church renews itself, it must necessarily look to a particular period in its history as somehow "normative." To renew means to become what we once were when we were at our best. That entails knowing when Christianity was at its "best." If we wish to renew, we must know when we were "new."

Most Christians would automatically and perhaps even huffily respond that, of course, Christianity was best when it *was* newest. The first century or even the first decades of Christianity must always be our model. Indeed is that not one reason why Christian Scripture is so valued, because it tells us what Christianity should be like for all time?

The answer to that question, however, is not as obvious as it first appears. Little was settled in those early years. How do we celebrate; how do we organize; what do we believe? What is essential? Even more radically, are we Jewish or are we something else? If something else, what else?

Most people would not really want to go back to those first decades of confusion alone, as much as they might wish to capture its enthusiasm. And, of course, we cannot go back. We may celebrate in remarkably similar ways, but not now in ways that the first centuries would easily recognize. We have chosen distinct patterns of organization and fought bitterly over them. Equally bitter battles have been waged over what we believe, and especially over what is essential to who we are. We cannot now go back and make believe none of this has happened.

In effect, we chose different periods to emulate along with our appreciation of the enthusiasm of the first decades. Orthodox Christians and many Anglican Christians see the fourth and fifth centuries as "normative," that is, as providing the best examples of liturgy and organization and self-understanding. Reformed Christians, while always attending closely to the first decades, recall those decades in light of the sixteenth century's understanding of them.

Roman Catholics, on the other hand, have often looked to the Middle Ages for normativity. This has even led some to identify the Middle Ages as "Roman Catholic." Such a claim is complex and hardly historical. You could not have Roman Catholics until there were Protestants, at least in the way we mean "Roman Catholic" now. What would the term mean? Roman Catholic as opposed to what? No, there were Western Christians of different varieties and Eastern Christians of many varieties, but no Roman Catholics in the Middle Ages, at least from a historian's point of view.

Roman Catholics (and indeed many others) may well be appalled to hear this. Aren't Roman Catholics the Christian group that deliberately decided to remain medieval? Well, yes and no. The Council of Trent

(1545–63) changed almost as much of late medieval Christianity as did Geneva, Wittenberg, or Canterbury. However, the church emerging from Trent deliberately identified those centuries as basically sound in Christian thought and practice, while Geneva, Wittenberg, and Canterbury did not.

In other words, Roman Catholics understand the Middle Ages to provide a model for Christian life in a way in which other Western Christian groups do not. This essay will suggest that indeed there are qualities in medieval Christian life that do make for excellent models. In short, Roman Catholics have much to recommend their fondness for this period, even if the qualities suggested here are not always those most closely associated with either Roman Catholicism or the Middle Ages.

I would love to discuss many of the great qualities of the church of the Western Middle Ages: its generosity to the poor; its concern for the entire community, living and dead; its optimism that most people can make it to heaven even if that means a stay in purgatory. But since my space is brief, I will discuss what I think is the most admirable, and also the most surprising, quality about the medieval Western church: its remarkable freedom. In this the Middle Ages is not at all what it appears to be. It is not, for example, any sort of unity. The period from roughly the fifth through the fifteenth century in Europe is wildly diverse. The thirteenth century probably has far more in common with the present than it has with the eighth century. All those centuries don't deserve to be lumped together as if they somehow fit some pattern of unity. The construct of the "Middle Ages" is purely political—a move on the part of early modern scholars who liked the classical period. They saw themselves as a continuation of that period, and so junked everything between the golden period of Greece and Rome and themselves as some vague "middle" when everyone sat around, dirty and stupid, waiting for the Renaissance.

At the very least, the first six hundred years of the Middle Ages (roughly 500 to 1100) was quite different from the last four hundred years (roughly 1100 to 1500). Western Christianity during the first of these periods was very much under episcopal and/or lay control. Bishops really ran the church and the papacy rarely had influence outside the immediate area of Rome. Emperors, kings, queens, lords, and ladies appointed bishops, abbots, abbesses, priests, deacons, and even popes.

Most importantly the distinction between "ordained" and "lay" persons was understood very differently than it would be by the thirteenth century. To be "ordained" during this period meant to move to another *ordo* (function or ministry) in the church or indeed in society. Ceremonies that celebrated and enacted such transitions were all designated "ordinations." Kings, queens, emperors, priests, deacons, deaconesses, abbots, abbesses, canons, canonesses, monks, and nuns were all considered ordained, and the ceremonies by which they were ordained were called ordinations.

According to the brilliant church historian, Cardinal Yves Congar, "instead of signifying, as happened from the beginning of the twelfth century, the ceremony in which an individual received a *power* henceforth possessed in such a way that it could never be lost, the words *ordinare, ordinari, ordinatio* signified the fact of being designated and consecrated to take up a certain place or better a certain function, *ordo*, in the community and at its service."[81] The separation, therefore, between clergy and laity was not as clear as in the second millennium of Christianity nor the clergy understood as a separate and higher form of being Christian.

Western Christians dramatically changed their understanding of ordination in the twelfth and thirteenth centuries. Henceforth only those who were ordained served at the altar, and only men could be considered truly "ordained." They made this change for several reasons, the most obvious being that the church had become completely controlled and even owned by the secular rulers. The church no longer had any independence from which to take a prophetic stance over against secular society.

The important point to make here is that the church did change. Two very different ways of governing the church mark the Middle Ages. This means the church felt free to change its form of governance. If we see the Middle Ages as a model, then we too are free to change the way we govern ourselves. The example of the change in the meaning of ordination is not the only one that could be given. One after the other of the great medieval saints were simply lay people who made up new ways of Christian living. Benedict of Nursia was a layman who thought we could do better as Christians if we gave up material possessions and lived in community. Francis of Assisi didn't even follow some earlier models, as Benedict did. Francis just started wandering around, begging and preaching. He thought he was doing what the apostles had done, but he was really making it up as he went along. The same goes for his friend, Clare. And there are other less well-known experimenters, such as Gilbert of Sempringham who decided women religious communities ought to rule over male religious in mixed communities. There were knights who wanted to live like monks, and friars who dedicated their lives to changing places with the slaves who rowed galleys in order to free them. Later on, most of these groups got organized and wrote rules to live by and became established, but this was not the plan of their "founders."

These marvelous people just started doing what they thought was right. Most often they didn't ask for permission or wait for some distant bishop or pope to act. They just went ahead, believing that the Holy Spirit was with them. Some were condemned; others became saints. They were not afraid to disagree with bishops or popes or even criticize them if they needed it. In the great medieval classic, Dante's *Divine Comedy*, popes are more often envisioned in hell than in heaven, yet Dante did not seem to feel any less Christian for suggesting it was so. Especially in the eleventh through the thirteenth centuries, examples abound of people, even ordinary people, who felt remarkably free to experiment, to change, to grow.

The Middle Ages ought to teach us that the present was not always the way it was, and so the future need not be the way the present is. We are free to imagine and create new ways of Christian living and that very freedom is our tradition. I imagine our medieval ancestors cheering us on from heaven: "Don't be so afraid; the future belongs to the Spirit. You can trust the Spirit just as we did. Laugh a little more; be a little more trusting. Don't wait for a new pope or another council; JUST DO IT!"

CHAPTER 28

The Church Is
Monastic

Francis Kline, OCSO

Father Francis Kline is abbot of Mepkin Abbey in Moncks Corner, South Carolina. He was born Joseph Paul Kline III on December 21, 1948, in Philadelphia, Pennsylvania, the oldest of three brothers. Music would soon come to define much of his early years.

Kline played his first organ recital in Philadelphia at age fifteen. He went on to study privately with Alexander McCurdy of the Curtis Institute before entering the Juilliard School as a student of Vernon deTar. During his last year at Juilliard, he presented the complete organ works of J.S. Bach in fourteen recitals, inspiring an editorial in the Christian Science Monitor *and a feature article on the twenty-one year old in the* New York Times. *The Philadelphia Musical Fund Society sponsored the Bach cycle the following year. The Columbia Records recordings of these fourteen recitals are still aired today.*

His musical career, which included appearances on the Voice of America and as a featured soloist at the Academy of Music in Philadelphia, came to an abrupt halt in 1972 when he entered the Trappist monastery of Gethsemani in Kentucky. There he took the name of Francis.

Following solemn profession at Gethsemani, Kline studied theology in Europe. He was sent to Rome to study at the Benedictine Athenaeum, Sant' Anselmo, where he earned a bachelor of sacred theology degree. Two years later he was ordained a priest and appointed novice master. On January 21, 1990, he was elected third abbot of Mepkin Abbey. He was appointed director of the Office of Prayer and Worship for the diocese of Charleston in March 1995. Under Father Francis's guidance, Mepkin Abbey has continued to flour-

ish as a spiritual sanctuary while simultaneously offering an open door to diverse spiritual seekers.

He has published works on patristics and the theology of St. Bernard, including Lovers of the Place: Monasticism Loose in the Church.

If we can talk about monasticism as one of the characteristic treasures of the church, we must describe its essence. I would call it an impulse coming directly from God and given as a gift to the church. That ecclesial impulse enlivens the way of salvation, enriches the reading of sacred Scripture, and alerts the church to an ever-ready vigilance for Christ's glorious coming. Poised for new life, it wants to be recognized in the church for what it is: one of God's most precious gifts to the marriage of Christ and the human family, and a storehouse of a continual stream of gifts coming from the Holy Spirit.

The monastic impulse is a claim God makes directly on the individual. Like a talent for music, art, or sport, it is incontrovertible and fathomless, in that the person can do little about it except develop it, if he or she is willing, and live with and by it.

Jesus called people in this way with an absoluteness that borders on the harsh. He also made it clear that only a certain few were to follow him in this way. None of the rest doubted his love for them and the other kinds of claims he made on their lives by his gospel. He said that only those to whom the grace was given could live that special kind of claim, to leave literally all to follow him (see Mt 19:27–30).

Monasticism in the Church Today

The call of the Lord to come apart and pray is still heard in the church. For what service in the church is the person called? To what ministry, to what mission? Here is where the contemplative vocation must redefine itself according to the ecclesiology of the Second Vatican Council (see *Lumen gentium*). It must take its place beside many other ecclesial groups and charisms, including the domestic churches, that is, household groupings. It is neither above them nor below them, as all share in the baptismal grace of Christ and receive his call to holiness. The redefinition of the contemplative and monastic in the contemporary church starts with prayer.

Here is what happens when Christ makes his monastic claim on an individual. The person is led to detach from the society, to leave one's identity in that society, that is career, position, status, etc. One is even called to leave one's ecclesial community to come apart and follow Christ into the "desert." One enters a community where everyone is equal and, according to the Rule of St. Benedict, the only seniority is the time of one's entrance into the community. This detachment amounts to a withdrawal and a marginalization so thorough that it allows one to live a radical interpretation of Christ's gospel, to leave all things to follow him, to form, with Christ at the center, a community, and within that community, to preach, to feed the poor, to live justly and chastely—all this, in order to remain rooted in prayer so as to come to that love that can turn the other cheek, and prefer another to oneself.

With this way of life, one begins the inner journey. One discovers in oneself layer after layer of resistance to God. One discovers a will that is corrupt and acts as a dysfunctional head of a household, controlling everything, but never honestly letting itself be confronted or questioned, but, sovereign even against God, hiding itself away in the self, as if in a black, airless, and sunless room (see Rom 7:14–26). The will needs correction and rehabilitation, and the person it controls needs salvation.

When the monastic arrives at this deep truth about himself or herself, he or she discovers that, all of a sudden, the situation of one's neighbor invites not judgment but compassion. For we are all together in this plight of non-salvation. And the monastic also discovers the Christ of his or her baptism waiting for him or her at this deep center. Christ invites the monk or nun to join him on the return journey out of slavery to sin and dysfunction, and into the joy, peace, and freedom of the children of God.

Christ gifts the monk and nun with the solidarity with all other persons for whom Christ died. Christ shares his own mission of intercession and mediation before God the Father for all the persons the Father has given him (see Jn 10:28; 17:11–12). Christ brings the monk or nun to the heart of himself, his saving will, which unites him to the Father and the Spirit, and with which he wishes to strengthen the monastic's own will. With that heart, the heart of the glorified Christ, the monk or nun stands, obviously at the heart of the church, for it is Christ's body.

The question for today is, can such communities exist, and if so, how do they function when a physical withdrawal from society is more and more impossible? What is their relation to the church, and how does the church consider them? Can a post-modern, and even post-Christian, society tolerate these communities, or ignore them, or condone them, or appreciate them?

Contemplative monastic communities today often exist according to a nineteenth-century model, where physical withdrawal is achieved through property boundaries and cloister walls. In our communities today, with increased demands for hospitality, due to the popularity of things "monastic," with the advent of ever-developing technology at the service of communication, with real estate practices bringing domestic dwellings closer and closer to the wilderness or rural areas dear to monasteries, the nineteenth-century model is no longer viable. The retreat movement, tourism, and the necessity of relating well to the surrounding area mean that contemplative communities must greet in some fashion the visitors who come for whatever reason. Telephone, internet, and other means of communication have put severe strains on our discipline of stability and enclosure. It makes no sense to shut oneself in a monastery only to ruin one's concentration on prayer and the inner journey with constant contacts by telephone and internet.

Even with the availability of easy communication, the monastic community is able to discipline itself from the inner core to the outward appearance, so that telephone access, internet use, and so on, all fall under a strict community observance, strengthened not by punishments as in the past, but by the careful discernment of motives and needs. A community can create a solitude and a detachment, made possible not by sheer willpower of individuals, but by the deliberate and loving and trustful framework of a determined group: the community itself.

Easy means of travel will demand a new understanding of the traditional vow of stability in the monastery. There have been and will continue to be more travel outside the monastery for various reasons. Yet, the inner discipline of the community, and the all-important network of accountability for each appointment beyond the monastery property, preserves and enhances the avenues of the inner journey. In this way, the enclosure becomes once again sacred ground, the place where the graces of prayer are given, and where the land itself breathes forth a peace and reconciliation, because a careful spiritual discernment has been made in the treatment of this time-honored spiritual discipline.

With this perseverance of an ancient tradition in the church of today, and its constant renewal and enhancement according to the grace of Christ, the contemplative vocation and monastery provide the church with an ancient and Spirit-filled charism of prayer, and manifest it among other charisms in the church. Monastic prayer takes the monk and nun to the heart of the church, that is, to Christ in his mission of reconciliation between God and humankind. One is not in the monastery for the sake of oneself, but for the sake of Christ, that is, for his body, both in the local church and the global church. As with all other charisms, without this monastic prayer the church is incomplete, lacking the full operation of the Holy Spirit.

Finally, we can say that monastic prayer reveals the all-consuming fire of God's love, which burns at all times for all that God has made. This revelation longs for and thirsts for a fitting response that it receives in the fidelity of Jesus Christ to the Father, and in his continual burning prayer of intercession to the Father. Monastic prayer, quite simply, is Christ drawing hearts to share his same zealous desire that all should be saved. This is Christ's claim on individuals, and his freedom to choose those whom he wills. His love is without compromise, without boundaries, without measure.

The church would not be the church if it did not keep alive in its memory and in its daily ministry this dimension of God's love without measure. The importance of contemplative communities to manifest and witness to this love cannot be over-estimated. The church is not whole, not itself, until the witness to God's unfathomable love has a voice and a presence. The contemplative monasteries are called into existence out of this ecclesial need.

The monastic tradition has grown conscious of its enormous heritage, which amounts to a treasure house from which the church may bring forth things new and old. But its most valuable jewel is the contemplative journey into the heart of the church, first elaborated many centuries ago, made palpable and newly attractive by St. Bernard and the Cistercian school, and still alive and present in monastic communities where all things converge on Christ, in whom are hidden all the treasures of wisdom and knowledge (see Col 2:3).

CHAPTER 29

The Church Is
Mystagogical

Harvey D. Egan, SJ

Harvey Egan was born on November 6, 1937, in Putnam, Connecticut. After attaining a bachelor of science degree in electrical engineering from Worcester Polytechnic Institute, he worked for the Boeing Airplane Company in Seattle. Entering the Society of Jesus in 1960, he earned master of arts and licentiate degrees in philosophy from Boston College. After obtaining his master of arts and licentiate degrees in theology from Woodstock College, Maryland, he was ordained. Father Egan then went on to receive a doctorate in theology under the direction of Karl Rahner at Westfälische Wilhelms-Universität in Münster, Germany. He also served as a part-time NATO base chaplain during this period.

Father Egan taught at Santa Clara University and later served as the Bannan Distinguished Professor of Religious Studies. From 1975 to the present, he has taught theology at Boston College where he was tenured and promoted to full professor of systematic and mystical theology.

He has translated or edited the following works: Karl Rahner—I Remember, Karl Rahner In Dialogue: Conversations and Interviews 1965–82, Faith in a Wintry Season: Conversations and Interviews with Karl Rahner in the Last Years of His Life, The Content of Faith: The Best of Karl Rahner's Theological Writings, *and* The Great Church Year: The Best of Karl Rahner's Homilies, Sermons, and Meditations. *He has authored* What Are They Saying About Mysticism?, Christian Mysticism: The Future of a Tradition, Ignatius Loyola The Mystic, An Anthology of Christian Mysticism, *and* Karl Rahner: Mystic of Everyday Life. *He has also published several articles in books, including "Rahner's Mystical Theology," in* Theology and Discovery, *"Essays in Honor of Karl Rahner,"* edited by *William Kelly, SJ, and "Christian Apophatic and Kataphatic Mysticisms,"* in Theological Studies. *The granting of the Robert H. Goddard Distinguished Alumni Award from Worcester Polytechnic Institute (1999) deeply pleased him.*

Baron Friedrich von Hügel, the distinguished Catholic intellectual, awakened Catholic Christians to the benign neglect of their own profound mystical tradition when he argued one century ago that every religion contains three perennial elements: the institutional, the intellectual, and the mystical. In more recent years, Karl Rahner, the great German theologian, focused sharply on Christianity's mystical dimension when he contended that every person's deepest, primordial experience—albeit often implicit and not verbalized—is of God-above-us (Mystery), God-with-us (enfleshed Word), and God-in-us (Holy Spirit).

The call of Mystery explains why our questions never cease, why we eventually must ask ultimate questions, and why we are never satisfied totally with anything in this life. Because we are historical persons, we search incessantly for that one person who fulfills us perfectly—whom Rahner calls the "absolute savior." The attraction of the Holy Spirit explains why our immense longing often lures us into our deepest interiority. Thus, we are essentially ecstatic beings summoned to God's mystery, worldly, and historical beings attracted to an absolute savior, and enstatic beings lured to our deepest interior by the fontal fullness of the Spirit of Love. Rahner deemed our implicit trinitarian consciousness to be the innermost human experience.

One should not even call it an experience because as the ambience in which all human experiences take place, it is beyond all particular experiences. It is the spiritual atmosphere in which we live, "more intimate to us than we are to ourselves," as the mystics were fond of saying. Just as we take our breathing, our beating hearts, or our own self-awareness for granted, so too might the ever-present experience of the triune God remain overlooked, repressed, or even denied. This universal experience of triune grace grounds Rahner's view that the human person is *homo mysticus* and contextualizes his avowal that in the future the devout Christian will either be someone who has experienced "something," i.e., a "mystic," or he will cease to be a Christian.

Rahner underscored that *everyone*—not only Christians—is called to a mysticism of everyday life. Unrequited loving; doing good or forgiving another, and having this goodness or forgiveness taken for granted; selflessly loving and forgiving without the compensation of feeling good about one's selflessness; remaining silent rather than striking back in the face of unjust treatment; patiently and mysteriously penetrating one's own and one's beloved's sinfulness and reaching a core of infinite goodness; patiently enduring God's silence—these are all ways to experience the mysticism of everyday life.

In addition to the mysticism of everyday life, Rahner speaks of a "mysticism in ordinary dress," or a "mysticism of the masses." This odd phrase refers to contemporary charismatic spirituality lived by Christians who claim to be intoxicated with the Holy Spirit. They often experience dramatic faith conversions, speak glossolalia, publicly and loudly proclaim their faith, prophesy, experience swooning or "slaying" in the Spirit, and heal others. Their mysticism occurs more ostentatiously than the mysticism of everyday life and more commonly than the extraordinary mysticism of the great saints. Because of their often unusual power to intensify the ever-present experience of God and to deepen the Christian faith, hope, and love of those in such movements, Rahner says that they are a profound expression of Christianity.

This provides the context for speaking of a mystagogical church, that is, one that leads the individual-social person into his or her own deepest mystery. This church must awaken, deepen, and make more explicit the mysticism of everyday life experienced by everyone. Also, it must purify and enrich what is best in the mysticism of the masses.

The mystagogical church actualizes its existence as the guru of the love of God, and brings to explicit awareness what we all know implicitly: that God does exist, that we exist for God—not God for us, that we can have a personal relationship with God, that we shall be judged after death, that we shall be raised bodily from the dead, and that we are people of eternity, of absolute longing, and of unlimited hope.

In this age of a wintry and troubled faith, the mystagogical church should assure the flock that faith often requires enduring God's silence and that the seeming diminution of faith is an actual mystical "thickening" of it. Despite what can be said of Christianity's content, faith is often as simple as remaining silent with respect to God ("Be still, and know that I am God!" [Ps 46:10]) and as complex as engaging in the struggle to recognize the Lord in the breaking of bread for strangers.

The mystagogical church has given birth to a host of mystical titans who can teach us much in this increasingly secular and self-sufficient age—an age in which God is seemingly absent. The church should strive to initiate Christians into their individual-social experience of God by using the classical masters as irreplaceable teachers for developing both a theology and a mystagogy that makes intelligible the personal experience of God. (Such a theology and mystagogy drawn from the experiences of the great Christian mystics would also help Christians in their dialogue with Eastern religions.)

The church's mystics purified and amplified with little distortion the often barely audible and distorted experience of God found in everyone. Because the classical mystics interpreted their experiences of God in the terms of their own day, the mystagogical church must transpose their writings for contemporary use—a transposition which would be highly fruitful because it would enable us to discover in ourselves the traces and whispers of these experiences.

However, the church must make it clear that both the mysticism of everyday life and the extraordinary mysticism of the saints occur in the "normal" realm of grace and faith. The extraordinary mysticism of the saints is not radically different from the ordinary life of grace. With Rahner, one must neither overestimate the extraordinary mysticism of the saints nor underestimate the real depths of the "ordinary" Christian life of faith.

The specific way in which the great saints experience God belongs to the person's natural ability for concentration, contemplation, meditation, submersion into the self, self-emptying, and other psycho-mental techniques often associated with Eastern mysticisms. These techniques help to root faith, hope, and love more deeply in the person's core. However, the gospels' teaching that feeding the hungry, giving drink to the thirsty, clothing the naked, and visiting prisoners are of extreme importance for salvation and must never be forgotten.

The mystagogical church must reject any elitist interpretation of life that holds that perfection can be reached only by a trained mystic. The New Testament awards to all who truly love their neighbor and therein experience God that final salvation in God's judgment that is not surpassed even by the highest ascent or the deepest absorption of the mystic.

Just as the Fathers of the church spoke profoundly of the hidden presence of the triune God and Christ in the liturgy, the sacraments, the Scriptures, and the events of daily life, so too must the contemporary mystagogical church. Exegesis properly done, for example, requires reading the Scriptures with faith's mystical eye, which the Fathers described as "mystical contemplation." The mystagogical church must guide its members through its liturgy into an invisible, objective world revealed by the Scriptures and founded by Christ ever-present in this church. Maximus Confessor, for example, explicitly called the Eucharist liturgy the "mystical service."

The mystagogical church should initiate people into what Karl Rahner calls the "liturgy of the world." The world and its history, to him, are the terrible and sublime liturgy which breathes of death and sacrifice. With his grace, God sustains this liturgy of the world which God celebrates and permits to be celebrated in humanity's free history of humanity. In the entire length and breadth of this immense history of birth and death—replete with superficiality, folly, inadequacy, and hatred (all of which "crucify")—on the one hand, and silent submission—fidelity both in living and in dying, in successes and failures—on the other hand, is the true liturgy of the world present.

It is present in such a way that the liturgy that the Son brought to its absolute fulfillment on the cross belongs intrinsically to world, emerges from it, and constitutes the supreme point of this liturgy from which all else draws its life, because everything else is always dependent upon the supreme goal and at the same time sustained by it.

Christians, therefore, should not understand the Eucharist as a sacral ghetto in the midst of a profane, pagan world but as the explicit coming-to-awareness of this tremendous drama—full of guilt and grace—that unfolds in the whole of world history, therefore also in our times and in our lives. The Eucharist peaks in that death in which Jesus—in the incomprehensibility of his death—surrendered in total confidence to the mystery of forgiving love, to the mystery we call God.

We do not always dwell at the core of our incomprehensible being but too often allow ourselves to be exiled to our humdrum, bustling everyday life. Yet once in a while, we too are thrown into the mystery of guilt, death, forgiveness, and unfathomable freedom that issues from God into the midst of our life. For example, when we endure the crucifixion of everyday life silently yet filled with radical hope, we celebrate the eucharist of everyday life, which finds its fulfillment in the church's Eucharist. And when we then celebrate Mass, we offer the world to the Father knowing that it itself is already ceaselessly offering itself up in rejoicing, tears, and blood to God's incomprehensibility.

CHAPTER 30

The Church Is Nonviolent

Thomas J. Gumbleton

Thomas Gumbleton was born on January 26, 1930. After completing elementary school and seminary high school in Detroit, he earned a bachelor of arts degree from Sacred Heart Seminary in 1952. Four years later he received his master of divinity degree from St. John's Provincial Seminary in Plymouth, Michigan. That same year he was ordained and began his ministry as an associate pastor in Dearborn, Michigan. While serving as assistant chancellor for the archdiocese of Detroit, he earned a doctorate of canon law degree from the Pontifical Lateran University in Rome. In 1968 he was ordained bishop and became auxiliary bishop and vicar general for the same archdiocese.

In addition to serving as pastor at several Detroit parishes, Bishop Gumbleton has been very active throughout his ministry in promoting peace and justice. He was a member of the U.S. Catholic bishops' committee that drafted the pastoral letter "The Challenge of Peace" and he initiated the bishops' pastoral letter "Always Our Children." He was the founding president of Pax Christi, USA and served in that capacity from 1972–1991. He was also president of Bread for the World from 1976 to 1984. In addition, he has served on the board of more than thirty socially engaged institutions. He has traveled around the world promoting peace and has received honorary degrees from eight academic institutions. For his outstanding work promoting faith and social justice, Bishop Gumbleton has received about fifty awards, including the Public Citizen of the Year from the National Association of Social Workers (1980), the Outstanding Service & Witness Award from Dignity/USA (1995), the Washington Theological Union Distinguished Service Award (2000), the Prophets of Peace Award (2000), and the Reconciler Award from the National Franciscan Federation (2003).

They don't teach "apologetics" anymore. And it's probably a good thing. Back then we Catholics were so sure we were the only true church, the one that Jesus founded. And in our apologetics classes we learned how to line up "irrefutable" arguments to overwhelm any opponent.

Actually it's embarrassing to think about the posture we took toward all those who in good faith did not belong to the true church of Jesus.

We knew we were the true church because we could show without the possibility of rebuttal that only the church of Rome had the four *marks* of the true church: one, holy, catholic, and apostolic. With an arrogance that hardly befitted a follower of the Jesus who embraced everyone—even those who were ritually unclean or who were not part of the "chosen people"—we easily established to our satisfaction our standing as God's true and only church.

Actually, if we look to the marks of the church from the very beginning, we find there was another that clearly "marked" Jesus' community: the theology of Christian nonviolence. But by the fourth century this mark of the church began to disappear. From that time till today this mark of the church has been apparent sometimes only faintly, sometimes more strongly.

John McKenzie, a well-known and highly respected Scripture scholar, puts it very clearly: "If Jesus did not reject violence for any reason whatsoever, we know nothing about Jesus." In other words, he says it is so plain when you look at the gospels, when you listen to the words of Jesus, when you watch how he acted, when you watch how he accepted being executed, when you watch what he did and when you listen to what he said, if you can't say that Jesus rejected violence, you may as well say "we can't know anything about Jesus of Nazareth." It's so clear if we are willing to listen, if we're willing to look and reflect on how he lived and how he died.

John McKenzie goes on to say, Jesus taught us how to die, not how to kill. There is nowhere in the gospel where Jesus teaches how to kill, how to use violence at all. He did show us how to die. You die loving, forgiving the one putting you to death. When you go back to the words of Jesus, you find it so clear, really. "You have heard that it was said to those of ancient times, 'You shall not murder.'" A very clear command: you shall not murder. But then Jesus asks even more: "But I say to you, you may not even have anger, vengeance in your heart toward a brother or sister. Even if you're coming to the altar to offer your gift and there you remember your brother or sister has something against you, leave your gift at the altar, go first and be reconciled. Only then come back and worship God" (see Mt 5:21–25). You cannot worship God if there is anger, hatred, and vengeance in your heart. You must be reconciled to your brother or sister. "You have heard it said,

'Love your neighbor, hate your enemy.' I say to you love your enemy." Love your enemy! Return good for evil! This is what Jesus said. It is so plain. "You have heard that it was said, 'An eye for an eye and a tooth for a tooth.' But I say to you: Do not resist an evildoer. But if anyone strikes you on the right cheek, turn the other also; and if anyone forces you to go one mile, go two. If anyone wants to sue you and take your coat, give your cloak as well" (see Mt 5:38–48). There is no limit to the love that you extend, even to the one who is attacking you, the one who is hurting you. You return good for evil, you love those who hate you.

The first community of disciples of Jesus lived according to his way of nonviolence for over 300 years. It was truly the most authentic mark of the church. "See how these Christians love one another." It was the radical dynamic "spirit force" which in the words of Ignacio Ellacuria, SJ, could "transform this world into as close an image of the reign of God as possible."

With the ascent of Constantine in the fourth century, however, the contradiction between being a follower of Jesus and practicing nonviolence was lost. Throughout the centuries that have followed, countless wars have been waged and other innumerable acts of violence have been perpetrated all in the name of Jesus. The context I find myself in today as both a U.S. citizen and a Christian is particularly painful. Our nation is at war in Iraq. Furthermore, U.S. military personnel are stationed in places that most of us are not even aware of. Our history resounds with the cries of deadly conflicts—Persian Gulf, Vietnam, Korea, World War I, World War II. Tragically, some might say inevitably, from the time of our Civil War we have been at war with ourselves. In a sense, it could be said that as a nation we were birthed in war—the Revolutionary War. Violence is the original sin of the United States. The question I have is when will this madness end? When will the solemn pledge offered by Pope Paul VI during his 1965 address to the United Nations General Assembly be realized: "No more war, war never again"?

Building upon the inspiration of Pope (now Blessed) John XXIII, the bishops gathered at the Second Vatican Council affirmed nonviolence as a way of truth for the church in the Pastoral Constitution on the Church in the Modern World (*Gaudium et spes*). Addressing the need to foster peace and a greater sense of international community, the council fathers wrote: "We cannot but express our admiration for all who forgo the use of violence to vindicate their rights and have recourse to those other means of defense which are available to weaker parties, provided it can be done without detriment to the rights and duties of others and of the community" (GS 78).

Interestingly, the mark of nonviolence is one the church can and has offered the world. I think here of the great Hindu and Indian independence leader, Mahatma Gandhi. Through his reading of the gospels, Gandhi was introduced to the person of Jesus and found strength in his model of "turn the other cheek." As the quote often attributed to him goes: "An eye for an eye only makes the whole world go blind."

When we fully reclaim this part of the message of Jesus and truly manifest it by rejecting all war and all violence, we will not have to engage in arguments to prove that we are the true church of Jesus. We will be the message, and the reign of God, which Jesus proclaims is at hand, will burst forth in its fullness.

CHAPTER 31

The Church Is Marked by Openness to Science

John Polkinghorne

John Polkinghorne was born on October 16, 1930, and grew up in a Christian home. He reports that he cannot recall a time when he was not part of the worshiping and believing community of the church. He studied mathematics at Trinity College, Cambridge, where he also earned a doctorate in theoretical physics. There followed twenty-five years of work as an elementary particle theorist, mostly at Cambridge. Dr. Polkinghorne became a professor and a fellow of the Royal Society (the British National Academy of Science). At the end of this period he felt that the time had come to do something else. He then trained for the Anglican priesthood and, after ordination, worked in the parish ministry for five years. Rev. Dr. Polkinghorne then returned to Cambridge, first as Dean of Chapel at Trinity Hall and then, for seven years, as president of Queens College. After retirement in 1996, he was made a Knight of the British Empire by Queen Elizabeth, and in 2002 he received the Templeton Prize for progress in research into spiritual reality. For the last twenty years his intellectual interests have centered on investigating the relationship between scientific understanding and Christian faith. He loves writing and among his many books have been his Gifford Lectures, The Faith of a Physicist, *his Terry Lectures,* Belief in God in an Age of Science, *and* The God of Hope and the End of the World.

Catholic Inclusivity

The church is called catholic, an adjective derived from a Greek word meaning "universal," as an expression of the all-embracing inclusivity of the body of Christ. In institutional terms, this description is made problematic by the divisions that, from the time of the Great Schism in 1054, have separated Christian from Christian. My concern here is not with these ecclesiastical matters, but with a different kind of inclusivity that should also be a mark of the church: its openness to and acceptance of all forms of truth and beauty. Scriptural warrant for this attitude can be found in the words of Paul to the Philippians, "Finally, beloved, whatever is true, whatever is honorable, whatever is just, whatever is pure, whatever is pleasing, whatever is commendable, if there is any excellence and if there is anything worthy of praise, think about these things" (4:8).

When we remember the way in which the church has inspired and encouraged artists and musicians we can see how splendidly this Pauline injunction has been fulfilled in relation to beauty. In relation to truth—and in particular, in relation to scientific truth—the record has been somewhat more mixed. Yet the founding figures of modern science, as it came to its first full fruition in seventeenth-century Europe, were almost all persons of religious faith, whether Roman Catholic like Galileo, or Protestant like Kepler and Newton. These great pioneers liked to say that God had written two books, the book of nature and the book of Scripture. Both were to be read and, if understood right, they could not contradict each other because they had the same author. It seems to me that the history of the mature interaction between science and religion fully bears this out, despite the undeniably fraught moments that there have been along the way.

The psalmist declares that "the heavens are telling the glory of God; and the firmament proclaims his handiwork" (Ps 19:1), and the church has good reason to welcome the insights offered to it by modern cosmology. I am thinking not so much of the fact that the universe is known to have originated in the fiery singularity of the big bang some fourteen billion years ago, as of the knowledge that we have gained of the structure of the universe and of the character of its long history. As scientists have been able to penetrate into the secrets of matter, through quantum theory and through elementary particle physics, they have uncovered a deep and beautiful order built into the very fabric of the cosmos. The world has proved to be both rationally beautiful and rationally transparent to human enquiry. "Wonder" is a word habitually used by physicists to describe their response to these profound discoveries, which provide the reward for all the labor involved in the endeavor of scientific research. We live in a universe whose marvelous order can readily be understood as a reflection of the mind of its Creator, partly revealed through the exercise of rational powers that form part of the image of God in which human beings have been created. Truly catholic Christianity can gratefully rejoice in these wonderful gifts.

The universe began extremely simple. Its initial state was just that of a ball of energy. Now the universe is rich and diverse, the home of saints and scientists. In itself, such a fruitful history is readily open to interpretation as the unfolding of the purposes of a divine Creator. Moreover, as physicists have studied that cosmic history and understood many of its processes, they have been led to a striking and most unexpected discovery. It has turned out that, though ten billion years elapsed before any form of life appeared, the possibility of that life had been built into the physical fabric of the world from the start. The cosmos was pregnant with the necessary potentiality from the era of the big bang onwards. We have come to realize that a universe that is capable of developing carbon-based life is not just "any old world," but a very special kind of universe indeed. The forces of nature at work in the world (which science treats as given and whose character it is unable of itself to explain) had to be just right—"finely-tuned" one might say—if life was to be an eventual possibility at all. For example, the only place where carbon is made is in the interior nuclear furnaces of the stars—we are all people made of stardust—and this process itself is only possible because the nuclear forces that control it are exactly what they are and no different. This remarkable precision does not look like simply a "happy accident." The Christian will see it as an expression of the fruitful will of the Creator.

Of course, the processes that turned that initial ball of energy into the world we inhabit today have been evolutionary in their character. It is historically ignorant to suppose that when Charles Darwin published his great work, the *Origin of Species*, in 1859, its appearance was greeted by unanimous acceptance in the scientific community and by unanimous rejection in the church. Reaction was, in fact, mixed on all sides. It is sad today to see some Christians still resisting the idea of evolution. They have no need to do so. God is the ordainer and sustainer of nature and works as much through nature as by any other means. Within a short time of the publication of the *Origin of Species*, an Anglican clergyman, Charles Kingsley, saw clearly how the church should think theologically about evolution. He said that God could no doubt have created a ready-made world, but instead God had chosen to do something cleverer than that by bringing into being an evolving world in which "creatures could make themselves." Evolution is the shuffling exploration of divinely endowed potentiality, a gift from the loving Creator that permits creaturely freedom in bringing to birth the inherent fruitfulness of the world. Accepting these deep insights can only enhance the church's affirmation of its belief in "the Father, the Almighty, maker of heaven and earth."

These gifts from science are all ones that should be accepted with gratitude by the church as it fulfills its catholic vocation to welcome and cherish all truthful accounts of reality. Ultimately, knowledge is one because God, the fount of all knowledge, is one. Those who are seeking to serve the God of truth should never fear truth from whatever source it comes. Those who are pursuing truth without reserve are ultimately searching for the One who is Truth itself, whether they know that or not. The catholic heritage of the church in this respect enables it to be open and liberal in relation to all human quests for understanding. Christians do not dwell in some ecclesiastical ghetto, but we live in an open relationship with all that is good and true in human culture.

The strain of Western Christian thought that stems from Thomas Aquinas has been particularly open to the embedding of Christian faith in a wide context of truth-seeking. I want to conclude with one of my favorite quotations, from a twentieth-century Thomist thinker, the Canadian Jesuit, Bernard Lonergan. He once wrote that "God is the unrestricted act of understanding, the eternal rapture glimpsed in every Archimedean cry of 'Eureka!'" Those fine words speak to both the scientist and the believer in me, and they express the foundation on which the catholic inclusivity of the church can safely rest.

CHAPTER 32

The Church Is Petrine

Richard P. McBrien

Richard McBrien was born on August 19, 1936, in Hartford, Connecticut, and was educated in public and parochial elementary schools, and at St. Thomas Seminary in Bloomfield, Connecticut, for both high school and the first two years of college. He pursued major seminary studies at St. John Seminary in Brighton, Massachusetts, where he received a master of arts degree in theology.

McBrien was ordained a priest for the archdiocese of Hartford, Connecticut, on February 2, 1962, and subsequently served as a parish assistant at Our Lady of Victory Church in West Haven and concurrently as chaplain to Catholic students at Southern Connecticut State University in New Haven. The next year he was loaned to the archdiocese of Boston for eventual service on the faculty of a new seminary for delayed vocations, and was sent to Rome to study for a doctorate in theology at the Pontifical Gregorian University. Father McBrien was there during two of the four sessions of the Second Vatican Council.

Father McBrien joined the faculty of Pope John XXIII National Seminary in Weston, Massachusetts, in the Fall of 1965, and was later appointed as its dean of studies. Beginning in 1966, he also began lecturing at Boston College on a part-time basis and then reversed the roles in 1970, going full-time at Boston College and part-time at the seminary. In 1975, he was appointed director of Boston College's Institute of Religious Education and Pastoral Ministry and served in that capacity, as well as professor of theology, until 1980, when he accepted an invitation to join the faculty of the University of Notre Dame as the Crowley-O'Brien-Walter Professor of Theology (later renamed as Crowley-O'Brien) and as chairman of its department of theology. He completed three terms as departmental chair in 1991.

Father McBrien was president of the Catholic Theological Society of America in 1974–75 and received its John Courtney Murray Award in 1976. His major publications include Catholicism, *which received a Christopher Award in 1981,* Lives of the Popes, Lives of the Saints, *and the general editorship of* The HarperCollins Encyclopedia of Catholicism.

Because I have specialized in ecclesiology and have written and lectured extensively on the papacy, or Petrine ministry, I have been frequently invited to offer commentary for the electronic and print media on current developments in the Catholic Church, especially as they relate to the pope and the Vatican. For so many millions of Catholics, the pope is exceeded in importance only by Jesus Christ himself and his Blessed Mother. For them (and for millions of non-Catholics as well), it is the pope who defines what it means to be Catholic, who enforces that definition without personal accountability to any other earthly authority, and who personifies the character and driving spirit of Catholicism.

Prior to the election of Benedict XVI in 2005, many under the age of forty knew no other pope than John Paul II, who was elected in 1978. If there was a comparable papal presence in my own younger life, it was Pius XII, who reigned from 1939 until 1958. When he died, I was in the first year of my major-seminary studies in Boston. Pius XII and John Paul II were alike in their manner of governing the church. Both adopted a highly-centralized approach to papal leadership, displaying little tolerance for pluralism and placing a high premium on loyalty to the Holy See and its policies. This was reflected especially in their appointments to the hierarchy.

Although John XXIII was in office less than five years, he had the deepest and most lasting impact of any pope upon my Catholic and pastoral consciousness. Paul VI (1963–78) had a more mixed effect. His shy, cautious manner was perceived as a sign of weakness and some took advantage of it by pushing him in one direction or another. That seems to have happened in the case of his eventual decision to reject the 2–1 recommendation of the Papal Birth Control Commission that the church's official teaching on contraception should be changed.

In July 1968 he issued his fateful encyclical, *Humanae vitae,* that proved to be among the most divisive papal initiatives in the modern history of the Catholic Church. But that same sense of self-doubt also kept him from moving precipitously against certain theologians. He is said to have written in the margin of a document critical of the Swiss theologian, Hans Küng, "Proceed with charity." John Paul II had no such inhibitions. Within a year of his election, he censured Küng and withdrew his canonical mandate to teach as a Catholic theologian. A similar fate would befall other theologians and even a few bishops.

Consequently, when one speaks of the papal or Petrine "mark" of the Catholic Church, one has to be clear about how one understands those terms. Is the church papal or Petrine in the Pius XII and John Paul II sense, or in the John XXIII sense? Whatever the difference, it is still the case that the Catholic Church is papal or Petrine in character.

Since the East-West Schism of the eleventh century and the Protestant Reformation of the sixteenth century, the Petrine ministry has distinguished the Catholic Church from all other Christian faith communities within the body of Christ. The Catholic Church alone holds that the bishop of Rome is the direct successor of St. Peter and, as such, exercises a primacy of jurisdiction over the universal church. On the other hand, he is, first and foremost, the bishop of Rome. As such, he is a bishop among bishops, not over and above and apart from the others.

But the bishop of Rome is not simply a *primus inter pares* ("a first among equals"). He has the distinctive ministry of strengthening the faith of his brother bishops and of sustaining the unity of the universal church (see Lk 22:31–32), although these are not his responsibilities alone. By reason of their membership in the college of bishops, all bishops are obliged to strengthen one another in the faith, including their brother bishop in Rome. Furthermore, it is not primarily—much less, exclusively—the pope who insures the unity of the universal church but rather the Holy Spirit, and, after the Holy Spirit, the Eucharist and the other sacraments.

In Reformation England, Catholics were distinguished from Protestants by the term "papist." In the mouths of Protestants, the epithet was a term of derision and contempt, carrying the possibility of imprisonment and even execution. Many contemporary English Catholics, however, embraced the term as a positive self-description, proud of their loyalty to the pope. They did not lapse under pressure, not even under the threat of torture and death. The "papists" saw themselves as confessors of the faith in the technical sense of the word (i.e., those who suffered for the faith, short of death), and many of them also became martyrs—racked, beheaded, hanged, or drawn and quartered.

Today there are many thousands of Catholics around the world who also glory in their allegiance to the pope, but it is toward a particular pope—like John Paul II or Benedict XVI—not popes in general. These Catholics are often closely identified with movements promoting the so-called "new evangelization": Opus Dei, the Legion of Christ, the Neo-Catechumenate, Focolare, and Comunione e Liberazione. Many converts to Catholicism entered the church during the pontificate of John Paul II for reasons not unlike those who became Catholic in the 1940s and 1950s, namely, to find religious certitude and to escape the errors of their past religious allegiances. These are the self-proclaimed "papists" of the early twenty-first century.

Then there are Catholics who have been formed in the Catholic Church from birth, and renewed in their faith by the Second Vatican Council. They, too, recognize the abiding importance of the Petrine ministry. They accept the bishop of Rome as the earthly head of the universal church, with a degree of authority greater than any other individual bishop. But then the lines become fuzzy.

Does the pope have the last word on everything that pertains to the life of the church? Does he alone have the right to appoint bishops? Are the bishops simply the helpers of the pope, or are they his true collaborators, with co-responsibility for the well-being of the universal church? Is the pope's personal theology and spirituality normative for everyone else in the church? Are his views on controversial topics always to be taken as definitive, against which the views of others are to be measured, critiqued, and censured? To what extent is papal authority limited, if it is limited at all?

The history of the papacy teaches us that there are many different ways of exercising the papal office and of exercising the Petrine ministry on behalf of the universal church. John Paul II has offered one model; John XXIII, another. And there have been many variations in between.

The problem with long papal reigns, like John Paul II's, is that they tend to distort this truth. People become so familiar with one occupant of the Chair of Peter and with his distinctive style of governance that they assume it to be what Jesus originally had in mind when he uttered the historic words, "You are Peter, and on this rock I will build my church" (Mt 16:18). Alas, the infamous Alexander VI was not the only corrupt pope. Most popes, in fact, have been mediocre and eminently forgettable. Few have been outstanding or great.

And yet the church has endured in spite of the papacy's actual historical record. For some forty years, in fact, the church survived without knowing who the legitimate pope was. Throughout the period of the Great Western Schism (1378–1417), there were two simultaneous claimants to the papacy and, toward the end, there were three, one of whom called himself John XXIII. It was not until the general Council of Constance (1414–18) that the rupture of unity was brought to an end. Significantly, that was a council at which the so-called lower clergy, religious, theologians, and laity were among its active participants, with full voting rights.

Can it be said, therefore, that the one, holy, catholic, and apostolic church is papal or Petrine as well? Yes, but not at the same theological level as those four classic marks, which are included in the historic Niceno-Constantinopolitan Creed. One would search in vain for references to the papacy in any of the historic creeds. The papacy may be a distinctive and highly important ministry within Catholicism, but it is not so essential to it that the church could not function in its absence. The experience of the Great Western Schism indicates otherwise, and, for that matter, much of Christian history itself.

Pope John Paul II's 1995 encyclical, *Ut unum sint* ("That All May Be One"), acknowledged that, while the Petrine office belongs to the essential structure of the church, the manner in which the Petrine ministry is exercised is always subject to criticism and improvement. Indeed, the pope invited his readers, especially those in the other Christian churches and ecclesial communities, to enter into dialogue with him about the manner in which his office is exercised and to recommend ways in which its exercise might conform more faithfully to the gospel.

The church is papal or Petrine, to be sure, but always with an asterisk.

CHAPTER 33

The Church Is Prayerful

Barbara Fiand, SNDdeN

Barbara Fiand is a sister of Notre Dame de Namur. She was born with an identical twin on January 16, 1940, in Soerabaja, Java, of German parents. She lived in both Germany and Canada before becoming a resident of the United States. She received a bachelor of arts degree from Anna Maria College in Paxton, Massachusetts, a bachelor of education degree from the University of Montreal, and a master of arts degree in philosophy from DePaul University in Chicago before earning, in 1980, her doctorate in philosophy at DePaul University, where she specialized in the foundational thought of Martin Heidegger.

Sister Fiand taught religion at the high school level in Montreal for many years, and taught spirituality as well as philosophical theology at the Athenaeum of Ohio in Cincinnati for seventeen years. She has published numerous articles on topics of both philosophy and spirituality, and has written seven books, all published with the Crossroad Publishing Company. Those titles include: Releasement: Spirituality for Ministry; Living the Vision: Religious Vows in An Age of Change *(which has been translated into French as well as Portuguese);* Where Two or Three Are Gathered; Embraced by Compassion: On Human Longing and Divine Response; Wrestling with God: Religious Life in Search of Its Soul; Prayer and the Quest for Healing; *and* In The Stillness You Will Know: Exploring the Paths of Our Ancient Belonging. *Her revised and greatly expanded version of* Living the Vision *is now available under the title:* Refocusing the Vision: Religious Life into the Future.

Sister Fiand lectures widely throughout the world and also gives retreats throughout the United States and Canada. Audio tapes of her lectures, given virtually every year at the Religious Education Congress of the archdiocese of Los Angeles, can be obtained from the archdiocesan office in Los Angeles.

Not long ago I was invited to give a mission for a large parish community in the greater Chicago area. The theme was "Transformation of the Heart," and I was invited to orient the community to this theme during the homily time at all the Sunday liturgies. All the readings were powerful that particular Sunday, but I decided to focus on the gospel, which happened to remember the wedding feast at Cana. A remarkable story, perhaps not so much in terms of water transformation, but in the role which it assigns to the mother of Jesus to be the catalyst for her son's public ministry. "Do whatever he tells you," Mary quietly instructs the servers at the feast (ignoring her son's reticence). And when they, in fact, take him seriously and do whatever he asks of them, he saves the party.

A priest friend of mine had mentioned to me just a few weeks prior to the parish mission that it is his belief that no Scripture story is complete until it becomes our story—until we walk into it and make it our own. So I reflected with the parishioners that day on how much easier it is to transform water into wine than to genuinely transform hearts. The mission of Jesus, and our own mission as baptized into his life and death, is clearly about heart transformation. That requires courage, trust, and willingness on our part—making the changing of water into wine easy in comparison. They say that Jesus could not work healing unless there was trust. That is why, I suppose, after he healed someone, we often hear him say: "Go in peace, your faith has made you whole." Somehow the love energies of healer and of the wounded soul have to connect for wholeness and transformation to happen, and even the most powerful person can do nothing for us if our "yes" is being withheld.

The present reflection focuses our concern on our call, as a church, to pray. "Do whatever he tells you," I hear the mother of Jesus say to us. "Take my son seriously; give him the 'yes' of your faith, and he will change you, just as he changed water into wine at the wedding feast in Cana long ago." Our question during this reflection is the meaning of this for us as individuals and, particularly, for us as church. It sounds strange to imply the need for prayer in an organization for whom the importance of prayer is a given. There is no doubt that as a church we have a long and distinguished history of prayer. Our various liturgies are second to none in both depth and beauty. Yet, are we a church in rapture, I wonder, a church lost in God, a church filled with and moved by the reality of God's unconditional Abba-love, and filled with the passion for God's reign that cannot but flow from that experience? What is it about the prayer life of each of us and about the prayer of the body of believers—the church—that would warrant even today a plea from the mother of Jesus to take her son seriously?

In my book *Prayer and the Quest for Healing*, I meditated at length on the "Prayer Jesus taught us." My concern was then, and is always, with the disposition that I believe it was intended to inspire—a disposition often lacking when the prayer is recited formula-style. It seems highly unlikely to me that Jesus, when asked by his followers to help them reach the depth of prayer they observed in him, offered them a fool-proof set of statements to recite. The exhortation not to "babble" when they pray (Mt 6:7) speaks for itself. God knows what we need, Jesus informs us. My sense is that he wanted his disciples to have the ingredients for union with God; that he showed them, and wants to show us still, a path that opens up to rapture.

The God of Jesus is not a God of protocol before whom we need to watch our language, speak the proper words, and take a position of sub-servience—stand at appointed times and kneel at others. His, I believe, is a God who envelops us, who yearns for us, in whom we want to "drown" our-selves, whose love is all-encompassing and never-ending. We do not need to "seek" the God of Jesus. God is our refuge—infinite and tender Presence. The story of the little fish comes to mind, which asks its mother where and when they would find the water. The answer? "Honey, you are in it." "In [God] we live and move and have our being." The question of worthiness and religious decorum was not at all primary for Jesus, nor should it be for his church. The God that Jesus enfleshed does not care for externals. Rumi, the poet, says it well when he has God tell Moses: "I am apart from all that."

> Ways of worshiping are not to be ranked…
> It's not me that's glorified in acts of worship.
> It's the worshipers! I don't hear the words
>   they say. I look inside at the humility.
> That broken-open lowliness is the reality,
>   not the language! Forget phraseology.
> I want burning, burning…
> Moses,
>   those who pay attention to ways of behaving
>   and speaking are one sort.
> Lovers who burn are another.
> (Rumi, Moses and the Shepherd)

The God enfleshed in Jesus of Nazareth had Zacchaeus the tax collector come down the tree and dined with him. God in Jesus forgave much because of the intensity of love in the sinner—society's reject—who washed his feet with her tears. His God promised paradise from the cross that very day. The God of Jesus is a God of compassion: the Abba whose reign he felt compelled to proclaim, whose will impassioned him. "If you want to pray in my way and experience my God," he told his disciples, "feel the Abba-love throbbing in your veins and allow yourself to be suffused in it."

A church who believes in this Abba and experiences the passion for God's reign, trusts that each day it will have what it needs to bring it about. Its prayer life assumes an attitude of care for those in need, since the enfleshing of God in the body places the welfare of those in need squarely into its hearts. "Christ has no body now but yours," Theresa of Avila rightly asserts. As Christians we do not choose to help the needy. As Christians we cannot do otherwise. Abba-love flows through us as the very embodiment of creative compassion. We are compelled into God's mercy even as it divinizes our hearts.

It is clear that forgiveness of our brothers and sisters—and even of our enemies—flows out of the same "flood gate." In addition, the prayer of Jesus gently reminds us to ponder our own need in this regard. To know that we've "been there and done that"—that we are sinners in need of mercy—helps our inner healing even as it opens us up to brotherly and sisterly love and forgiveness. We belong to each other, Jesus instructs us, and the prayer that arises out of a deep inner awareness of the human condition and our interconnectedness there heals us because of its unmitigated honesty and truth. Last, but not least, placing our prayer life squarely into the waters of God's mercy helps us also accept our own vulnerability and need for protection.

"Deliver us from evil, not least of which is our own arrogance and blindness," we pray out of our experience of total surrender. A church who prays the prayer Jesus taught and allows itself to be permeated with its message, absorbed by its vision, and penetrated with its conviction is a church at one with his mission. It is clearly a church that is here and, also, is not yet, a church that is still to come, that we are all called to help bring about. It is the church of our longing—embraced and loved by the Holy One because it is ablaze with God's endless love and compassion.

When I finished the mission at St. Margaret Mary Parish in Naperville, Illinois, where we had pondered together the rapture of Jesus and prayed into its revelation for us, a woman came up to me as we were saying goodbye. "Barbara," she said, "I want to thank you for helping me move away from the 'babbling' into the 'dwelling,' and for making me proud of my God." As I pondered her words "Mary-style"—in my heart—it occurred to me that, above all, we are called to think "big" and to love "big." The God of Jesus is ever ahead of us, calling us to grow hearts as wide as the world.

CHAPTER 34

The Church Is Priestly

Robert Barron

Robert Barron was born in late 1959, and came of age in the decade after the Second Vatican Council. He reports that he was a fairly disinterested Catholic until, in freshman year in high school, he was introduced to the works of Thomas Aquinas. This encounter changed his life and placed him on a path that he has never abandoned. He pursued studies in philosophy at The Catholic University of America, obtaining his master's degree. Then he attended Mundelein Seminary outside of Chicago, where he received a licentiate in sacred theology. That same year he was ordained to the priesthood by Joseph Cardinal Bernardin. After serving for three years as a parish priest, he commenced doctoral studies in theology at the Institut Catholique de Paris and received his doctorate in sacred theology, having written a dissertation comparing Thomas Aquinas to Paul Tillich. He then returned as a professor to Mundelein Seminary, where he has been teaching ever since.

Fr. Barron has written six books, including Thomas Aquinas: Spiritual Master, And Now I See: A Theology of Transformation, Heaven in Stone and Glass, *and most recently,* The Strangest Way: Walking the Christian Path. *The main focus of his writing has been the integration of theology and spirituality. He follows the church Fathers and the great medieval doctors in holding that theology is meant not simply to inform the mind, but to transform the soul.*

When I was coming of age in the late 1970s, and attending seminary in the 1980s, the dominant description of the priest was "the one who organizes other people's ministries." Now, I will grant you that the ordering of the charisms of ministry is one of the tasks of the priest, but I would argue that few of my contemporaries found that bland and rather functional definition of the essence of priesthood especially inspiring. Midway through my theological studies, while purusing an essay by the great French Jesuit Teilhard de Chardin, I came across an image of the priesthood that took my breath away. Teilhard said that the priest, standing on the border between heaven and earth, offers the prayers, striving, and suffering of the people upward to God and then, in an accompanying move, calls down the divine fire for the transformation of the world. Now that, I thought, is a description to stir the heart and move one to action. Teilhard's image, of course, is deeply rooted in the New Testament characterization of Jesus.

Christ said, "I came to bring fire to the earth, and how I wish it were already kindled!" (Lk 12:49). What is that fire? His forerunner, John, gave us a clue: "I baptize you with water; but one who is more powerful than I is coming....He will baptize you with the Holy Spirit and fire" (Lk 3:16). Jesus came in order to torch the world with the heat and light of the divine Spirit, which is none other than the love shared by the Father and the Son, the very inner life of God. Jesus is a prophet because he teaches; he is a king because he leads and shepherds; but he is a priest because he is the spreader of the sacred fire. Every one of the baptized shares in the priesthood of Christ and is therefore obligated to be a conduit of holiness, a bearer of the divine life. But according to the Vatican II document *Lumen gentium,* there is a coterie of people specially set aside, graced, and ordered for the task of sanctification in the Church: these are the ordained priests, the keepers of the holy fire.

There are two images that further specify the Teilhardian characterization of the priesthood: the caller of the divine fire is a mystagogue and he is a doctor of souls. Let me discuss each of these in turn.

The priest is a mystagogue in the measure that he leads others on a journey into the mystery who God is. Augustine said, "If you understand, it is not God that you understand," and Thomas Aquinas remarked that we only know God as someone unknown, and when Moses asked the one who addressed him out of the burning bush to reveal his name, he heard the strange response, "I am who I am" (Ex 3:14). For our great tradition, God is not so much a being in the world, but the sheer act of Being Itself, the Mystery that undergirds, suffuses, and transcends all things; and all of the Christian spiritual masters agree that our lives are meaningful and rich to the degree that we surrender to the lure of this Mystery. The priest/mystagogue is the one who facilitates, to borrow Bonaventure's phrase, "the mind's journey into God."

How does the mystagogue go about his work? He uses the full treasury of the Catholic heritage: doctrines, dogmas, creeds, architecture, spirituality, poetry, drama, the lives of the saints, and prayer—all of those prolongations of the energy of Jesus. It is worth noting that the earliest theologians of the church, people such as Justin the Martyr, John Chrysostom, Athanasius, Augustine, and Origen, were not academics in our sense of the term, nor were they writing for publication and tenure. They were pastors, catechists, priests, and bishops whose primary concern was the salvation of those whom they were shepherding. Thus Augustine wrote theological treatises and composed homilies, not to captivate graduate students, but to lead people deeper into the divine reality. Athanasius fought tooth and nail for the formulas of the Council of Nicea, not so much because he was a stickler for conceptual precision, but because he was passionate to save souls. So the doctrines and teachings of the church are signposts, pathmarks on the route into God's mystery. In *Divine Comedy*, Dante is led through the arduous paths of hell and purgatory by the ghost of Virgil, and when he comes to the spheres of heaven, he is conducted by Beatrice and finally by St. Bernard. All of these Dantean mystagogues use the wisdom that is available to them—for Virgil, poetic and philosophical insight, and for Beatrice and Bernard, the illumination of theology and mysticism. So the priest uses whatever pathfinding devices the incomparably rich Catholic tradition makes available to him, those icons which reflect the primordial Icon of Christ Jesus himself.

We could perhaps sum up the mystagogue's role as follows: he is an interpreter of the patterns of grace. God's grace is mysteriously at work in all that is and in all that happens, but in order to discern that grace we require a visionary. Picasso once said that the key to his artistic genius was his capacity to see visual analogies: the curve of a woman's body is like the contour of a guitar; that apple is redolent of the moon; an electric light is like the sun. So the priest/mystagogue is trained to notice the analogies that obtain between the archetypes of biblical revelation and the dynamics of ordinary experience: the leadership of Moses shapes the leadership of a good parent; the suffering of Christ on the cross sheds light on the suffering of an innocent child; David's repentance gives hope to us sinners.

The second great image for the priest is *doctor animarum*, doctor of souls. In the Catholic tradition, soul is not so much a spiritual substance set over and against the body as it is the deepest center of the entire person. It corresponds to what the church Fathers called the *imago Dei* (the image of God), to what Teresa of Avila called the "interior castle," and to what Blaise Pascal referred to as "the heart." It is that point in a person that is, in Thomas Merton's phrase, "here and now being created by God"; it is that energy that grounds and orients all of the powers of the mind, will, imagination, and passion. We have doctors who care for practically every aspect of the self, but who is it who practices *cura animarum*, care of souls? Though any baptized person can practice this delicate art, it is the priest who is specially ordered and graced for the task of doctoring souls.

What does he use in his work? Once more he can bring to bear any and all the dimensions of Catholic life from doctrines to saints to Gothic cathedrals, but his essential medicine is Jesus Christ himself. One of the earliest descriptions of Jesus was *soter* (healer), rendered in Latin as *salvator*, which means simply "the bearer of the *salus* (health)." Interestingly, the closest word in English to *salus* and *salvator* is "salve," healing balm. In the story of the man born blind, Jesus spits on the earth and mixes the mud, which he then rubs on the blind man's eyes. In his magnificent commentary on this narrative, Augustine says that the spittle of Christ represents his divinity, while the earth symbolizes his humanity and thus the coming together of the two, the "salve," stands for the healing power of the Incarnation. And so the doctor of souls brings to bear on a suffering humanity the living Jesus Christ, both God and human.

Can we see this process more clearly? In the third chapter of his gospel, John recounts the story of the woman at the well. A Samaritan woman coming to fetch water encounters Jesus, who tells her that he is prepared to give her living water that will permanently quench her thirst. Once more Augustine's gloss is illuminating. He says that the well represents the various objects of errant desire—money, sex, power, the esteem of others, sensual pleasure—all those things that necessarily fail to satisfy our infinite thirst for God. Jesus, God in the flesh, is the living water, the Good that alone is great enough to correspond to the capaciousness of human desire. The doctor of souls, operating in the spirit and person of Jesus, offers the same water to people caught in similar patterns of frustrated desire. It is in the sacraments above all, especially reconciliation and the Eucharist, that the soul doctor offers this water, or to shift the metaphor, rubs in the salve of the Incarnate Son of God.

It is Jesus Christ himself, the High Priest, who is the most authentic mystagogue and the most efficacious healer of souls. But his priests, inasmuch as they share in his office, partake of his mystique and his power. It is Christ's will that, through the agency and fidelity of priests, his holy fire will continue to spread until it engulfs the world.

CHAPTER 35

The Church Is Marked by Its Relationship with Judaism

Mary C. Boys, SNJM

A native of Seattle, Washington, Mary Boys was born on November 4, 1947. Since 1994 she has been the Skinner and McAlpin Professor of Practical Theology at Union Theological Seminary in New York City. Prior to that appointment, she served for seventeen years on the faculty of Boston College. Boys also serves as an adjunct faculty member of the Jewish Theological Seminary of America and Teachers College, Columbia University.

Boys is the author of four books: Biblical Interpretation in Religious Education, Educating in Faith: Maps and Visions, Jewish-Christian Dialogue: One Woman's Experience, *and* Has God Only One Blessing? Judaism as a Source of Christian Self-Understanding. *She has published over seventy articles in books and journals such as* Concilium, Horizons, Religious Education, Biblical Theology Bulletin, Cross Currents, SIDIC, *and the* Journal of Ecumenical Studies. *Boys received her master's and doctoral degrees from Columbia University in a joint program with Union Theological Seminary, and has done advanced study at the Ecumenical Institute for Theological Research in Jerusalem, Israel. She is also the recipient of the doctor of humane letters degree,* honoris causa, *from Hebrew Union College-Jewish Institute of Religion. She has served as visiting lecturer of religious education at Princeton Theological Seminary, Claremont School of Theology, John Carroll University, Villanova University, and St. Mary's College (London, England).*

Dr. Boys is a member of the editorial boards of the Journal of Religious Education *(Australia),* Teaching Theology and Religion, *and* Religious Education. *Boys served as co-director of the Lilly Endowment-sponsored Religious Particularism and Pluralism project involving Jewish and Catholic educators and academics, and is a member of the boards of the Tanenbaum Foundation for Interreligious Understanding, the Suenens Foundation, and the National Catholic Center for Holocaust Education. Since 1965, she has been a member of the Sisters of the Holy Names of Jesus and Mary, a congregation of Roman Catholic women.*

A Right Relationship with Judaism

I would have first learned about the marks of the church from our elementary religion textbook, *Baltimore Catechism*. The answer to question 154 ("What do we mean by the marks of the Church?") defined the marks of the church as "certain clear signs by which all men can recognize it as the true Church founded by Jesus Christ." It adds: "Jesus Christ willed that the true Church should have these marks, which would distinguish it from all false religions." I suppose we must have been taught that Protestants were to be categorized as adherents of a "false religion," but in my Seattle neighborhood, most of our neighbors were either Protestants or religiously unaffiliated, as was (and is) my father. I don't remember worrying about their salvation.

In those days, I knew only one Jew, Pauline Lee, a close family friend. While my grandmother, mother, and maternal aunts were practicing Catholics, they had no interest in seeking Pauline's conversion. Perhaps their respect for Judaism was the reason I took little notice of another question in the *Baltimore Catechism*: "Why did the Jewish religion, which up to the death of Christ had been the true religion, cease at that time to be the true religion?"(#391). The answer reads: "[B]ecause it was only a promise of the redemption and figure of the Christian religion, and when the redemption was accomplished and the Christian religion established by the death of Christ, the promise and the figure were no longer necessary."

Looking back, it seems that my upbringing as a child of a "mixed" marriage in the religiously diverse Pacific Northwest left a lasting impression. When my first-grade teacher, whom I otherwise adored, told us that only Catholics went to heaven, I knew she was wrong. If heaven did not include my father, a man of enormous integrity who was a loving husband and father, then something was very wrong with heaven. What kind of a god would consign non-Catholics to hell or limbo?

Vatican II, which coincided with my high school years and energized my interest in religion, put ecumenism and interreligious exchange on my personal map. Yet I did not set out to work in the realm of interreligious dialogue, but rather to educate Catholics. An interest in Judaism had, nevertheless, taken root. During the years of my graduate study in New York City in the mid-1970s, I learned both a more complex understanding of Christian origins and something of the vitality of contemporary Jewish life—learning now enriched by years of teaching and research, membership in a study group (The Christian Scholars Group on Christian-Jewish Relations), involvement in dialogue at various levels, and, most importantly, friendships with many Jews.

I can no longer imagine practicing my Catholic faith without loving Judaism. My Jewish friends have become my study partners in discerning God's voice amidst the cacophony of life. Their commitment to live the Way of Torah enlivens my commitment to live the Way of Jesus Christ. A church marked by holiness must do justice to Judaism, from which it originated and with which it has had a long and difficult history.

Establishing a Right Relationship with Judaism

Because so much of Christian self-understanding has been premised on inadequate understandings of Judaism and simplistic notions of Christian origins, establishing a right relationship with Judaism requires a three-step approach. First, Christians must be willing to set aside preconceptions about Judaism—and do not underestimate the difficulty of this renunciation. For most of us, oversimplifications about Judaism were embedded in our education in Christianity, whether about the alleged legalism of post-exilic Judaism, the hypocrisy of the Pharisees, or the responsibility of the Jews for the crucifixion. Setting aside preconceptions thus entails learning to interpret the gospels in more perceptive ways, and situating texts in their historical, religious, and literary contexts. This is a monumental educational challenge in itself, one that in my experience has barely begun in the churches despite an abundance of resources and many committed teachers.

The second step in the process of reworking our self-understanding is the willingness to grapple with the shadow side of Christian proclamation. Until we face our history with relation to the Jewish people, and examine our collective Christian conscience about our unjust attitudes and actions for nearly two thousand years, any dialogue will be shallow. Yet it is no small matter to face this history honestly; it is deeply disillusioning to learn of the church's hostility to and harsh treatment of Jews over so many centuries—a history that poses serious questions to the church's mark of holiness. Most Christians are blissfully ignorant of the "teaching of contempt," in Jules Isaac's memorable phrase, and of the terrible consequences it has wrought.[76] Therefore, care must be taken in helping persons understand the rivalry that accompanied the partings of the ways, and the factors that hardened the rivalry into disputation, denunciation, and persecution.

A third step involves a commitment to reconstruct and revitalize our understandings of Christianity in light of deepened knowledge about our origins and history in relation to the Jewish people. For example, the Pontifical Biblical Commission's 2001 document, "The Jewish People and their Sacred Scriptures in the Christian Bible," contributes to further thinking about how to articulate the relationship between the Testaments.[77] This text is unwieldy, imperfect, and often tedious, but with some fine insights. It proposes, for example, that we understand Christianity's appropriation of the "Old" Testament as a rereading, a "retrospective perception." Moreover, the document says that it is not that Jews do not see what the Old Testament texts proclaim, but rather that "the Christian, in the light of Christ and in the Spirit, discovers in the text an additional meaning that was hidden there" (II.A). We are invited to read the Bible without the template of a simplistic promise/fulfillment schema, and with appreciation for Jewish modes of reading texts.

Christians, in fact, enrich their self-understanding by engaging in dialogue with Jews. By explicating the way the respective communities understand and use key theological concepts, such as salvation and messiah, each will come away with enhanced self-understanding. Self-understanding is best achieved in the presence of the knowledgeable other.

In light of the tragic history in our relationship with Jews, we Christians need to open ourselves to learning about Judaism from Jews, and to engage in dialogue with them. Because dialogue is much harder than it sounds, we need the wisdom of thinkers such as Martin Buber, Paulo Freire, and Nicholas Burbules.

Martin Buber's work, most notably *I and Thou*, has exercised considerable influence on the interreligious realm. While both monologue (self-centered conversation) and technical dialogue (information-centered conversation) are inevitable ways of communication in the modern world, the "I-it" relationship they constitute is far removed from the community of relation that "I-Thou" represents. Buber's lament that much conversation is "false dialogue," with no true turn to the other and no real desire to foster mutuality, hovers over all interreligious (and intra-religious) encounter. Yet in my experience too often the atmosphere established and the processes employed do little to enhance mutuality.

Paulo Freire, the late Brazilian lawyer, philosopher, and educator, places humility at the center of dialogue. "How," he asked, "can I dialogue if I always project ignorance onto others and never perceive my own?...How can I dialogue if I consider myself a member of the in-group of 'pure' men and women, the owners of the truth and knowledge, for whom all non-members are 'these people' or the 'great unwashed'?...How can I dialogue if I am afraid of being displaced, the mere possibility causing me torment and weakness? Self-sufficiency is incompatible with dialogue."[78] Freire's questions may be modified as Christians anticipate dialogue with Jews. How can I dialogue if I approach Jews with questions such as "Why don't you believe Jesus was the messiah?" and have not myself grappled with why I believe he is? How can I dialogue if I believe only Christians of my belief and practice are saved? How can I dialogue if I fear confronting the shadow side of my church?

Educational philosopher Nicholas Burbules offers a complementary perspective in his contention that dialogue is best characterized by a commitment that joins interlocutors in a continuing relationship. To be successful, a dialogue depends on cooperation, particularly when disagreements, misinterpretations, and difficulties beset it. Persistence necessitates "a relation of mutual respect, trust, and concern—and part of the dialogical interchange often must relate to the establishment and maintenance of these bonds."[79] For this, perseverance is indispensable. Dialogue is not a mere method. It is a way of life that demands attentiveness to our emotions and to nurturing virtues and skills that foster relationships.

We must be attentive to our emotions because every serious interreligious exchange, especially that between Jews and Christians, exposes our vulnerabilities as we open our beliefs, practices, and values to the scrutiny of another. It takes time to develop trust, time to develop an atmosphere in which persons need not feel defensive or apologetic. Sufficient time is an essential dimension of genuine dialogue; mutuality grows slowly. Yet time alone will not suffice. We need also to practice what Burbules calls the "communicative virtues": patience, tolerance, openness to receive as well as give criticism, willingness to admit one may be mistaken, desire to translate or reinterpret one's concerns so as to make oneself comprehensible to others, imposition of self-restraint, and the commitment to listen thoughtfully and attentively.[80]

These considerations also need to be at the forefront so that our leaders can create conditions conducive to genuine dialogue. While the Catholic tradition has many fine recent statements on its relationship with Judaism, it has less skill in fostering dialogue *within* the church, thereby unintentionally muting the effect of its theological reflection since Vatican II. We will best witness to what the church has learned in the past forty years of scholarship and dialogue with Jews by teaching in a dialogic manner— thereby embodying the marks of one, holy, catholic, and apostolic church in new ways.

CHAPTER 36

The Church Is Marked by Ritual

John B. Foley, SJ

John Foley, SJ, is founder and director of the Center for Liturgy at St. Louis University where he is also a faculty member of the Department of Theology as Distinguished Liturgical Theologian. Born in 1939 in Peoria, Illinois, he entered the Society of Jesus in August 1962. He received his doctorate in theology with a specialty in liturgy and aesthetics from the Graduate Theological Union (Berkeley, California) in 1993. He is a noted lecturer and speaker throughout the United States on the topics of liturgy, spirituality, theology and music.

Fr. Foley has published widely on liturgical and musical topics with articles appearing in both scholarly and popular journals and books. He is perhaps best known as one of the composing coalition called the "St. Louis Jesuits," who after the Second Vatican Council became one of the prime influences on American and Roman Catholic worship music through their compositions. In this regard, he has published and recorded numerous collections of music, most recently God Among Us, *and he has nearly 150 liturgical pieces in print. He has also written church dramas such as* River of Light *and* Like Winter Waiting, *as well as classical music.*

In 1998 Foley founded the National Liturgical Composers Forum, which is planned and executed by the Center for Liturgy. He has served on the Board of Directors of the National Liturgical Conference (1984–93) and is presently a member of the North American Academy of Liturgy.

Knowing by Heart: How Ritual Affects Our Lives

One distinguishing mark of the church is so quietly present that most people never advert to it. It is called "ritual." Without ritual there could be no full and active participation by all the people in the liturgy, and thus the primary and indispensable source from which we are to derive the true Christian spirit would disappear! Yet most of us have only a vague idea of what ritual is. This chapter is one attempt to shed some light on this interesting subject.

Allow me to begin with a day-by-day example. My friend asked me as I passed, "How are you?"

I replied, "Fine, how are you doing?"

"Great," my friend affirmed. Actually she looked unhappy, and as for me I was trying to get over the cold that was going around, so maybe the exchange was not very truthful.

Of course, my friend could have responded, "Actually not so good. My mom is sick, I creased the fender of my car going sixty as I hit a police car, and I think I am going to lose my job. How are you?" A much more honest sentiment. But is such a detailed reply really in place? *I did not ask for an inventory of your troubles,* I say to myself. Yet in fact I *did* ask. What is going on here? What is the meaning of this strange everyday activity? The answer will tell us about ritual.

Imagine what would happen if I refused to engage in the "How are you?" exchange. What would I say to you instead when we meet? "Jane…uh…hi." But "hi" is not allowed, since it is a contraction of "hiya," which is short for "How are you?" How about "What is going on?" or "What have you been doing?" and so on. But these also accomplish the same thing as "How are you?"—they ask something general about the person. With all these omitted there is not much left to say. Our mouths open and nothing comes out.

Does this mean that we must stuff meaningless words into an otherwise embarrassing moment? A bit of a magic trick to take our attention away? No, ritual is not meaningless, it is meaningful in a different way.

When I ask someone how they are, I am really making an underlying statement that is very important: I am signaling that I care about their state of health in a general way and expect them to care about mine. A mugger does not ask the muggee how he or she is. But friends set up a positive basis for their conversation by asking about the other's health.

Strange to say, if we spoke such wishes explicitly the setup would not work. If I said, "I have a positive attitude toward you, and therefore we can relate safely," you would wonder what is wrong with me. Did I think you would be afraid of me? Because you did not have an active, explicit fear, my explicit words reassuring you seem out of place. But I code this meaning into a set formula of words and deeds. I smile and repeat the formula. I tell you at a level at which you will receive it. In other words, I do it by ritual.

The Characteristics of Ritual

Ritual is always *interpersonal*. It happens between or among people. I do not ask after the doorknob's health. And I must listen to the answer the other person gives. Someone asked me yesterday how I was but then looked at their watch as I replied. The ritual failed.

Ritual is *repetitive*. The formula can be spoken every day, many times a day. In fact it has to remain more or less the same each time. I could not say "Where is Timbuktu?" instead of "How are you?" But I could say, "How are things?" and accomplish the same thing. Or "'Sup?" which is a contraction of "What is up?" The repetitiveness does not bother anyone; in fact most of us like that feature. It is comfortable.

Ritual is *value-oriented*. We are telling one another, in a subliminal way, that we value each other. Even if the exchange may seem trivial, we are really saying "I care about you, and that is a good basis for our conversation."

Finally, ritual is *done without explicit thought*. I am not in a quandary about the other person's health which I solve by asking. I ask by instinct, as I carry out all rituals by instinct. Ritual is like a stairway worn smooth, showing the age-old tread of feet before me, needing no complicated thinking in order to get to the top.

So what does ritual have to do with liturgy? Take the formula we hear often at Mass, "The Lord be with you." This is probably the way early Christians greeted each other instead of saying "How are you?" It is the same kind of ritual formula we have been looking at. It is a greeting that sets up a positive framework for what follows. Notice that many presiders do not realize this fact and add another greeting on top of the first: "Good morning," they say, which does the same exact thing as "The Lord be with you" and so is redundant.

The ritual intent is not to state a fact (as the variant still used by many presiders, "The Lord is with you" does) but to express a desire on the part of the speaker. I desire the Godly good for you, just as "How are you?" is an expression of good will. Presiders are not implying that God is absent from the person; they are giving a deeper message to you.

Another example of ritual is the Eucharistic Prayer. No one is surprised to hear the presider say "The night before he died he took bread and gave you thanks and praise." We have already heard the exact same words many hundreds of times, and they reside at a very deep level within us.

Then why does the presider say them? Because human beings live by ritual, by the repetition of formulas between people that affirm, at a subliminal level, matters of great worth. The Eucharistic Prayer expresses through thanksgiving and memory the inner truth of Christianity. Our interior path has already been formed by the many re-hearings. We are not learning something; we are watching as our own inner Christian soul is played out again ritually. To put it another way, the Spirit of Christ's action is already within us at root level and needs to be teased out by ritual prayer. This is like the child who asks for the same story to be read for the tenth time, or who intently watches the same movie for the thirtieth time. The very formulaic nature of such repetition is what they seek.

This smooth-worn stairway, this repetition of the already known, guards great truths through time. We might doubt or gradually forget otherwise. In fact, all great truths must have ritual status if they are to last beyond the present generation. Ritual is a vessel that holds and preserves these truths, pours them out carefully to the centuries and eons to come. Not only "The Lord be with you," but also "This is my body which will be given up for you."

A Postscript

If there were space, we could discuss liturgical music as fitting into the ritual pattern. One would have to be cautious, of course, but still, the characteristics I listed above do seem to describe aspects of liturgical music: interpersonal, able to be repeated, value-oriented, not invoking explicit thought. Liturgical music, even with the "message" found in the words, could never be called a communication of ideas. The most favorite hymns are ones during which the congregation does not really pay much attention to the words. As in ritual, their meaning has long since been ingested and assimilated and is merely activated by the new singing of the hymn. Notice also that there is always a formality about the production of music. Listeners become quiet. They sit or stand differently than they would in a conversation. The performer creates an aura, speaking figuratively, from which the music emerges. There is an "informal formality," even in a rock concert or a performance by a folk guitarist/singer, so that, even if the music is wild, which of course, church music is not, there is still a contemplative quality. Can church music be defined literally as a ritual? I admit that I do not know, but from what this chapter has touched upon it starts to seem likely.

In any case, it is easy to see that ritual—particularly ritual that contains such foundational values—is intrinsic to human life. Most important among these values is the expression of the Christian assembly's very identity as the people of God, in Christ, through the Holy Spirit. Ritual carefully carries our identity as Christians and wraps it about us regularly so that we will never forget.

CHAPTER 37

The Church Is Sacramental

Peter E. Fink, SJ

Father Peter Fink is professor of sacramental-liturgical theology at the Weston Jesuit School of Theology in Cambridge, Massachusetts, where he has taught since 1975. Born July 16, 1938, and a graduate of Regis High School and Fordham University, a Jesuit from the New York Province, he was ordained to the priesthood in 1969, and presides in both the Roman and Maronite Catholic Churches.

Father Fink has taught at Creighton University, The Catholic University of America, Boston College, and St. Bernard's Institute in Rochester, New York. He holds master's degrees in physics (Rensselaer Polytechnic Institute) and theology (Woodstock College), and received a doctorate in systematic theology from Emory University in Atlanta. He is author of Worship: Praying the Sacraments, *and was editor of* The New Dictionary of Sacramental Worship *and of reconciliation and anointing volumes in the Alternative Futures for Worship series. Some of his more recent articles are "Theoretical Structures for Liturgical Symbols," in* Liturgical Ministry, *"Future Choices for Ordained Ministry" in* The Way Supplement, *"Human Imagination and the God it Reveals," in* The Way Supplement, *and "The Human Ways Of God," in* The Way Supplement. *One article on the paschal mystery and two articles on the sacrament of reconciliation appeared in* Liturgical Ministry, *and the article "Preaching at Penance Services" was published in* Preach.

His areas of interest include sacramental/liturgical theology, with a special focus on Eucharist, Christian initiation, orders, and reconciliation; liturgical praxis and spirituality; myth, symbol, ritual, and imagination; and, theolog-

ical anthropology. He is a charter member of the North American Academy of Liturgy, and was president of the academy in 1995. He is also a member of Societas Liturgica, and Jesuits for the Christian East.

Many years ago, while I was still a graduate student in Atlanta, I offered a series of talks on the sacraments. Most of them were simply verbal, discourses about the Eucharist, reconciliation and healing, marriage, orders, and Christian initiation. One of them, however, was entitled, "Communicating through Symbols," and I knew I could not simply talk about such communication. I had to "speak" using the prayers and symbols of our sacraments.

I asked the people first to stand in a circle, facing outward, with only a lighted candle set behind them in the center of the circle. I prayed an Advent prayer, asking the Lord to come into our midst. Then, sprinkling some with water, I invited a few to turn around, now facing the candle. Those who did received a smaller candle lighted from the central candle. Then we read the text from Paul to the Romans (10:14–15): How can they believe if they have not heard; how can they hear if no one preaches? Those with the candles invited the others to turn, and presented them with a candle as well.

The crowd then sat down. Bread and wine were passed among them while a brief prayer of blessing was prayed. We said the Lord's prayer together, and greeted each other in peace. At that point, the central candle was extinguished. The people, still holding their candles, stood again facing outward, this time themselves being the candle of Christ to the world.

The meaning of the event was simple. It followed the pattern of Christian initiation, where Christ invites us, Christ gives us shape as his body, and then sends us out to be ministers of his word to the world. Christ, the light, was first a single candle. At the end, Christ the light was a circle of candles, facing out, still seeking those who have not yet heard.

Several insights struck me that night that I knew in my head but not yet fully in my heart. All of them had to do with the church as sacramental, and with my own commitment as priest and theologian to the sacramental life of the church. The first is that God uses symbol at least as much as word to communicate to us. Symbol is the language of mystery. Symbol appeals to our freedom and invites us to engage the mystery that is communicated. Word, too, can appeal to our freedom, provided it is spoken to invite us and not simply to give us rules and declarations.

The second insight, which was later articulated by both Edward Kilmartin and Aidan Kavanagh in books on liturgical theology, was that ritual enactment of a community at prayer is at least as important as theological reflection when it comes to understanding sacraments, and may in fact be primary. People do not always perceive the niceties that theological reflection requires. But sacraments are of little value unless they sanctify men and women, build up the body of Christ, and give worship to God, and unless the faith of people is nourished, strengthened, and expressed (Constitution on the Sacred Liturgy 59). Such achievements will only happen when a community gathers to celebrate the sacraments.

The third insight had to do with my own future ministry, which has now unfolded through thirty excellent years. I was learning to understand the innerworkings of sacraments. This was not just the internal structure of the ritual, though that was important, but what it was like to bring people into the mystery that was enacted. Years later I wrote a number of pieces on liturgical spirituality, in particular what was required to preside and preach. I knew I would serve best in seminary work, helping seminarians, and later lay women and men, to understand and serve the church at prayer. As the 1983 Code of Canon Law put it, sacraments are not to be considered merely "things of grace" entrusted to the church, but rather as liturgical actions belonging to "the sanctifying mission" of the church.

My commitment to the sacramental life has kept me at Weston Jesuit School of Theology since January 1975. While I have published modestly, the primary witness of my ministry is the women and men I have invited into the mystery of Christ as it is set forth in our sacramental life. My ministry has been not only to teach sacramental theology, but to witness the mystery of Christ through preaching, presiding, and reconciling.

If there is a single word that operates in me as a general methodology it would be *mystagogy*—a catechesis of illumination made prominent again through the Order of Christian Initiation and a re-emphasis on the Easter season. Mystagogy is something other than a catechesis based on allegory, a classic distinction in liturgical studies between a catechesis of doers versus a catechesis of watchers. It is also different from a catechesis of correlation, such as used by Paul Tillich or Geofrey Wainwright. Mystagogy is very close to what I see as the method of Karl Rahner: let me show you what I have seen so that you can see it as well.

Mystagogy is itself a liturgical concept. It refers to how we learn after we have undergone our baptism. Unfortunately, we are still more enamored of the preparatory catecheses of Lent, and less focused on living as baptized people. Mystagogy focuses on the imagination as a theological and pastoral tool. It sees empathy as a theological and pastoral goal. And it embraces symbol as the proper language of mystery and myth as a particular way of telling the truth.

Because I see mystagogy as my prime theological method, there are two questions that guide me. The first: What must I do if I am to do this venture well, whether the venture is understanding, presiding, and preaching at liturgical functions, or engaging in interaction proper to pastoral advice (e.g., spiritual direction, counseling, confessional advice)? The second follows from the first: What might happen to me once I do this venture well, whether the venture is understanding, presiding, and preaching at liturgical functions, or engaging in interaction proper to pastoral advice?

Since my major ministry is teaching sacramental theology, this mystagogical approach comes through in everything I teach. For example, for the course on Eucharist, I set forth two purposes. The course is about the major doctrines of eucharistic faith: institution of the Eucharist by Christ; the real presence of Christ; the enduring sacrifice of Christ; and the promise of eschatological fulfillment. The first purpose is to explore this tradition and to receive it in forms appropriate to the contemporary church. The second purpose is to deepen one's participation in the Eucharist and to aid in one's preaching, prayer, and liturgical ministry.

A similar thing can be said about all of my sacramental courses, whether they are on Christian initiation, healing or vocation sacraments, and whether they are for the presider or the other members of the assembled church. What must I do if I am to do this venture well; what might happen to me once I do this venture well? It is equally important to teach people how to participate in the worship of the church as it is to help them to understand it. It is equally important to illustrate how people are affected by their participation in the sacraments of the church.

This reflection is about the sacramental nature of the church. Even more, however, it is a statement of one who trains men and women to be part of a sacramental church. It is part of Christian initiation. That journey moves from the grace of God that comes even before baptism, through the whole sacramental life of the church, culminating in Christian death and burial, a final movement which enacts in fact what we have enacted in sacrament all our lives.

CHAPTER 38

The Church Is Marked by Sexuality

Christine E. Gudorf

Christine Gudorf was born in Louisville, Kentucky, in 1949. She attended parochial grade and high schools, and received a bachelor of science degree from Indiana University in religion, classics, and secondary education. She has also received master of arts, master of philosophy, and doctor of philosophy degrees in religion from Columbia University in a joint program with Union Theological Seminary. Her dissertation was published (Catholic Social Teaching on Liberation Themes), *followed by six other books and dozens of journal articles and book chapters. She taught at Xavier University (Cincinnati, Ohio) from 1978 to 1993. Presently she is professor and chair of the religious studies department at Florida International University. She is also at work on a doctorate in comparative sociology concentrating on social theory and international development. She is presently co-editor of* The Journal of Christian Ethics. *Her latest book, co-authored with James Huchingson, is* Boundaries: Cases in Environmental Ethics; *some of her latest journal articles are "The Erosion of Sexual Dimorphism: Challenges to Religion and Religious Ethics" in* Journal of the American Academy of Religion; *a review article on Susan Frank Parsons'* The Ethics of Gender, Blackwell Companion to Feminist Theology, *and "Feminism and Christian Ethics" in the* Journal of Religious Ethics, *and a response to Mary Hobgood in* Journal of Feminist Study of Religion.

I think I have always understood the church as sexual, even though I was never fond of the symbol of the church as the bride of Christ. Interpretations of that symbol placed too much emphasis on Christ as ruler and the church as obedient to be attractive to me, who expected to be a bride someday. I grew up the oldest of nine children in a Midwestern Catholic family, married my high school sweetheart when we were both nineteen, and remain happily married to him thirty-six years, three children, and two grandchildren later. My understanding of sexuality as a mark of the church has little to do with the theological tradition and everything to do with my personal experience of Catholic life and faith. It seemed to me that comparisons of sexuality as creating souls for the church and evangelization as converting souls for the church were entirely too focused on numbers, and missed what was the essential connection between church and sexuality.

The sexual attitudes of my parents were perhaps not common among their generation; certainly their behavior in our home did not reflect the reticence and suspicion that commonly surrounded anything to do with sexuality among Catholics, or, for that matter, among our Protestant neighbors. My father was a doctor and my mother was a middle school science teacher who had been a tomboy all her life. I learned to cook because my father fairly frequently came home from his office, tiptoed up behind my mother at the stove, tickled her, and carried her off to their bedroom as she giggled and called back to me: "Don't let the dinner burn!" One Christmas when the grandparents, aunts, uncles, and cousins were all at our house for dinner and the adults were making teasing toasts, my father, who could get tipsy on a single glass of wine, made my mother crimson with embarrassment with his toast: "To Lucie and her multiple orgasms!" After dinner that night, as every night, we all said a family rosary.

Growing up, it seemed to me that the obvious delight my parents took in their sexual relationship was as important for the faith of us children as was the nightly rosary. Their very sexual love surrounded us with warmth and love, and like the nightly rosary created a firm foundation for our family life. My parents made sure we all had basic sex education rather young; my sisters and I felt they went into much too much detail at the time, but looking back I am not so sure. Until I was in high school (when my father finished medical school and internship and began a family practice) we had only one bathroom for all eleven of us, and so we were rather casual about nudity and semi-nudity. It helped that the oldest five children were girls, so the boys were still rather young when they finally got their own bathroom. Until I was married, I thought that such open casual attitudes about sexuality were typical.

While my husband fell in love with me at least in part because I did not conform to gender stereotypes any more than my mother had (I was a

National Merit Scholar who worked for eight summers as a beach life-guard, often as the only female), he found my attitudes toward sex initial-ly scandalous. Hesitant to make love when we visited either set of parents on vacation from the university lest they hear the bedsprings (or my moans), he resisted my dismissal of such concerns: "We're married! They have to know we make love. Why should it be different in their home than in ours?" Slowly I wore him down on this point. The big discussions came a few years later, when I suggested one night that for us sex was a sacra-ment. I think he expected me to be struck dead by lightening on the spot. He disliked the whole idea, saying it made him feel like the pope was in bed with us, which rather dampened his ardor. It seemed to me, though, that our lovemaking was certainly a channel of grace for both of us. It not only expressed our love for each other, but it made us love each other more. The pleasure in shared sex rewarded us both so much that it made us even more generous with each other, and with everyone around us. It created a warm atmosphere in our home, a fact that was not lost on our children. One Saturday when my husband and I had one too many household chores turn difficult and had begun to snap at each other, the tension in the house grew over a couple hours, with the kids trying to avoid both of us. Finally, our oldest son, who was about nine at the time, came to me and suggested, "Mama, why don't you and Dad go take a little nap?" In our family "a little nap" was our euphemism for a half hour retreat to bed to make love in the middle of weekend or holiday afternoons. Our sons did not know exactly what we did, but they did recognize the effects. Our lit-tle naps frequently produced a call to get everyone together to play a game, go out for ice cream, rent a movie and make popcorn, or invite another family over for dinner. I think it was the kids who convinced their Dad that our sex was, indeed, sacramental.

The experience of shared sexual pleasure in a committed relationship creates joy. Like all forms of pleasure, it affirms the worth of the person pleasured.[82] Shared sexual pleasure also bonds people together. We like to be with people with whom we are happy, people with whom even the suf-fering and misery that come our way seem less onerous and more bear-able. But more than this, as the authors of *Embodied in Love* noted, shared sexual pleasure acts as a school for love.[83] When we make ourselves physi-cally and emotionally vulnerable to our partner in sex, we are rewarded with overwhelming pleasure, which teaches us that risking vulnerability to the partner in other areas is worthwhile, and may also be rewarding. Time after time of risking ourselves with our spouse and being rewarded with reciprocal trust, openness, and vulnerability (not to mention the pleasure these bring) encourages us to risk ourselves with yet other persons in non-sexual relationships. As my great-aunt Nellie once told me about her own marriage: "I was over six feet tall, and in the 1920s, that made me a freak. Simon was at least a foot shorter than me, but he didn't care how we looked. He loved me and my body, and he loved me so well that I came to love myself, and that let me begin to make friends. He loved my voice, and signed us up for two parish choirs. We were asked to sing lots of weddings and funerals, and over forty years we made lots of friends in those choirs and in the Knights of Columbus who didn't think I was a freak at all." Nellie lived to ninety-nine, and is the best-loved person I have ever known—by five generations of family, hundreds of friends and neighbors. She attributed the joy that radiated from her, her kindness and generosity, all to Simon's loving her so well that she could reach out to others.

Once my husband and I were visiting our son and his wife and their children for a few days, and I had wandered into the kitchen one morning, not knowing anyone was up. My son and his wife were standing in the middle of the kitchen, coffee makings lying on the counter, locked in a deep, very sexual kiss. I backed out of the doorway, and bumped into my six-year-old granddaughter, who peeked around me at her parents, covered her mouth to smother a giggle, and led me back into the dining room, whispering with a big grin, "They do that mushy stuff sometimes, but it makes them happy." Clearly, it made her happy, too.

Sometimes shared sexual pleasure helps us bear tragedy. In the face of accident, disaster, chronic illness or death of a loved one, when there are no effective words of comfort, we share our pain and our love in the bittersweet pleasure of sex, and the shared pleasure strengthens us to resume our responsibilities again. Such sex is not simply a "time out" from the pain and misery, but is a necessary reminder that behind the immediate pain and darkness, human life is not only worthwhile, but even joyous. Is this not grace?[84]

Today Catholics all around the world are affirming the value of sexuality—of mutual sexual pleasure—for its own sake and for the benefit of marriage, the family, and the wider church community, and not only as a permitted but undesirable by-product of reproductive activity. For most couples, the sexual experience that is most enhanced by the procreative potential of sex is not the sex during which a child is conceived (which most couples do not know at the time), but sex during and after pregnancy, when the couple glories not only in the pleasure of sexual love, but also in the new love object that the creative power of that sexual love has brought about. The very welfare of children demands that they be the product of mutually pleasurable sexual love, rather than sexual pleasure being an incidental byproduct of creating children. When children are born, the pleasure by which they were begotten enhances our joy in them, and helps us love them even amid sleepless nights. The very love and care of children that is so essential to their well-being begins with conception within sacramental sexuality—mutually pleasurable sex that connects us with not only each other but also with the divine love at the center of existence. Is this connection with the divine presence not the primary function of the church?

CHAPTER 39

The Church Is Sinful

Charles E. Curran

Charles Curran was born on March 30, 1934, the third of four children to Gertrude Beisner Curran and John F. Curran. He went to the seminary in Rochester, New York, graduating with a bachelor of arts degree from St. Bernard's College and Seminary in 1955, before going to study theology in Rome. After receiving a doctorate in sacred theology from the Gregorian University in 1961 and a doctorate in sacred theology with a specialization in moral theology from the Accademia Alfonsiana, Curran returned to teach moral theology at St. Bernard's Seminary in Rochester, New York, from 1961 to 1965. His teaching career at The Catholic University of America from 1965 to 1988 was marked by three significant events: in 1967 the faculty and students went on strike and successfully overturned the original decision of the board of trustees not to renew Curran's contract; in 1968 he was the spokesperson for a group of over 600 Catholic scholars who issued a statement of dissent from the major conclusions of the encyclical Humanae vitae; *in 1986, after a seven-year investigation, the Congregation for the Doctrine of the Faith concluded that Curran was neither "suitable nor eligible to exercise the function of a professor of Catholic theology." After losing a lawsuit to retain his right to teach Catholic theology at The Catholic University of America, Curran ultimately accepted the Elizabeth Scurlock University Professorship of Human Values at Southern Methodist University in 1991.*

Curran has served as president of three national academic societies—the Catholic Theological Society of America, the Society of Christian Ethics, and the American Theological Society. The Catholic Theological Society of America in 1972 named him the first recipient of the John Courtney Murray Award for Distinguished Achievement in Theology. In 2003 the College

Theology Society gave Curran its Presidential Award for a lifetime of scholarly achievements in moral theology. Curran has authored and edited over fifty books; the latest ones are Catholic Social Teaching 1891–Present: A Historical, Theological, and Ethical Analysis, *and* The Moral Theology of John Paul II: An Appraisal.

"There are five marks of the church—one, holy, catholic, apostolic, and sinful." I made this statement my first year teaching theology in 1961. Docile pre-Vatican II seminarians resisted accepting my five marks of the church. I have the feeling that the students I taught in 1961, after the experience of life in the church in the last forty plus years, have come to recognize sinfulness as a fifth mark of the church!

To explain what I meant, I used the analogy with venial sin and the need to keep all five marks of the church together in tension. If sinfulness were the only mark of the church, it would be like saying the church is in mortal sin and has totally failed its commitment to live the life of the Spirit. But sinfulness, as one of the five marks of the church, is like venial sin— the church is never as one, holy, catholic, and apostolic as it should be. The whole church begins the eucharistic liturgy with a confession of sins and a plea for God's mercy. Why does the eucharistic liturgy pray for the bishop of Rome and the local bishop if they are totally sinless?

How could we as a church ever have forgotten about the sinfulness of the church? The theological reason comes from an exaggeration of what I think is a very strong and even distinctive aspect of Catholic theology. I use the word "mediation" to describe this reality. Others have talked about the incarnational principle, the sacramental principle, or the analogical imagination.

Catholic theology sees the divine as mediated in and through the human. The best illustration of this is the Eucharist that is the heart and the center of our church life. God is present to and with us in a celebratory meal. Celebratory meals are the primary way in which human beings celebrate their love and share their joys and sorrows with family and friends. Even in the midst of our growing reliance on fast food, we still have celebratory meals on important days like Thanksgiving and Christmas, and also to mark important events such as baptisms, marriages, and even funerals. So we as a church took over the way in which human beings celebrate their love and share their lives and stories with one another as the way in which God's love and presence comes to us.

Catholic moral theology well illustrates mediation. How do we decide what to do? Do we knock on God's door and ask? No. The Catholic natural law tradition (I have some problems with aspects of that tradition) recognizes that our God-given reason reflecting on the nature and creation that God made can come to understand how God wants us to live and act. God's law is mediated to us in and through the natural law.

Our theology of the church illustrates mediation. God comes to us in and through a visible human community with human leaders. For many Protestants, the church is primarily invisible and God is primarily present in the heart and soul of the individual believer. But, for Catholics, God comes to us in and through the visible human community of the church.

But the Catholic problem has been to associate the human too closely to the divine or even to identify them. Such an exaggeration constituted the theoretical basis for the triumphalism of the church. The church was pure, holy, without spot, and was identified with the reign of God. But the church at best is a sign or sacrament pointing toward the reign of God but can never totally be identified with the reign of God. Vatican II correctly reminded us that the church is the pilgrim people of God, always under the imperative to grow in faith, hope, and love.

To his credit, Pope John Paul II apologized and asked forgiveness for many past failures in the church. But, unfortunately, he was not willing to say the church itself did these wrong or sinful acts. They were done by some members of the church. But if the church is the pilgrim people of God, these were truly actions of the church. John Paul II did not want to accept sinfulness as a fifth mark of the church, but theology and experience remind us of this truth.

Some important consequences flow from accepting sinfulness as the fifth mark of the church. First, the church as a whole and all its members are called to continual conversion—to grow in our multiple relationships with God, neighbor, world, and self. The flip or negative side of this call to conversion and growth is the sinfulness that affects the church and all its members. We do not live out as faithfully as we should the gospel message of Jesus. We always fall short. The church must publicly confess how often it hides rather than manifests the reign of God. This call to conversion has been expressed in the axiom *ecclesia semper reformanda*—the church is always in need of reform.

Second, this call to reform also refers to the structures of the church. The recognition of the sinfulness of the church not only calls for a constant scrutiny of the structures and institutional aspects of the church, but also gives some indication of the type of structures we need. Here, as in other areas, we can learn from the human wisdom we have acquired. The tendency to sinfulness calls for a balance of power. The imperfection and sinfulness of any one person or group calls for some institutional structure to dialogue with and perhaps even challenge it. I am not saying here that the church should adopt a total democratic system, but I am definitely saying the church is not a monarchy.

In this area, church structure can learn much from the Catholic Church teaching on the structure of civil society with the important role given to the principle of subsidiarity. The principle of subsidiarity recognizes there are different levels within society and maintains that the higher level should provide whatever help (*subsidium*) is necessary so that the lower levels can do all they can on their own. The higher level takes over only when the lower level cannot do it on its own even with help. In this light, subsidiarity develops proper roles for individuals, societies like families, all types of voluntary societies ranging all the way from the press and academic institutions to professional groups to voluntary groups helping the poor and the needy, and local, regional, and national governments. But the higher group or the highest group, such as the national government, cannot and should not usurp the power and functions that can be carried out on lower levels. The Catholic Church today is still too centralized, but all we have to do is to put into practice existing Catholic teaching on the collegiality of bishops, the role of the local church, and the God-given role of the individual believer in the church.

The terrible clergy sex abuse scandals and the response to them well illustrate the need for a balance of power. Many bishops hid the problems of clergy sex abuse and failed to protect the youngest and most vulnerable people in the church. A good part of the problem was structural. There was no one to raise objections to what they did.

To help solve the clergy sex abuse problem, the national conference of bishops has appointed a review board, which in general is a very good move. But review boards should not be appointed only after the horse has left the barn. Review boards or similar structures should exist in every diocese and parish with regard to all important realities.

Third, the church and its leaders must recognize the sinfulness of the church and be more modest and honest in our rhetoric and understanding. Take as an example the teaching office of the church. The papal rhetoric at the present time goes something like this. The church, "the pillar and bulwark of the truth" (2 Tim 3:15), continues the teaching role of Jesus with the "task of authentically interpreting the word of God…entrusted only to those charged with the church's living magisterium, whose authority is exercised in the name of Jesus Christ."

But, as the church is a pilgrim church, so too is the teaching office in the church a pilgrim magisterium. Even the most conservative theologian acknowledges that the most solemn teaching in the church is not perfect. Our imperfect human words can never fully grasp the divine mysteries. A very large category of church teaching is called noninfallible, which means that it is fallible. Some of this teaching in the past has been wrong. Think, for example, of slavery. Sinfulness is by no means the only reality affecting the pilgrim teaching office in the church. Human imperfection, finitude, and the lack of eschatological fullness also contribute to the pilgrim nature of the church and its teaching office, despite the presence of the Holy Spirit.

The Catholic Church needs to accept in theory and in practice sinfulness as a fifth mark of the church. All of us who belong to the church must constantly be on our guard against a self-righteousness that fails to recognize our own sinfulness as well as that of the church.

CHAPTER 40

The Church Is Marked by Suffering

M. Shawn Copeland

M. Shawn Copeland, a Roman Catholic laywoman, was born in Detroit, Michigan, and educated in parochial and private schools in that archdiocese. In 1991 she received a doctorate in systematic theology from Boston College, where she now holds a tenured appointment in the department of theology. In addition, she is (adjunct) associate professor of systematic theology, and associate director for the master's program in pastoral theology at the Institute for Black Catholic Studies of Xavier University of Louisiana (New Orleans).

Her academic research and publications include the areas of theological and philosophical anthropology, political theology and philosophy, and embodiment, with special attention to gender and race. At the same time, she has been recognized as one of the most important influences in North America in drawing attention to issues surrounding African American Catholics. Dr. Copeland has served as Convener of the Black Catholic Theological Symposium and is a former president of the Catholic Theological Society of America.

Copeland has taught theology at Yale University Divinity School and Marquette University. She has authored more than a hundred articles, reviews, and book chapters, and along with Elisabeth Schüssler Fiorenza, has co-edited two volumes of the international theological journal Concilium: Violence Against Women *and* Feminist Theologies in Different Contexts *which have been translated into Dutch, French, German, Italian, and Spanish.*

I am now rejoicing in my sufferings for your sake,
and in my flesh I am completing what is lacking
in Christ's afflictions
for the sake of his body, that is, the church.
(Col 1:24)

A mark identifies, indicates position, signifies status, specifies a boundary. A mark can account for absence as well as presence, as it includes even as it excludes. As a mark of the church, suffering defies the constraint of definition, for suffering is a universal and inescapable fact of the human condition: Despite age, socio-economic status, education, race, gender, religion, physical prowess, moral development, *all* human beings suffer.

The *ekklesia*, the assembly or community we call church, emerges in and on the Spirit-moved recognition, assent, and confession of Jesus of Nazareth as *Messiah*, as Lord, as the Christ of God. Yet the human persons who make this confession do so from within particular historical, cultural, and social (i.e., political, economic, and technological) situations. To be sure, neither they nor their confession are determined by historical circumstance, but the force of history cannot be ignored. Indeed, the concreteness of human particularity contributes to the richness and the poverty of the church. It also contributes to its engagement with social suffering.

The notion of social suffering expresses the escalation of human anxiety and anguish and pain through massive public events such as torture, genocide, extermination, ethnic cleansing, "disappearance," enslavement, cultural decimation, even protracted systemic racism. Such events, as theologian Rebecca Chopp has written,

> have no completed meaning in history; they cannot be fully explained, understood, or represented [and] this suffering cannot be forgotten or ignored in history's interpretation or construction; once progress has shoved the masses of humanity onto life's margins, history is broken, its end forever in question, and its purpose lost in suspension.[85]

Such massive suffering silences its victims, disarms them with pain, drives them to the borders of hopelessness and despair. Yet, oppressed, poor, and marginalized, the victims of history confound the sheer horror of their suffering through seizing their inner power, discovering righteous anger, and struggling against the evil manifest in cruelty and injustice. Enduring such grotesque suffering alongside the poor, despised, and excluded children, women, and men as well as standing in solidarity with them in their struggle constitutes a mark of the church of the crucified. For the church must authentically bear the marks of its Lord.

Some days after the death of the rabbi Jesus from Nazareth, the author of the fourth gospel depicts his disciples as gathered behind locked doors, hiding in fear of persecution from their relatives, friends, and neighbors. Jesus enters this gloom and anxiety; he stands boldly, bodily in their midst. "Peace be with you" is his greeting. The Johannine writer then tells us that Jesus, unasked and unbidden, *shows* the disciples his hands and his side. The wounds reveal the identity correspondence between the crucified and the risen one: He is one and the same. The disciples rejoice (see Jn 20:19–23).

But Thomas, one of the twelve, was not with them at the time of this appearance. When the others insisted that they had seen the Lord, he would not brook such a wonder. He wanted evidence—dispassionate, disinterested, clear: "Unless I see the mark of the nails in his hands, and put my finger in the mark of the nails and my hand in his side, I will not believe." A week later, again the disciples are gathered in the same house, again the doors are shut, again Jesus appears among them. Once again he greets them: "Peace be with you." This time Jesus turns to Thomas and commands, "Put your finger here and see my hands. Reach out your hand and put it in my side. Do not doubt but believe." Thomas cannot but reply, "My Lord and my God" (20:24–28).

We are encouraged, particularly by the Johannine writer (20:29), to read this story in honor of all who will not have seen, but who shall believe that Jesus of Nazareth is the Christ of God. We tend to cast a suspicious or pitying eye on Thomas. Yet, there is something cautionary, perhaps wise in his protest and behavior. Thomas grasps that the risen Lord must always be identical to the crucified man whose passion for God and compassion for human others resulted in death on the cross. The community that shall confess Jesus of Nazareth as Lord, as the Christ of God, that shall call itself church ought to bear the mark of the nails, the mark of the lance—the mark of suffering.

Hence, the community of believers, the *ekklesia*, the church ought to be recognizable in its willingness to stand beside the poor, injured, despised, and excluded sufferers in history, in its willingness to suffer.

Like Jesus, the church must move from intention to action. What Jesus says, he does. He brings to life, he performs his words; indeed, *he* is the performative Word who brings God to life in and for the community of the dispossessed. We who constitute the community of believers are called to scrutinize the relation between our words and our deeds, our speech and our acts.

Like Jesus we seek a new and deeply loving relationship with God; moreover, that relationship brings about a new determination in real relations among ourselves. We initiate a new community of brothers and sisters who *belong* to a merciful, loving, and compassionate God who gives us life, who nurtures us, who sustains us, who holds us in divine embrace. Indeed, our community must be an authentic community—attentive to particularity, to location in place and time, to the griefs and sorrows of all. To belong to God is to belong to an open and non-exclusive community; to belong to God is to realize in history a new relationship of creativity, fidelity, and freedom. Our converted relationships are the basis for a new society in the concrete. Women and men heal, create, and love concretely in history, but heal and create and love so well as to realize in all their relationships that eschatological or absolute future which opens out into God.

In this new community, the memory of the crucifixion and resurrection are public. This memory is critical and liberative: breaking the spell cast by the prevailing consciousness and injecting the dangerous freedom of Jesus into modern society.

The creating that takes place in history seeks the concrete transformation of the world as this has been determined by God in Jesus. A redemptive aesthetics struggles to overcome those psychic, social, and moral alienations that give impetus to irrationality, chaos, and evil. The creative Christian social praxis that emerges to confront social suffering does not depend upon the prevailing social, cultural, historical modes of operation, nor upon utopian schemes for liberation. Rather, such praxis engages in the project of creating a new and totally different future: to be sure, one in which oppressive economic, social, political, gender, and racial paradigms are eliminated, but one which embraces the challenges of suffering as part of the lot of those who follow the Crucified and Risen One, for the Risen Lord goes before us to the poor, to the oppressed, to the outcast.

Like Jesus, the church must have a vision of the gracious, compassionate reign of God. If the church is to fulfill the vision of the reign, then the broken-hearted must be welcomed among us with an embrace and a kiss. Above all, these children, women, and men must be welcomed not as objects of pity or mercy, but as equals, as necessary partners, as human subjects—persons capable of discernment, understanding, decision, and action; persons with whom we have a future and without whom we have nothing.

Like Jesus, the church must be a place of refuge and healing, where the abused and tortured are nourished and healed by love. Above all, these children, women, and men must be greeted with warmth and tenderness, with regard and respect.

Like Jesus, the church must be willing to risk fortune and future for the sake of those who are abandoned to the scrap heap of history. Above all, these children, women, and men must be loved, for in their suffering they bear the mark of the crucified Jesus, who is no one else than the Resurrected Lord.

Like Jesus, the church must be willing to work and fight and die, to suffer in history for the abundant life that Jesus has promised.

The church must be willing to "complete what is lacking in Christ's afflictions" for the sake of his "little ones" who are church (after Col 1:24).

Like Jesus, the church must be willing to invite and withstand our scrutiny: "See the mark of the nail, touch the mark of the lance. Take refuge in the suffering church of Christ."

CHAPTER 41

The Church Is World-Embracing

Monika K. Hellwig

Monika Hellwig was born in Breslau, Silesia (then a German city) in December 1929, three years before Hitler came to power. At the age of six she fled with her family, first to the Netherlands and three years later to Scotland, where she and her sisters spent the better part of World War II. After a pre-medical course in the Sixth Form, she changed direction and obtained her bachelor of laws degree and a post-graduate diploma in social sciences from Liverpool University in England. Some years spent in religious life and further studies at The Catholic University of America resulted in a master of arts degree and a doctorate in theology with a minor concentration in cultural anthropology, enhanced with studies in cultural linguistics at the University of Oklahoma and in South Asian area studies at the University of Pennsylvania.

Her work experience included general social work, teaching theology (three decades at Georgetown University), retreat work, radio broadcasting, ghost writing, and research. During most of Vatican II she was in Rome following the reported speeches of the council, the documents as they were published, and the conferences given by the various periti. *From 1996 until her death in 2005 she directed the Association of Catholic Colleges and Universities. She authored some dozen books, including* Understanding Catholicism, The Eucharist and the Hunger of the World, Guests of God: Stewards of Creation, *and* Public Dimensions of a Believer's Life. *She held a number of honorary degrees and awards, including the John Courtney Murray, SJ, Award of the Catholic Theological Society of America and the Theodore M. Hesburgh, CSC, Award of the Association of Catholic Colleges and Universities.*

She was also the single adoptive mother of three now grown children, Erica Hellwig Parker, Michael Hellwig, and Carlos Hellwig, and the grandmother of Miles, Sterling, and Quincy.

The church is world-embracing; it is concerned with this world in which we live in all its many dimensions. It is concerned with the natural world— with its ecology, its beauty, its resources, its great potentialities that need to be tended, valued and cherished. But the church is also concerned with this world of people—people with their languages, cultures, histories, people with their needs and interdependence, people with their gifts and talents, skills and knowledge. Finally, the church is concerned with this world as it is organized by human beings over the course of the centuries—with the interactive economies around the globe, with the political structures at the local, national, and international levels, and particularly with the structures that can create peace and harmony, that transcend natural rivalries and hostilities by building wider communities of fellowship and collaboration.

This world-embracing concern has always characterized the church, but as we look back through history it is not always as evident to us. As we read the New Testament it may seem that Jesus is entirely other-worldly and apolitical. But this impression is due to the fact that, unless we have spent some time and energy studying the context of the gospels, we are not familiar with the society in which Jesus lived, and we do not always catch the implications of his actions and his words. Even when we become aware how much the life, actions, and words of Jesus were shaped by his Hebrew heritage, we may not know the extent to which the laws of Leviticus, for instance, reflect ecological wisdom and practice. We may not realize that the laws protecting the dignity and needs of the poor, the powerless, and the alien were such as would look to us like radical socialism. All this has to be seen as assumed by the stories and teachings of the New Testament. Moreover, as we read the gospel accounts of the actions and words of Jesus we need to take into account the context to see how politically provocative and socio-critical these actions and words really were in their own context.

Throughout the centuries there have been mystics and missionaries, prophets and activists who have grasped this characteristic of Christianity: Paul in the letters to the churches; Irenaeus in his interpretation of history as community building; Macrina and her grandsons, Basil and Gregory, in their leadership of Christian participation in the wider community; Ambrose and Augustine of Hippo about the structuring of human society; Pope Gregory I and Augustine of Canterbury about relations with pagans and their traditions; Hilda of Whitby and Hildegarde of Bingen about the natural and the human world in which we live; Bridget of Sweden and Catherine of Siena about the need to challenge misuse of power, even in the church; and many others.

But in between these giants there have always been the shrunken and faint-hearted, who withdrew into separation from the world and condemnations of it. There have been resulting condemnations of the great thinkers of the world, including: Thomas Aquinas for his use of Aristotle; the whole range of modern scholarship in the Syllabus of Errors of 1864 and again in the Decree against Modernism of 1907; Teilhard de Chardin for his serious engagement of religious thought with modern science; Karl Rahner for the logic of con-celebration (which was later endorsed), a matter closely linked to the under-standing of grace; Yves Congar for his understanding of the role of the laity and the call to ecumenism (both later endorsed); and many others.

Such condemnations were issued not only in relation to writings but also with reference to practice: concerning democracy in the governance of nations; concerning the adaptations of liturgy and catechesis to non-European cultures, ever since the time of Matteo Ricci and Robert de Nobili; concerning dress and names in African cultures; and much more. Vatican II, and particularly its Pastoral Constitution on the Church in the Modern World, *Gaudium et spes*, has brought the attention of the whole church back to the realization that Christianity is essentially world-embracing because the redemption is essentially world-transforming.

The council brought us back from a Catholicism of condemnation to a Catholicism of engagement. But this has not been fully appreciated by all. There are still many among the laity who want the clear-cut certainties and sense of always being right that goes with the Catholicism of condemnation, and who even attack the bishops when the latter do not issue the desired condemnations. It must be admitted that the church as it had shaped itself in the time between the Council of Trent, 1545–63, and the time after the Second World War, mid-twentieth century, offered a very internally coher-ent way of living, and there was much that was good about it, but it was out of touch with the big human questions and challenges of modern times.

Already before Vatican II there were movements within the church com-munity that responded to these challenges, such as the convergence of lay initiatives that came to be known as Catholic Action. And there were movements outside the Catholic Church that engaged and challenged the church, such as the League of Nations and subsequently the United Nations, the World Council of Churches, and the World Parliament of

Religions. And within the Catholic Church, even within its official structures, there were moves to respond to these challenges.

There were scholars like Yves Congar and great church leaders like Cardinal Suenens who pointed the way to a truly world-embracing church. But the great breakthrough came with the Second Vatican Council of 1962 to 1965, and especially with its Pastoral Constitution on the Church in the Modern World, *Gaudium et spes* (GS).

Gaudium et spes, elaborating on principles already stated in *Lumen gentium*, the Dogmatic Constitution on the Church, and in *Apostolicam actuositatem*, the Decree on the Apostolate of Lay People, sets out at length and very practically how this world-embracing character of the church is first and foremost the task of all the people of God, of the baptized as such, and therefore of the laity in general. The quest for the reign of God demands that the Christian community be actively involved with all who are poor and suffering, and therefore with the structures of human society that shape the conditions for human lives (GS 1). This means responsibility for the global inequalities, cultural uprootedness, and migration problems that cause so much suffering (GS 6–10). It means a global concern for the common good and a just social order, based on the dignity of all human beings (GS 12–32). Therefore it means finding ways of restraint on the greed of the rich and powerful (GS 33–39). Further, it means creating and maintaining structures of real support for the relationships created by marriage and family. Finally, this epoch-making document points to the urgent responsibility of the community of the baptized for the building of just and universally supportive economic structures (GS 63–72), for a wholesome political order (GS 73–76), and above all for establishing peace in the community of nations (GS 77–93). The document does not leave it to individual interpretation to flesh out what each of these terms means, but is quite specific and exigent in spelling out what is intended.

Hearing the claim that a mark of the church is that it is world-embracing, some thoughtful and well-instructed Catholics will say that that is already included when we proclaim the church is catholic, i.e., universal. This is true if "catholic" is understood to mean more than that membership is open to all people. It is true if "catholic" is understood as having to do with all aspects and components of our life in the world. But because this last often gets little or no attention, the Second Vatican Council gave 100 pages to spelling this out beyond question, leaving us a much longer document than on any other topic. It may take both time and deep conversion for all of us truly to accept the reality that the church is essentially world-embracing.

CHAPTER 42

The Church Is Youthful

Robert J. McCarty

Robert McCarty has been the Executive Director for the National Federation for Catholic Youth Ministry (NFCYM) since 1997. The organization provides networking, resources, conferences, and leadership for the development of youth ministry within the Catholic Church. He has been in professional youth ministry since 1973, serving in diocesan, parish, school, and community programs. McCarty offers workshops and training programs in youth ministry skills and issues internationally, providing consultations and training in Australia, New Zealand, Samoa, Germany, and Canada.

Born in August 1951, McCarty received his bachelor of science degree in sociology and theology from Saint Joseph's University in Philadelphia, Pennsylvania, his master of arts degree in religious rducation from LaSalle University in Philadelphia, and a doctor of ministry degree from the Graduate Theological Foundation in Indiana.

His teaching experiences include adjunct staff positions with La Salle University, Christ the King Seminary in Aurora, New York, Saint Mary's Seminary and University in Baltimore, St. John's University in Collegeville, Minnesota, and Loyola University in New Orleans. He has authored numerous articles and several books, including: Training Adults for Youth Ministry; Meeting the Challenge: Resources for Catholic Youth Evangelization; Survival in Youth Ministry; Teen to Teen: Responding to Peers in Crisis *through Saint Mary's Press, and* Tips for Raising Teens: A Primer for Parents.

The NFCYM awarded Dr. McCarty the National Youth Ministry Award for Training in 1994. McCarty is also a volunteer in his parish youth ministry and catechetical program at St. Francis of Assisi Parish in Fulton, Maryland.

The Young Church of Today: Called and Gifted

I had the privilege of attending World Youth Day in 1993, when Pope John Paul II welcomed 80,000 young people in Mile High Stadium as they chanted, "John Paul II, we love you." This was a remarkable experience given the perception of young people as being disinterested in organized religion. However, even more significant was the pope's response, "John Paul II, he loves you." The youthful crowd erupted in cheers, applause, and even tears. I remember wondering if perhaps this was the first time our young people had heard that the church, through the person of the pope, loved them.

Actually, Pope John Paul II first revealed his special affection for young people when he became pope in 1978. "You are the hope of the church and of the world," he told them. "You are my hope." More recently, in his apostolic letter "On The Coming of the Third Millennium," he wrote to and about youth: "The future of the world and the church belongs to the younger generation....Christ expects great things from young people" (#58). He has identified the gifts they bring to the church: their enthusiasm and joy, their commitment to justice, their idealism, and their search for Jesus.

This love affair between the pope and young people deepened through the various World Youth Day gatherings and the pope's many visits to countries around the globe. In every instance we heard, "John Paul II, we love you," and his response, "John Paul II, he loves you." In our own country we have witnessed tens of thousands of our Catholic young people participating in regional and national gatherings and conferences. Over 24,000 young people attended the 2003 National Catholic Youth Conference. Even more are participating in diocesan, parish, and school youth ministry programs. These experiences have ushered in a new relationship, a renewed commitment—not just of the church to young people, but of young people to the church. And in so doing, an indelible, youthful mark has been left on the church.

At the 2000 World Youth Day in Rome, Pope John Paul II challenged young people to "open themselves to God's love and to accept the plan or mission that he has for each individual life." Further, "Do not be afraid to accept your responsibilities: the church needs you, she needs your commitment and generosity; the pope needs you, and at the beginning of this new millennium, he is asking you to take the gospel on the paths of the world."

The present generation of young people may well be one of the most spiritual generations ever. They are searching for a faith that makes sense, that provides direction and meaning and that challenges. Young people are looking for a language to help them understand their experiences of God, searching for ways to deepen their experiences of the sacred, and seeking a community of people with whom to journey.

Indeed, young people are a gift to the church—and that is an important shift in perception. Despite media characterizations, young people are interested in justice and service, in volunteering in the community, and in addressing global issues. They are optimistic, desire to succeed in academics and in their chosen occupations, want to be close to their parents, and are convinced they can make a difference in the world. A significant mark for our church—*young people are not a problem to be solved, they are a gift to be shared.*

But are they a gift we are ready to accept? Those of us who are parents and many others in the church often wonder and worry: will our children have faith? But the real issue facing the church is: will our faith have children? Will the Catholic Church feed that spiritual hunger of today's young people for an authentic experience of God, for justice and service, for meaning and purpose, and for a spiritual home?

This is a challenge today because young people are believers first, and "belongers" second. Though young people are interested in spirituality and issues of faith, they can quickly become disinterested in institutional religion unless they experience the church as welcoming, supportive, and accepting of their gifts. What an interesting dilemma! Our church is blessed with young people who want to share their gifts within the faith community and all that is required is for the community to accept their gifts and welcome their participation.

Truly, young people are looking for a worthwhile adventure and living as disciples of Jesus Christ is an adventure. The pope outlined this adventure when he said: "Today, you have come together to declare that in this new century you will not let yourselves be made tools of violence and destruction; you will defend peace, paying the price in your person if need be. You will not resign yourselves to a world where other human beings die of hunger, remain illiterate, and have no work. You will defend life at every moment of its development; you will strive with all your strength to make this earth livable for all people" (Pope John Paul II, 2000).

Too often young people receive the message that their time has not yet come, that they are too inexperienced, and that youth is a time of education and training in preparation for a future role in the church and in the community. Yet, the pope was abundantly clear that youth is not a stage of life oriented to what will be later; rather he challenged them to live as disciples now. The pope echoed the prophet Jeremiah who says, "Say not, 'I am too young.' To whomever I send you, you shall go; whatever I command you, you shall speak. Have no fear before them, because I am with you to deliver you, says the Lord" (Jer 1:7–8).

The U.S. bishops in their 1997 pastoral letter *Renewing the Vision: A Framework for Catholic Youth Ministry* (RTV) state that discipleship is at the heart of the church's mission. If young people are to have genuine opportunities for exploring what discipleship involves, they must be exposed to situations in which they experience "the demands, excitement, and adventure of being a disciple of Jesus Christ," experiences that "tax and test their resources and…stretch their present capacities and skills to their limits" (RTV p. 10). The call to discipleship demands a response now, not in some distant future.

Thus a second significant mark for our church—*youth are not the church of tomorrow, they are the young church of today.* Young people are not Christians in training. Through their baptism young people are called to "responsible participation in the life, work, and mission of the faith community" (RTV p. 11) and to use their gifts on behalf of the community. The young church is called to become participants, not mere spectators, in the adventure of discipleship.

Fostering this youthful character requires a communal commitment. Pope John Paul II challenged the entire church when he said, "What is needed today is a church which knows how to respond to the expectations of young people. Jesus wants to enter into dialogue with them and, through his body which is the church, to propose the possibility of a choice which will require a commitment of their lives. As Jesus with the disciples of Emmaus, so the church must become today the traveling companion of young people" (World Youth Day, 1995).

To be traveling companions of young people, to recognize their giftedness, and to celebrate the young church of today—that is both a blessing and a mark of the church.

Endnotes

1. *The New Saint Joseph Baltimore Catechism* (New York: Catholic Book Publishing Co., 1964, revised 1969), 62. Though said to be revised in 1969, after the Second Vatican Council (1962–65), it appears that little has changed. When speaking of the marks of the church it reads: "We know that the Catholic Church is the one true Church established by Christ because it alone has the marks of the one true Church."

2. Richard P. McBrien, *Responses to 101 Questions on the Church* (Mahwah, NJ: Paulist Press, 1996), 12.

3. Joseph Cardinal Ratzinger, the former prefect of the Congregation for the Doctrine of the Faith, admits as much in his book, *Introduction to Christianity*, trans. J.K. Foster (New York: Herder and Herder, 1969), 261–68.

4. Søren Kierkegaard's *Journals and Papers*, ed. and trans. Howard V. Hong and Edna H. Hong (7 Volumes). Quote taken from *Provocations: Spiritual Writings of Kierkegaard*, compiled and edited by Charles E. Moore (Farmington, PA: The Plough Publishing House, 1999), 176.

5. Denise Lardner Carmody, *An Ideal Church* (Mahwah, NJ: Paulist Press, 1999), 16.

6. Taken and adapted from *The Good You Do Returns: A Book of Wisdom Stories* by J.P. Vaswani (Liguori, MO: Liguori Publications, 1995), 66.

7. In Teutonic—German and Anglo-Saxon—cultures, people used this word (*circe, Kirche, Kerk*) to render the Greek term *kyriakon*, which refers to the "assembly" (*ekklesia, ecclesia*) that had gathered around Jesus the Lord (*Kyrios* is the Greek word for Lord).

8. Berard L. Marthaler, *The Creed* (New London: Twenty-Third Publications, 1993), 312.

9. *Creeds of the Churches*, ed. John H. Leith, 3rd ed. (Louisville: John Knox Press, 1982), 23.

10. The Apostles' Creed is so named because, according to legend, it was composed by the apostles, with each one writing a specific article of the creed. Lorenzo Valla (1406–57) demonstrated the legendary character of this version of the creed's authorship and his work was supported by subsequent scholars. John Leith says, however: "The creed does have a legiti-

mate claim to its title on the basis of the fact that all of its articles are to be found in the theological formulas that were current around A.D. 100." *Creeds of the Churches*, 22. The earliest appearance of the received text (*textus receptus*) of the Apostles' Creed dates from the early eighth century. The Creed was adopted by Rome and became the common creed of Western Christianity.

11. Marthaler, *The Creed*, 308.

12. John 14:25–26: "I have said these things to you while I am still with you. But the Advocate, the Holy Spirit, whom the Father will send in my name, will teach you everything, and remind you of all that I have said to you." Matthew 28:18–20: "And Jesus came and said to them, 'All authority in heaven and on earth has been given to me. Go therefore and make disciples of all nations, baptizing them in the name of the Father and of the Son and of the Holy Spirit, and teaching them to obey everything that I have commanded you. And remember, I am with you always, to the end of the age.'"

13. "Where the bishop appears, there let the people be, just as where Jesus Christ is, there is the Catholic Church." Ignatius of Antioch, "Letter to the Smyrnaeans," 8:2; in *Epistles of St. Clement of Rome and St. Ignatius of Antioch*, trans. James A. Kleist (Westminster: The Newman Bookshop, 1946), 93.

14. See Cyril of Jerusalem, Catechetical Lecture 18:23 in *A Select Library of Nicene and Post-Nicene Fathers of the Christian Church*, 2nd series, ed. by Philip Schaff and Henry Wace (Grand Rapids: Eerdmans, 1978), VII:140.

15. Marthaler, *The Creed*, 314.

16. The bishops gathered at Nicea probably began with a baptismal creed that had already been in use in Syria or Palestine. They then added to it statements that clearly presented a desired alternative to the claims of the presbyter Arius (ca. 250–336), who, in his teaching, subordinated the Son to God the Father. The majority at Nicea inserted into their creed two elements directly opposed to Arius' position: the declaration that Christ is the "only begotten" Son of God and the declaration that the Son is "of the same substance" (*homoousios*) as the Father. The first declaration sought to make clear two points: first, that the Son, and only the Son, comes directly from God, whereas all creatures come from God in the sense that they were created by the Father with the Son; second, that the Son was not a creature, contrary to the Arian assertion, because he was "begotten, not made." The second declaration sought to emphasize the Son's essential equality with the Father.

17. Cyprian of Carthage, bishop of Carthage in the early third century, gave powerful expression to the interconnection of the different marks of the church. For him there is no salvation outside the one visible church because the Holy Spirit was bestowed by Christ upon the church of the apostles and its heirs. See his "The Unity of the Catholic Church," 6, reprinted in *Early Latin Theology*, ed. S.L. Greenslade (Philadelphia: Westminster Press, 1956), 127–28.

18. Bede the Venerable, Exposition of I John, in *Patrologia Latina* (Paris: 1878–90), 93:106, cited in Jaroslav Pelikan, *The Christian Tradition: A History of the Development of Doctrine*, vol. 3: *The Growth of Medieval Theology (600–1300)* (Chicago: The University of Chicago Press, 1978), 44.

19. The Cathari critique went beyond criticism of the institutional church's apparent lack of apostolic poverty. The Cathari also advocated a dualistic understanding of God, reminiscent of Manicheism; they denied the full humanity of Christ; and they rejected the traditional doctrine of the resurrection of the body. See Pelikan, *The Growth of Medieval Theology*, 237–42.

20. Thomas Aquinas, "Exposition on the Apostles' Creed," in *Theological Texts*, trans. Thomas Gilby (New York: Oxford University Press, 1955), 340–43.

21. J. Derek Holmes, *A Short History of the Catholic Church* (New York: Paulist Press, 1983), 76–77.

22. In response to the point that the church contains the good and the bad (the wheat and the tares), Hus said: "Now for the right understanding of these things and the things to be said, we must lay down out of the apostle's words that Christ is the head of the universal church, that she is his body and that every one who is predestinate is one of her members and consequently a part of this church, which is Christ's mystical body, that is, hidden body, ruled by the power and influence of Christ, the Head, and compacted and welded together by the bond of predestination." John Hus, *The Church*, trans. David S. Schaff (Westport, CT: Greenwood Press, 1974), 17–18. See also 22–23.

23. See Pelikan, *Reformation of Church and Dogma*, 75.

24. Hus, *The Church*, 21.

25. For a brief description of the issues, see Clyde L. Manschreck, *A History of Christianity in the World*, 2nd ed. (Englewood Cliffs: Prentice-Hall, 1985), 130–32. See Pelikan, *Reformation of Church and Dogma*, 87–90.

26. Heinrich Kalteisen, *On the Free Proclamation of the Word of God*, cited in Pelikan, *Reformation of Church and Dogma*, 92.

27. Augsburg Confession, section VII, in *Creeds of the Churches*, 70.

28. "Wherever we see the Word of God purely preached and heard, and the sacraments administered according to Christ's institution, there, it is not to be doubted, a church of God exists (see Eph 2:20)." John Calvin, *Institutes of the Christian Religion*, Book IV, ch. 1, sect. 9 in *Calvin's Institutes* in two volumes, ed. John T. McNeill (Philadelphia: Westminster Press, 1977), 1023.

29. See Article XIX, according to the American revision of 1801, in *Creeds of the Churches*, 273.

30. The Second Helvetic Confession (1566), in *Creeds of the Churches*, 149.

31. Augsburg Confession, Article VII: "For it is sufficient for the true unity of the Christian church that the Gospel be preached in conformity with a pure understanding of it and that the sacraments be administered in accordance with the divine Word. It is not necessary for the true unity of the Christian church that ceremonies, instituted by men, should be observed uniformly in all places. It is as Paul says in Ephesians 4:4, 5, 'There is one body and one Spirit, just as you were called to the one hope that belongs to your call, one Lord, one faith, one baptism.'" *Creeds of the Churches*, 70.

32. See, for example, Calvin, who declared: "The church is called 'catholic,' or 'universal,' because there could not be two or three churches unless Christ be torn asunder (cf. 1 Cor 1:13)—which cannot happen! But all the elect are so united in Christ (cf. Eph 1:22–23) that as they are dependent on one Head, they also grow together into one body, being joined and knit together (see Eph 4:16) as are the limbs of a body" (Rom 12:5; 1 Cor 10:17; 12:12, 27). John Calvin, *Institutes of the Christian Religion*, Book IV, ch. 1, sect. 2 in McNeill ed., 1014. See the Second Helvetic Confession (1566), which states: "Also, there is but one head to the body, which has agreement with the body; and therefore the Church cannot have any other head besides Christ. For as the Church is a spiritual body, so must it needs have a spiritual head like unto itself. Neither can it be governed by any other spirit than by the Spirit of Christ." *Creeds of the Churches*, 143.

33. The Westminster Confession, Chapter XXV, *Creeds of the Churches*, 222.

34. The Schleitheim Confession (1527), composed by Michael Sattler and one of the earliest statements of belief of the Swiss Brethren, states: "To us then the command of the Lord is clear when He calls upon us to be separate from the evil and thus He will be our God and we shall be His sons and daughters....From this we should learn that everything which is not united with our God and Christ cannot be other than an abomination which we should shun and flee from. By this is meant all popish and antipopish works and church services, meetings and church attendance, drinking houses, civic affairs...." *Creeds of the Churches*, 286.

35. Dordrecht Confession (1632), Article VIII, in *Creeds of the Churches*, 299.

36. Robert Bellarmine, De Ecclesia (On the Church), III, ii, 9: "*Nostra autem sententia est, Ecclesiam unam tantum esse, non duas, et illam unam et veram esse coetum hominum ejusdem christianæ fidei professione, et eorumdem sacramentorum communione colligatum, sub regimine legitimorum pastorum et præcipue unius Christi in terris vicarii romani pontificis.*" *In Disputationum Roberti Bellarmini Politani, Opera Omnia* (Naples: J. Giuliano, 1837), 2:75.

37. "Unity," *The Catholic Encyclopedia*, ed. Charles Herbermann et al. (New York: Robert Appleton Co., 1912), 15:181.

38. "The Call to Unity," Faith and Order Conference (1927), in *Creeds of the Churches*, 568.

39. "Affirmation of Union," Faith and Order Conference (1937), in *Creeds of the Churches*, 573.

40. "The Unity We Have, the Unity We Seek," Third World Conference on Faith and Order, in *Creeds of the Churches*, 577–78.

41. Pius XI as cited in Williston Walker et al., *A History of the Christian Church*, 4th ed. (New York: Charles Scribner's Sons, 1985), 686.

42. See Xavier Rynne (pseud.), *Letters from Vatican City*, 77.

43. In the original draft, the council "teaches and solemnly professes that there is only one true Church of Jesus Christ, namely the one we celebrate in the creed as one, holy, catholic, and apostolic...which, after his resurrection, he entrusted to St. Peter and his successors, the Roman pontiffs, to be governed; therefore only the Catholic Roman has a right to be called the Church." Quoted by Giuseppe Ruggieri, "Beyond an Ecclesiology of Polemics: The Debate on the Church," in *History of Vatican II.* Vol. 2: *The Formation of the Council's Identity*, ed. Giuseppe Alberigo and Joseph A. Komonchak (Maryknoll, NY: Orbis Books, 1997), 286.

44. *Lumen gentium*, 8. Austin Flannery, ed., *Vatican Council II*, 9. The Decree on Ecumenism repeats this same idea. See *Unitatis redintegratio*, 3, Flannery, 503.

45. *Lumen gentium*, 15 asserts that the church "has many reasons for knowing it is joined to the baptized who are honored by the name of Christian, but do not profess the faith in its entirety or have not preserved unity of communion under the successor of Peter." See Flannery, 20–21.

46. *Unitatis redintegratio*, 3, Flannery, 502–03.

47. Dr. Oscar Cullmann, a Protestant observer at the Council, rightly commented at the time: "This is more than the opening of a door; new ground has been broken. No Catholic document has ever spoken of non-Catholic Christians in this way." Cited by Walter Abbott in *The Documents of Vatican II* (New York: Guild Press, 1966), 338.

48. *Unitatis redintegratio*, 3, Flannery, 503.

49. See *Catechism of the Catholic Church* (Libreria Editrice Vaticana, 1994), #815.

50. *Catechism of the Catholic Church*, #820.

51. *Catechism of the Catholic Church*, #827.

52. See *Catechism of the Catholic Church*, #830–31.

53. *Catechism of the Catholic Church*, #836.

54. See *Catechism of the Catholic Church*, #849–51.

55. See *Catechism of the Catholic Church*, #863.

56. *Catechism of the Catholic Church*, #865.

57. John 14:18.

58. Catherine Mowry LaCugna, *God for Us: The Trinity and Christian Life* (San Francisco: HarperCollins, 1991), 402.

59. LaCugna, 403.

60. Excerpt from *The Catholicity of the Church* (1985), 21–25. Used with permission of Oxford University Press.

61. Excerpt from *Confessions of a Catholic* (1983). Used with permission of Sterling Lord Literistic, Inc.

62. Yves Congar, "My Path-findings in the Theology of Laity and Ministries," *The Jurist* (1972), 32:181.

63. See Leonard Swidler, *Toward a Catholic Constitution* (New York: Crossroad, 1996), 118–25.

64. Pope Paul VI, "Apostolic Exhortation on Evangelization in the Modern World" (*Evangelii nuntiandi*), (Washington, DC: USCC, 1976).

65. Pope John Paul II, "Apostolic Exhortation on the Family" (*Familiaris consortio*) Origins 11 (December 24, 1981): 437–68.

66. See Jean Vanier, *Community and Growth* (New York: Paulist Press, 1989); Michael Downey, *A Blessed Weakness: The Spirit of Jean Vanier and l'Arche* (San Francisco: Harper & Row, 1986).

67. NCCB, "Follow the Way of Love," *Origins* 23 (December 2, 1993): 436.

68. "We have to be catholic, that is to say, not bound by so much as a thread to any created thing, unless it be to creation in its totality." *Waiting for God*, trans. Emma Craufurd (New York: Harper & Row, 1951), 98.

69. "Cosmic Life," *Writings in Time of War*, trans. Rene Hague (New York: Harper & Row, 1968), 13–71.

70. A.M. Ramsey, "Catholicism," *The Westminster Dictionary of Christian Theology*, ed. Alan Richardson and John Bowden (Philadelphia: Westminster Press, 1983), 87.

71. See Chapter 1 of *Theology of Nature* (Philadelphia: Westminster Press, 1980).

72. *Nairobi World Council of Churches Assembly*, 1975.

73. For a longer account of his experiences as a refugee and its impact on his theology, see "Betwixt and Between: Doing Theology with Memory and Imagination." In *Journeys at the Margin*, ed. Peter Phan and Jung Young Lee (Collegeville: The Liturgical Press, 1999), 113–33.

74. On migration as a source of theology see "The Experience of Migration as Source of Intercultural Theology in the United States," in Peter C. Phan, *Christianity with an Asian Face: Asian American Theology in the Making* (Maryknoll, NY: Orbis Books, 2003), 3–25.

75. On this triple dialogue, see Peter C. Phan, *In Our Tongues: Perspectives from Asia on Mission and Inculturation* (Maryknoll, NY: Orbis Books, 2003) and *Being Religious Interreligiously: Asian Perspectives on Interfaith Dialogue* (Maryknoll, NY: Orbis Books, 2004).

76. See Jules Isaac, *Has Anti-Semitism Roots in Christianity?* (New York: National Conference of Christians and Jews, 1961), 57.

77. For a complete online text of the commission's document "The Jewish People and their Sacred Scriptures in the Christian Bible" go to http://www.vatican.va/roman_curia/congregations/cfaith/pcb_documents/rc_con_cfaith_doc_20020212_popolo-ebraico_en.html. Excerpts and commentary may be found at http://www.bc.edu/cjlearning.

78. Paulo Freire, *Pedagogy of the Oppressed* (New York: Seabury, 1970); original Portuguese, 1963.

79. Nicholas C. Burbules, *Dialogue in Teaching: Theory and Practice* (New York: Teachers College Press, 1993), 19–20.

80. Burbules, *Dialogue in Teaching*, 42.

81. "My Path-findings in the Theology of Laity and Ministries," *The Jurist* (1972) 32:180. The emphasis is the author's.

82. Partricia Beattie Jung, "Sanctifying Women's Pleasure," in Patricia Jung, Mary Hunt, and Radhika Balakrishnan, eds., *Good Sex: Feminist Perspectives From the World's Religions* (Piscataway, NJ: Rutgers University Press, 2001).

83. Charles Gallagher et al., *Embodied in Love: Sacramental Spirituality and Sexual Intimacy* (New York: Crossroad, 1986).

84. Christine E. Gudorf, *Body, Sex and Pleasure: Reconstructing Christian Sexual Ethics* (Cleveland: Pilgrim Press, 1994), 103–18.

85. *The Praxis of Suffering: An Interpretation of Liberation and Political Theologies.* (Maryknoll, NY: Orbis Books, 1986).